# Claiborne County Tennessee

# COURT OF PLEAS AND QUARTER SESSION

## 1819–1821

WPA RECORDS

**Heritage Books**
**2024**

**HERITAGE BOOKS**

*AN IMPRINT OF HERITAGE BOOKS, INC.*

**Books, CDs, and more—Worldwide**

For our listing of thousands of titles see our website
at
www.HeritageBooks.com

A Facsimile Reprint
Published 2024 by
HERITAGE BOOKS, INC.
Publishing Division
5810 Ruatan Street
Berwyn Heights, MD 20740

Originally published 1939



International Standard Book Number
Paperbound: 978-0-7884-9041-5

# TENNESSEE

## RECORDS OF CLAIBORNE COUNTY

## MINUTES OF COURT OF PLEAS & QUARTER SESSIONS
## 1819 - 1821

Prepared By
The Historical Records Survey
Transcription Unit
Division of Women's and Professional Projects
Works Progress Administration

Mrs. John Trotwood Moore
State Librarian and Archivist, Sponsor

T. Marshall Jones
State Director

Mrs. Penelope Johnson Allen
State Supervisor

Mrs. Margaret Helms Richardson
District Supervisor

. . . . .

Nashville, Tennessee
The Historical Records Survey
February 2, 1939

Prepared By

Mrs. Ommie Gilbert
Mrs. Grace C. Chadwell

Indexed By

Mrs. Ommie Gilbert

Typed By

Miss Edith McVey

The Historical Records Survey

Luther H. Evans, National Director
T. Marshall Jones, State Director

Division of Women's and Professional Projects

Florence S. Kerr, Assistant Administrator
Elizabeth D. Coppedge, State Director

WORKS PROGRESS ADMINISTRATION

F. C. Harrington, Administrator
Harry S. Berry, State Administrator

RECORDS OF STATE OF TENNESSEE

$1.00

COUNTY COURT RECORDS FOR THE YEAR 1819-1821

RECORD BOOK FOR CLAIBORNE COUNTY

BEGIN NOVEMBER 1819

---

STATE OF TENNESSEE

CLAIBORNE COUNTY

NOVEMBER 8TH 1819

# MINUTE BOOK

# 1819 - 1821

## NEW INDEX

**Note: Page numbers in this index refer to those of the original volume from which this copy was made. These numbers are carried in the body of the manuscript within parenthesis, as (p 124)**

# ORIGINAL INDEX

## Index for November Term 1819



## Index for February Term 1820

## Index For February Term 1829



## Index For February Term 1829

Index For February Term 1820 Reverse

Index for Feby. Term 1820 Reverse



Index for May Term 1820



Index For May Term 1820

Index for May. Term 1820



Index For May Term 1821

Index for May Term 1821



Index for August Term 1820

Index for August Term 1820



Index for August Term 1820

Index for August 1820



Index for August Term 1820

Index For November 1820

Index for November 1820



Index for Nov. Term 1820

Index for November 1820



February Term 1821 Indexed

Index for Feby. Term 1821 page

Index for Feby. Term 1821



Index for Feby. Term 1821

Index for May Term 1821

Index May Term 1821 Reverse



Index for May Term 1821

Index for May Term 1821



Index for August 1821



Index for August 1821

Index for August Term 1821

Index to find beginning of Each Term

# CLAIBORNE COUNTY

## MINUTE BOOK
## 1819 - 1821

(p 1) 1st Monday November 8th 1819

At a Court of Pleas and Quarter sessions began and held for the County of Claiborne at the court house in Tazewell on Monday it being the 8th day of November 1819 present the worshipful John Evans John Brock, Mercurous Cook, John Neal John Huddleston, John Lynch Aaron Davis, John Hurst, Alexander Campbell, and Archbold Bailes, Equires.

On motion Sally McNew and William McNew was admitted to administer all and Singular the goods and chattels rights and credits of John McNew Deceased and thereupon entered into a bond of one thousand Dollars with William Rogers as Security and returned an Inventory sworn to and was sworn as administratrix and administrator which Inventory was Received by the Court ordered to be filed and recorded and it is futher ordered that an order of sale Issue and on motion the court appoint Joel Bayse Henry Long and John Sharp commisseoners to set appart so much of the stock crop and provesions now on hand of the estate of the decedents as will be of value suffecent to support the widow and orphans for one year from the death of the Decd. and make returns to next court

(p 2) Monday November 8th

Ordered by the court a majority of the acting Justices present that, Abraham Cadle and Polly Cadle be placed on the poor lists of Claiborne County and be allowed to recive of the trustee of said county twenty Dollars each for the term of one year and that certificates Issue to Colo. John Lea and Betsy Cadle to see to the collection of the same John Lea, Peter Huffaker Lewis Huffaker William Ely John Roddye and Aaron Davis who were appointed a Jury of view at the last term of the court to veiw and lay out a road from the Powels Vally road to Roddys ferry do report that they have veiwed and marked the road begining at William Elys runing a long the vally road to the mouth of a hollow and up said hollow along the old path to the Kentucky Road and from thence to roddys ferry It ordered by the court a majority of the acting Justices present that the above reporte be confermed and that Peter Huffaker be appointed overseer of said road from the mouth of the Hollow to where the Lane Intersects the Kentucky Road and have for hands as follows to wit all from Gap Creek begining at Wallens Mill then up said creek to Wyatts Mill then up the fork of said creek so as to Include Mark Shumaker Theophelus Miller then along the Poor Vally Ridge to Kentucky Road then along said Road to Powels river

(p 3) Monday November 8th 1819

Ordered by the court that John Whitaker be appointed overseer of the road from the top of the Hill on the north side of Russels creek to the Kentucky Road at Blairs Creek in Room and Stead of Thomas Pyttmein and have the same hands and bounds of hands said Pyttman had.

---

Ordered by the court that Allen M. Carly be appointed overseer of the road leading from Tazewell to Lee court House from Tazewell to Wallens old field in room and stead of Jesse Neil and have the same hands and bounds of hands said Neil had

---

Ordered by the court that Joseph Jenings be appointed overseer of the Bullard upper ferry road from the old garrison to Tazewell in room and stead of John Claypoll and have for hands Isham Jenings Dickerson Jenings, John Harper John Lebow and all the hands in said bounds

---

Ordered by the court that John Streevle be appointed overseer of the big vally road from the forks of the road where Peter Lewis new road Intersects the same Down to Hunting creek in room and Stead of Hardy Hughs and have for hands Hardy Hughes Edward Burk William Lewis John Whitehead Samuel Broff James Maples Jr. William Maples James Devidson Charlie Powers William Whitehead Semil Shelby and all the hands that may hereafter Leve in the said bounds of the above named hands

(p 4) Monday November 8th 1819

Ordered by the court that the Sheriff of grainger County take into his custody a feemale bastard child by the name of Musteen of which Susannah Musteen has been delivered and of which Joseph Jenings stands charged as the reputed father and bring her into court at the next Term of this court or so provide that she may be here on the first day of the Term to be bound out as the Law derects

---

Ordered by the court that Joseph Walker be appointed overseer of the road leading from the Big spring to Mulberry Gap begining at the seven mile tree and thence to the ten mile tree in room and stead of John Condray and have the hands and bounds of hands said Condry had

---

John Keck produced in open court the scalp of a wolf and was sworn that he killed said wolf with in the conferms of Claiborne County Sence the year 1811 and that the said wolf was supposed to be over four months old

It is therefore ordered by the court five Justices present that he be allowed to recive of the treasure of East Tennessee three Dollars and that the Sheriff of said county burn said scalp

(p 5) Monday November 8th 1819

Ordered by the court that William Cook Executor of James Johnson Deceased be allowed thirty seven Dollars fifty five cents for his expence and trouble of the management of the Estate of the Decendents according to his account filed

---

Ordered by the court a majority of the acting Justices present that

Benjamin Cloud clerk of this court be allowed to recive of the trustee of Claiborne County

---

A Deed of conveyance from Levi Kenny to Neal McNeal for fifty acres of Land which was in part proven at May Term 1818 by the oath of John McNeal is now proven by the oath of Joel fairchild admitted to record and ordered to be Registered

---

A Deed of conveyance from William Inglebargo to Neal McNeal for Twenty five acres of Land which was in part proven at May Term 1818 by the oath of John McNeal is now

(p 6) Monday November 8, 1819

fully proven by the oath of Joel Fairchild admitted to record and ordered to be registered

---

A Deed of conveyance from Joseph Williams by his attorney in fact Thomas L. Williams William Condry for six hundred and forty acres of Land was proven in court by the oath of Stephen Cocke and ordered to be filed for farther probate.

---

A Deed of Conveyance from William Hord to William Jones for two hundred and fifteen acres of Land was proven in court by the oath of Elijah Jones and Aaron Davis witnesses there to and admitted to record and ordered to be certfied for registration

---

A Deed of conveyance from Thomas Adkins to Jesse Kain for fifty acres of Land was duly proven in in court by the oath of John and Alfred Lynch subscribing witnesses thereto admitted to record and ordered to be certfied for Registration

---

A Deed of conveyance from David James to Valentine Boroff for one hundred and fifty three acres of Land was proven in court by the oaths of Samuel Boroff and John Lynch witnesses thereto admitted to record and ordered to be registered.

(p 7) Monday November 8th 1819

A power of attorney from William Lane to Aaron Davis to sell the Butcher spring Land in Powels vally was proven in court by the oaths of George W. Craig and Samuel Lane the subscribing witnesses thereto admitted to record and ordered to be certfied

A Deed of conveyance from George Yoakum to Dennis Condry for four Town lots in the Town of Tazewell was proven in court by the oaths of Tidance Lane and John Huddleston subscribing witnesses thereto admitted to record ordered to be registered

---

Mary Cadle administraterix of the estate of Mark Cadle Deceased Returned a Supplementerl Inventory of sales of the estate of the Decetents which was Recived by the court and ordered to be filed and recorded

---

On motion the court appointed John Whitehed a constable in the bounds of Captain Henry Moyers Company who entered unto bond in the sum of five hundred Dollars together with Hardy Hughs as Security and was quallfied as the law directs.

(p 8) Monday November 8th 1819

Court adjourned till tomorrow morning 9 o clock

John Evans
John Lynch
Aaron Davis
Mercious Cook
John Neil

Tuesday November 9th 1819

Court met according to adjournment present the worshipful John Evans John Lynch Aaron Davis Mercureus Cook and John Neil Esquires Dennis Condrey Sheriff of Claiborne County returned the venirefacias Executed on the following named person to wit William Lanham A Peter Neal Jr., William Henderson Charles Shearmon Thomas Jinkens Christian Sharp Mathew Ousley James Rogers John Berry James McBroom James Davison William Lewis James Carpenter Harod Hopson William Cuninghem Huram Hunt Frasur Brundley Jesse Carpenter Isham Cloud Samuel Going George Hopkins John Parrott Hezekiah Runyon Luke Parker Gidon Brooks and John Harris out of which the following named persons was ballotted a Grand Jury to the present Term to wit
Huroin Hurst, foreman

| | |
|---|---|
| Herod Hopson | William Henderson |
| John Berry | John Parrot |
| Jesse Carpenter | James Carpenter |
| Luke Parker | George Hopkins |

(p 9) Tuesday November 9th 1819

| | |
|---|---|
| Charles Shearmon | Christain Sharp |
| William Lanham | James McBroom |

who was sworn and recived their charge by Stephen Cocke Solicitor protem for the Sheriff returned William Bullard as a constable of the Grand Jury who was sworn as the Law dericts

---

A Deed of conveyance from Isham Stinnet to James Henderson for one hundred Sixty and a half acres of Land was proven in court by the oaths of of George Vanbebber and John Bery too subscribing witness and is admitted to record and ordered to registered

---

---

A Deed of conveyance from Isham Stinnet to James Henderson for three quarters of an acre of Land was proven in court by the oaths of George Vanbebber and John Berry two subscribing witnesses thereto admitted to record and ordered to be regestered.

---

---

the court appointed Stephen Cocke solicitor protem for at the Present Term

---

---

Ordered by the court one third of the acting Justices present that Benjamin Cloud Clerk of this Court be allowed to recive of the trustee of Claiborne County Eighty seven Dollar Sixty three and a half

( Written in margin of original book ) Certificate Isd.

(p 10) Tuesday November 9th 1819

cents, for Ex offices services makeing out Tax list stationary & & for the year 1819 according to his acounts filed and that he make out a certifecate accordingly

---

---

On motion William Bullard is appointed a constable of the Sandlick Company for the ensueing two years and was sworn as the law derścts and thereupon entered into bond with John Hunt and Jeremah Cloud as his Security in the sum of five hundred Dollars

---

---

Caleb Dobbs resigns his appointment as constable

---

---

On motion Aaron Hurst is appointed a constable in the bounds of Captain Joseph Hursts Company for the ensueing two years and was sworn as the Law dericts and thereupon Entered into bond with Joseph Hurst and Reuben Harper as his Security in the sum of five hundred Dollars

---

---

After making proclamation the court proceeded to the Election of a constable in the bounds of Capt. John Rogerses Company and after counting and commairing the votes it appeared that Reuben B. Rogers was duly and constitutionally Elected constable of said bounds who was sworn as the Law dericts and Entered into bond together with William Rogers and William Maddy Jr. as his Security in the sum of five hundred Dollars

---

---

The juors of the origenal Pannel Present James Devedson Mathew Ousley William Lewis William Cunninghem and Gedion Brooks

(p 11) Tuesday November 9th 1819

Ordered by the court a majority of the acting Justices Present that John Bullard be allowed to recive of the Trustee of Claiborne County Twenty seven Dollars fifty cents for supporting and clothing and furnishing Mary Aldredge one of the poor of said county with money in the year 1818 and that the clerk make out certifecate accordingly

---

---

Benjam Cloud and William Graham Executors of the estate of Christopher Damron Deceased returned an account of sales of the personal and part of the real estate of the said decendants which was Recived by the court Examined and ordered to be filed and recorded

---

---

Ordered by the court that Andrew Hurst be appointed overseer of the Road leading from Tazewell to the court house in the room and stead of Barney Campbell and have the same hands and of hands that said Campbell had.
Isd.

---

---

John Hunt Deputy Sheriff of Claiborne County Reports to court that he has let to support for the Term of one year to Drury Herrel three of the poor of this county agreeable to an order made at last Term,

(p 12) Tuesday November 9th 1819

for one hundred three Dollars seventy five cents he being the lowest bidder it is therefore ordered by the court that he be allowed in manner and form as the before receted order and that the clerk make out a certeficate
Isd. sept. 1819 & 1820

---

---

Ordered by the court that Huran Edwards be appointed overseer of the road leading from the big spring to Mulberry Gap that is from the Spicewood Spring to Fitchpatricks mill path in room and stead of John Mason and the same hands and bounds of hands said Mason had Isd.

---

---

Ordered by the court that Tennessee Margraves be appointed overseer of the Kentucky road from Tazewell to the top of Wallens Ridge in room and stead of Lewis Morris and the same hands and bounds of hands said Morris had.
Isd.

(p 13) Tuesday November 9th 1819

A Deed of conveyance from William Dobbs William Graham & Company for ninty acres of Land was duly acknowledged in court by the said Dobbs and is admitted to record and ordered to be registered

---

A Deed of conveyance from Thomas R. McClary to Robert W. McClary for Twenty five acres of Land was duly acknowledged in open court by the said Thomas R. McClary admitted to record and ordered to be registered

---

A Deed of conveyance from Robert W. McClary to William Lanham for seventy acres of Land was duly acknowledged in open court by the said Robert W. Mc Clary admitted to record and ordered to be Registered

---

A Deed of conveyance from Thomas Henderson To John McCarty for Twenty five acres of Land was duly proven in open court by the oaths of John Hurst and Luke Parker subscribing witnesses thereto admitted to record and ordered to be registered

---

With leave of the court William Lanham records his Stock marke as follows a Smoth crop and under bit out of Each ear

(p 14) Tuesday November 9th 1819

A Bill of sale from William Graham to Zachariah McCubbins for three negros was duly acknowledged in open court by the said William admitted to record and ordered to be Registered

---

A Deed of conveyance from William Condry Isaac Cloud and Nancy Perryman to George Richardson for one hundred acres of Land was Duly proven in open c court by the oaths of John Condray and John Bartlet two subscribing witnesses thereto admitted to record and ordered to be registered

---

A Deed of conveyance from Jesse Neil to William Weaver for Twenty seven acres of Land was duly acknowledged in open court by the said Neil admitted to record and ordered to be registered

---

The State<br>vs<br>Elijah Clenton } Scerefaceas

Personally appeared in open court Elijah Clenton and confessed Judgment for the costs in the above cause

It was therefore considered by the court that the forfeiture heretofore entered up against the aforesaid Elijah be set aside and that

(p 15) Tuesday November 9th 1819

the State recover a Judgment against the said Defendant in manner and form aforesaid confessed and that Execution Issue for the same

---

James Campbell
vs
William Maddy Jr. &
George Yoakum

This day came the parties by their attorneys and thereupon also came a jury to wit:

James Davidson
William Lewis
Mathew Ousley
Hezekiah Brooks
Thomas Bray
James Pyttman
Richard Powell
Drewry Herrel
Tidance Lane
Bryant Breeding
Robert Vanbebber and
William Lea

who being Elected tried and sworn well and truly to try and the truth to speak in the matter in Desputе wherein James Campbell is plaintiff and William Maddy Jr. and George Yoakum or defendants upon their oaths do say they find for the plaintiff seven Dollars and fifty cents besides his costs It is therefore considered by the court that the plaintiff recover of the Defendant the sum aforesaid in manner and form as aforesaid by the Jurors aforesaid and assessed together with the costs in this behalf Expended and the Defendants in mercy & &

(p 16) Tuesday November 9th 1819

Court adjourned untill tomorrow morning 9 oclock

John Evans
Josiah Ramsey
John Neil
<u>Mercurius</u> Cook
John Brock

Wednesday November 10th 1819

Court met according to adjournment present the worshipful John Evans John Brock John Neil Mercurous Cook and Josiah Ramsey- - - - - - - - - - - -

The State
vs
Isaac Vanbebber

Indictment

this day came the State by her <u>Solecetor</u> protem Stephen Cocke and the Defendant in his own proper person and being charged upon the bill of Indictment for plea says he is not Guilty and thereupon also came a Jury to wit

James Davidson
Mathew Ousley
William Lewis
Tidance Lane
Chesly Dobbs
Edward Ashley
Caleb Dobbs
Jesse Prechard

(p 17) Wednesday November 10th 1819

| William Shumate | Robert G. Parks |
| --- | --- |
| Peter Niel | Richard Powell |

who bein Elected tried and sworn well and truly to try and the truth to speak upon the Issue Joined wherein the state is plaintiff and Isaac Vanbebber is Defendant upon their oaths do say they find the defendant not Guilty in manner and form as charged in the bill of Indictment

It was therefore considered by the court that the Defendant be discharged and that Judgement be entered up against the county for all Lawful costs and that the clerk make out certificate to the trustee of said county

A Deed of Relinquishment from John Lea to John Roddy for a certain peace of Land in the County of Claiborne no of acres not known was duly acknowledged in open court by the maker thereof admitted to record and ordered to be Registered

A Deed of Relinquishment from John Roddy to John Lea for a certain Peace of Land in the county of Claiborne number of acres not Known was Duly acknowledged in open court by the maker thereof admitted to record and ordered to be Rigistered.

(p 18) Wednesday November 10th 1819

A Deed of Conveyance from James Hemphill to Robert and Andrew Crockett for one hundred Sixty acres of Land was duly proven in court by the oaths of Elijah & Sqire Hurst two Subscribing witnesses thereto admitted to record and ordered to be registered.

A Deed of conveyance from David C. Jones by his attorney in fact John W. Jones to Andrew and Robert Crocketts for three hundred Eleven and three forth acres of Land was proven by the oath of Robert Gibson a witnesses thereto and ordered to be filed for futher probate.

A Deed of conveyance from David C. Jones by his attorney in fact John W. Jones to Andrew and Robert Crockett for Ten acres of Land was proven by the oath of David Cosbey and ordered to be filed for farther probate

A Deed of conveyance from Jesse Ward to Andrew and Robert Crockett for Sixteen acres of Land was duly acknowledged in court by the maker thereof admitted to record and ordered to be registered

A Deed of conveyance from John McCrary to Robert and Andrew Crockett for one hundred and Sixty acres of Land was proven by the oath of James Courm and ordered to filed for further probate

(p 19) Wednesday November 10th 1819

A Deed of conveyance from George Gibson to Samuel Jones for thirty one acres of Land was proven in court by Isaiah Jones and John Steakly two subscribing witnesses thereto admitted to record and ordered to be registered

---

A Deed of conveyance from Isaiah Jones to John Steakly for fifty two acres of Land was acknowledged in court by the maker thereof admitted to record and ordered to registered

---

A Deed of conveyance from George M_ Neal to David Pugh for one acre of Land was proven in open court by the oaths of Isaiah Jones and John Steakly witnesses thereto admitted to record and ordered to be Registered

---

A Deed of conveyance from Abraham Jones, to John Steakly for Twenty seven acres of Land was proven by George Hopkins and Isaiah Jones witnesses thereto Admitted to record and ordered to be registered

---

A Deed of conveyance from George McNeal to John Steakly for five acres of Land was proven in court by the oaths of Isaiah Jones and admitted to record and ordered to be registered

---

A Deed of conveyance from Ambrose Bryant to William Ritter for fifty acres of Land was acknowledged by the maker thereof admitted to record and ordered to be Registered

(p 20) Wednesday November 10th 1819

A Deed of conveyance from James McBroom to George Brock for Sixty acres of Land was acknowledged in court by the maker thereof admitted to record and ordered to be Registered

---

With leave of the court William Ritter Records his ear mark a crop off each ear and a crop stitch in the under side of the right ear

---

The State
vs } Indictment
Jesse Anderson

Ordered by the court that nole prorguy be entered in the above cause and that Judgment be entered up against the County of Claiborne for the costs of the above prosecution and that the clerk make out certificate accordingly

The State }
vs }
John Bundren }

This day came the State by his solicitor Protem Stephen Cocke and the Defendant in his own proper person and being charged upon the bill of Indictment for plea says he is guilty

It is therefore considered by the court that he be fined for such his offence one Dollar besides cost and that Execution Issue

(p 21) Wednesday November 10th 1819

The State }
vs } Indictment
William Boyd }

This day came the state by his Solicitor protem for Stephen Cocke and the Defendant in his own proper person and being charged upon the bill of Indictment pleaded thereto guilty

It is therefore considered by the court that he be fined five Dollars besides costs and be Imprisioned thrity days for such his offence and remain in prison till the fine and costs are paid or otherwise discharged by due course of Law and the Defendant is therefore prayed in custody of the sheriff

The State }
vs } Indictment
Bennett Arnold }

This day came the State by her Solicitor protem Stephen Cocke and the Defendant in his own proper person and being charged upon the bill of Indictment pleaded thereto Guilty

It was therefore considered by the court that the said Defendant be fined in the sum of five Dollars besides costs and be Imprisoned Ten days for such his offence and thereto remain till fine and costs are Satisfied and that the State recover Judgment against him the said Bennett the sum of five Dollars fine together with the costs of this procecution, and said Defendant is prayed in C of Shff

(p 22) Wednesday November 10th 1819

On motion leave is granted Joseph McClary to Keep a house of public Entertainment for one year at his own house in the Town of Tazewell who was sworn according to Law and Entered into bond together with Dennis Condry as his Security in the sum of five hundred Dollars and thereupon it is ordered that a Licence do Issue

---

The State }
vs } Bastardy
Josiah Price }

On motion a rule is Granted to shew cause why the capias should be quashed and after agurment of counsel being heared as well in support of said motion as against it and the matter and things therein contained being Duly considered and fully understood by the court

It was therefore considered by the court that the capias was <u>unsufficient</u> that the same be quashed and that the Defendant be discharged from his recognizance and it is further ordered that an alias capias Issue to bring the said Josiah in at the next Term of this court -

Peter Neil one of the origenal pannel is in court and ordered to be sworn as a Jurior to attend at the present Term

(p 23) Wednesday November 10th 1819

Court adjourned untill tomorrow morning 9 oclock

John Evans
Josiah Ramsey
John Brock
Mercenrens Cook
John Neil

Thursday November 11th 1819

Court met according to adjournment present

John Campbell
vs
Arthur L. Campbell } original attachment

In this cause it is ordered by the court that all further proceedings be stayed for Six months - it appearing to the court that said defendant is a citizen of Kentucky

The State
vs
Reuben Day

There came the state by the Solicitor Protem Stephen Cocke and the Defendant in his own proper person and being charged upon the bill of Indictment pleaded thereto not Guilty and thereupon came a Jury to wit

(p 24) Thursday November 11th 1819

James Davidson
Mathew Ousley
William Lewis
Peter Neil
Gidion Brooks
Wm. Cunningham
Spencer Edwards
Jacob Vanbebber
Reuben Harper
Robert Yoakum
William Perant
Chesly Dobbs

who being Elected tried and sworn well and truly to try and the truth to Speak upon the Issue Joined wherein the state is plaintiff and Reuben Day is Defendant upon their oaths do say they find the Defendant not Guilty in manner and form as charged in the bill of Indictment

It is therefore considered by the court that the Defendant be Discharged and that the County of Claiborne pay the costs & c

The State
vs
Kenny Grady } this day came the state by the solicitor protem and the Defendant in his own proper person and being charged upon the bill of Indictment pleaded thereto Guilty

therefore it was considered by the court that he be fined one Dollar and pay the costs of the above cause for such his offence

(p 25) Thursday November 11th 1819

The State
vs
Robert Gibson

Personally appeared in open court Robert Gibson and John Hunt and acknowledged themselves Indebted to the State of Tennessee in the sum of five hundred Dollars to be levied of them goods chattels Lands and Tenments that is to say the said Gibson the sum $250 and the said Hunt in sum of $250 Dollars void on condition that the said Robert make his personal appearance before the Justice of our court on the Wednesday after the Second Monday of Feby. next to answer a charge of the state against him in a bill of Indictment doth not Depart the court without leave

---

The State
vs
John Eads

Personally appeared in opent court Robert Gibson and acknowledged himself Indebted to the state of Tennessee in the sum of one hundred and Twenty five Dollars to be levied of his goods and chattels lands and Tenements void on condition he make his personal appearance before the Justices of our said court on the Wednesday after the second Monday in Feby. next to give evidence on behalf of the state against the said John in a bill of Indictment and doth not Depart the court without leave

(p 26) Thursday November 11th 1819

The State
vs
Robert Gibson

Personally appeared in open court Henry Cartor and acknowledged himself Indebted to the state of Tennessee in the sum of one hundred and Twenty five Dollars to be levied of his goods and chattels lands and Tenments void on condition that he make his personal appearance before the Justices of our said court on the Wednesday after the second Monday in Feby next to <u>proxecte</u> and give evidence on behalf of the State against the said Robert in a charge of the state in a bill of Indictment and doth not Depart the court without leave

---

The State
vs
John McClary

Personally appeared in open court Mathew Russle and acknowledged himself Indebted to the State of Tennessee in the sum of one hundred and Twenty five Dollars to be Levied of his goods and chattels Lands and Tenuments void on condition that he make his personal appearance before the Justices of our court on the Wednesday after the second Monday in Feby. next to prosecute and give Evidence on behalf of the State against the said John & &

(p 27) Thursday November 11th 1819

The State
vs
Saml. Dodson

Indictment

Ordered by <u>by</u> the court that a nole prosegur be entered and that the county be Taxed with the costs of the above prosecution and that the clerk make out certificate & &

George Vanbebber
vs
Wilson W. Martin

On motion of the Plaintiff and for Reason appearing to the Satisfaction of the court by af a filed a commission is Granted him to take the Deposetion of George Robert Vanbebber a witness on behalf the plaintiff on the 11th day of November 1819 at the courthouse in Tazewell before any and Justice also a commission Granted the Defendant to take the Deposition of Powell Sharp a resodent of Knox County Kentucky on behalf of the Defendant in the above cause before any Justice of said county and Defendant giveing plaintiff fifteen Days notice of time and place of taking the same

---

A Deed of conveyance from David Chadwell to John Chadwell for two hundred and Sixty acres Land was duly acknowledged in court by the maker thereof admitted to record and ordered to be certified

(p 28) Thursday November 11th 1819

A Deed of conveyance for one hundred acres of Land and a bill of sale for one negro & one mare from William Rogers to John Evans was proven in open court by the oathes of Wm. Grham and Cavenaugh Boylston two subscribing witnesses thereto admitted to record and ordered to be Registered

---

Pleasant McMiller
vs
William Norvell

Fa Fa

John Hunt Deputy Sheriff haveing returned said F_ Fa into court Levied on five Horse beasts to late for to advertise in time to sell and make his returns to court at this Term.

On motion it is ordered by the court that an order of sale Issue to the said Sheff to sell the aforesaid Horses according to Law and make his Return to next Term

Isd.

---

William Bullard a constable Summoned to attend on the Grand Jury at this Term proves three Days for which he is allowed three Dollars

Isd.

(p 29) Thursday November 11th 1819

George Hopkins proseded in open court a wolf Scalp and was sworn that he killed the wolf in the conferms of Claiborne County Since the year of 1811 and that the same was over four months old

It was therefore ordered by the court five Justices present that he be allowed to recive of the treasurm of East Tennessee the sum Stipulated by Law Isd.

---

Joel Jones produced in open court a wolf scalp and was sworn that he killed said wolf within the conferms of Claiborne County Sence the year 1811 and that the same was over four months old

It was therefore ordered by the court five Justices present that he be allowed to recive of the treasure of East Tennessee the sum Stepulated by Law

Isd.

---

---

the Grand and petit Jurors are discharged from further attendance at this Term

---

---

A Deed of conveyance from John McCrary to Andrew and Robert Crockett 160 acres of Land which was yesterday proven by the oath of James Counn is now proven by the oath of Abraham Roger admitted to record and ordered to be Registered

(p 30) Thursday November 11th 1819

A Power of attorney from William Evans to John Cocke was acknowledged in open court by William Evans and ordered to be recorded and certified

---

---

Thomas Jackson<br>vs<br>Frazur Bundley } certiorari

Justices in court John Evans John Brock Jonah Ramsey and Mercurous Cook Esqr. on motion of the Plaintiff by his attorney Dismisses the petition for writs of certiorari and supercedeas and the Defendant Frazur Bundley being called to come into court and prosecute his said appeals as he was bound to do came not but made default

It was ordered by the court that said petition and writs be dismissed therefore on motion of the plaintiff by atto. Frazur Bundley and Abner Hatfield his security have the sum of Eighteen Dollars the amount of the Judgement of the Justice in this cause

It was therefore considered by the court that the plaintiff that the plaintiff Recover of the Deft. Frazur Bundley and Abner Hatfield his Security the sum of Eighteen Dollars the amount of the Justices Judgment in this case with Interest from the date of Judgment together with all costs and the Defendants in mercy & &

Isd.

(p 31) Thursday November 11th 1819

Stephen Hopkins<br>vs<br>John Hurst }

this day came the plaintiff by his attorney and moved the court to Enter up Judgment by Default in the above cause award a writ of Inquiry returnable to the next Term of this court

Ordered by the court that the following named persons be appointed Jurors to the next Cercuit Court to wit

Jacob Vandevanter
Eli Davis
John Baker
Alexander Campbell
John Rhea
Micheal Camron
John McDowell
James Overton
Joseph Walker
William Barnwell
Bryant Breeding
Bruford B. Woodall
Tidance Lane Jr. X
John Simmons
Daniel Coffett
Joseph Hunter
Thos. Dunn
John Huddleston
Samuel Cloud
Lewis Morris
James Vanbebber
Thomas Clark
Jacob Castle
John Graves
Robert Crockett
Peter Ausmus

Issued

(p 32) Thursday Nov. 11 1819

Ordered by the court that the following named persons be appointed a Jury to the next Term of this court to wit

Lewis Rice
Robert Mann
Levi Jones
John Condray
Frances Patterson
Jeremiah Hunderson
Elisha Bice
William Ritter
James Williams
Isaac Bullard
Thomas Whitehed
Elijah Harp
George Ford
Wm. Gideon
And. Davis
John Hodges
Joseph Hurst
James Dobbs
John Bunch
George Shults
John Bowman
John Harris
John Carr
Martin Sharp
Manis Maddy
Emanuel Sowder

Issued

---

The State
vs
William Boyde

It ordered by the court that the Imprisonment of William Boyde be resided to ten Days and that he remain in prison till the fine and costs are paid.

(p 33) Thursday November 11th 1819

Ordered by the court that William Walles be appointed overseer of the new Road from Powells Vally to Tazewell that is to say from the forks of the Hollow below George brooks to Tazewell and have the same hands and bounds of hands heretofore allowed him in former orders

---

Ordered by the court that John Simmons Thomas Hurst Ransom Day be appointed commissioners to set apart so much of the stock crop and provisions of William Jenings Deceased as will be Suffocent to support the widdow for one year from the Death of the Deceased and make report to next court

Court adjourned untill next Term John Neil

John Evans
Jonah Ramsey
Mercuries Cook

(p 34) Monday February 14th 1820

At a court of pleas and Quarter Session began and held at the courthouse in the County of Claiborne on the Second Monday of February 1820

Present the worshipful William Graham John Evans John Huddleston John Neil John Brock George Brock John Lynch John Wallen Aaron Davis Johah Ramsey Mercureous Cook Archa Bales Alexander Campbell and John Hurst Esquires

William Savage Robert and John McClary Christopher Robinson and John H. Lea produced in open court a commission from his Excellency Joseph McMinn Governor of the state of Tennessee appointing them Justices of the peace of Claiborne County who severally took an oath to Support the constitution of the United states the constitution of the state of Tennessee and also the oath of office as and an oath more effectually to prohifet dueling Justices of the peace and thereupon took their seats

(p 35) Monday Feby 14th 1820

After makeing proclamation the court prodeeded to the Election of the court of decorum for the year 1820 and after counting and compairing the votes it appears that John Evans John Huddleston John Brock John Neil and Jonah Ramsey was duly Elected a court decorum to hold the courts of pleas and quarter sessions for thetrial of causes in the county of claiborne for the year 1820

On motion John Hodges and Elizebeth Todd are appointed as administrator and administratrix of all and Singular goods and chattels rights and credits of William Todd Deceased who was sworn as such and Entered to bond with John Hunt as their Securities in the sum of Six hundred Dollars

---

Ordered by the court a majority of the acting Justices present that John Grey be allowed fifteen Dollars for supporting Isaac Childress one of the poor of Claiborne County for the Term of Three months and that a certificate Issue - Issued Feby 24 1820

(p 36) Monday Feby. 14th 1820

John Deavenport
vs
Martin Fugate

Samuel Coffett the Security of the Defendant surrenders him in Discharge of himself as Bail and thereupon David Kain appeared in open court and acknowledged himself Indebted to the said plaintiff in the sum of two thousand Dollars void condition that the defendant in this action be cast he shall pay the cost and condemnation money or surrender himself in person or that he will pay it for him

---

On motion the court appointed Henry Lower as a constable in the bounds of Captain Henry Moyers Company who Entereds into bond in the sum of five Hundred Dollars with Peter Lower as security and thereupon was sworn as the Law Dericts

---

Ordered by the court a majority of the Justices present that Dennis Condray Sheriff of Claiborne County be allowed fifty Dollars for his Exoffices service for the year 1819

(p 37) Monday Feby. 14th 1820

Ordered by the court a majority of the acting Justices present thereby Sterling Cocke Solicitor General be allowed fifty Dollars for his Exoffice Services up to November Session 1819

Isd.

---

Ordered by the court a majority of the Justices Present that Dennis Condray Sheriff of the County of Claiborne be allowed a company credit of fifty five Dollars ninety Eight cents out of the county Tax on Delinquent Land and polls for the year 1819 as per his Return filed - which is as follows to wit

I Dennis Condry by my Deputy John Hunt do report to court that the Taxes remain due on the following polls and Tracts of Land and there is no goods and chattels whereon I came distress to make said Taxes cts.

| | cts. |
|---|---|
| Charly Payne 1 poll Tax | 60 |
| William Wilson | 60 |
| William Boyds | 60 |
| Isham Cloud | 60 |
| Thomas Jackson | 60 |
| Isaac Godfrey | 60 |
| Ambrose King | 60 |
| Elen Parton | 60 |
| Samuel Smith | 60 |

Isd.

(p 38) Monday Feby. 14th 1820

| | |
|---|---|
| William Burges | 60 |
| John Brumnets | 60 |
| John Edington | 60 |
| James Martin | 60 |

---

| | |
|---|---|
| William Buck C 500 acres of Land | $42.25 |
| Alexander Chadwell 820 acres of Land | 5.43 |

It was therefore considered by the court that Judgment be Entered up against Said owners of the Land before mentioned severally for the Taxes and costs severally Due thereon and that the clerk Issue a copy of said order and Judgment to the printer for publication and that an order of sale issue as the Law derects

Issued Feby. 23, 1820

---

Ordered by the court that Miles Hodges be appointed overseer of the Kentucky road from the top of Wallens Ridge to the big Spring in room and stead of Russel Lane and have the same hands and bounds of hands that said Lane had.

---

Ordered by the court that Isham Jennings be appointed overseer of the road from Bullards upper ferry from the old garrison to Tazewell in room and stead Joseph Jennings and have for hands the same bounds that Joseph Jennings had to wit Dickinson Jennings John Harper John Lebo and all the hands in said bounds.
Isd.

(p 39) Monday Feby 14th 1820

Ordered by the court that Ralph Shelton be appointed overseer of the Jennings ferry Road from the river hill to the Holt ford In Clinch river in room of William Jennings and have the same hands and bounds of hands Jennings had.
Isd.

---

Ordered by the court a majority of the acting Justices present that John McCarty Thomas Henderson Jeremiah Henderson Abel Lanham and William Condrey be appointed a Jury of view to view and lay out a road leading from Tazewell to Lee courthouse so as to leave out part of Robert Suthern Timber Land that the present old road now runs through and make report to next court.
Isd.

---

Ordered by the court a majority of the acting Justices present that John Neil Henry Gratner Jesse Carpenter Chistopher Robinson George Barnard Robert Graham and Sammel Dodson be appointed a Jury of view to view the Cainy Vally Road from the Kentucky road to Cocks old ferry the nearest and best way Injuring the farm of Indeviduals as little as possible and make report to next court
Isd.

(p 40) Monday Feby. 14th 1820

Ordered by the court a majority of the Justices present that John Riely Henly Fugate Enos Hobbs John Overton and Nathan Lawson be appointed a Jury of view to view and lay out part of the Lee County road leading by the plantation of Hugh Montgomery (viz) beginning at the lower end of the rob camp race paths and to Intersect the old road opposite the Dwelling house of said Montgomery and make report to next court
Isd.

---

John Whitehed Tenders to court his resignation of his appointment of constable in the bounds of Captain Henry Moyers Company which was Recived by the court

Ordered by the court a majority of the acting Justices present that John Evans be allowed to Recive of the County of Claiborne six Dollars for his services as a commissioner for four Days services in the year 1812 and 1813
Issued 24 Augst 1820

---

The assignment of a plat and certificate of survey from John Barnard to Samuel Dodson for Twenty five acres of Land was duly acknowledged in open court and ordered to be certified to the surveyor General
Isd.

(p 41) Monday Feby 14th 1820

A Deed of conveyance from Thomas Johnson and Samuel Nicholson by their attorney in fact Ashael Johnson to Joseph Cloud for one hundred acres of Land was duly acknowledged in open court admitted to record and ordered to be certified

---

A Deed of conveyance from David C. Posey to David Chadwell Sern. for Sixty two acres of Land was duly acknowledged in court by the maker thereof admitted to record and ordered to be registered

---

A Dead of conveyance from William Jones to Aaron Davis for one hundred and Eighty one acres of Land was duly acknowledged in court by the maker thereof admitted to record and ordered to be registered

---

A Deed of conveyance from Jesse Anderson to David Lay for one hundred acres of Land was Duly proven by the oath of Hardy Hughs and Thomas Anderson admitted to record and ordered to be Recorded

---

A Deed of conveyance from Thomas Anderson to Martin Miller for one hundred and twenty three acres of Land was proven in open court by the oaths of John Brock and Peter Lower admitted to record and ordered to Register

(p 42) Monday Feby 14th 1820

A Deed of conveyance from Walter Evans and John Casey to William Blackwood for one hundred acres of Land was proven by the oath of John and Isaac Bullard admitted to record and ordered to be registered

---

A Deed of conveyance from William Baily by his attorney in fact William Condrey to Zachariah Givens & Thos. Givens for six hundred and forty acres of Land was duly acknowledged in open court admitted to record

---

A Deed of conveyance from Thomas Anderson to Martin Miller for thirty acres of Land was proven by the oaths of John Brock and Peter Lower admitted to record and ordered to be Registered

---

A Deed of conveyance from James Glasgow by his attorney John Adair to William Blackwood and John Casey for one hundred acres of Land was proven by the oath of Ralph Shelton a Subscribing witness and also proven that he saw the other Subscribing Martin Bunch who is dead witnesses said Deed and that the Signature thereto belives to be the

(p 43) Monday Feby. 14th 1820

hand writing of the said Martin thereupon the same was admitted to record and ordered to be Registered

---

A Deed of conveyance from Dennis Condray sheriff of Claiborne County to John Condray for two hundred acres of Land was duly acknowledged in open court by the maker thereof admitted to record and ordered to be registered

---

A Deed of conveyance from Thomas Hopper Rhoda Hopper Jesse Hopper Betsey Hopper George Biggle and Huram Edwards to Spencer Edwards for two hundred acres of Land was duly acknowledged in open court by the makers thereof admitted to record and ordered to be Registered

---

A Deed of conveyance from John Casey and Walter Evans to John Bullard for five hundred acres of Land was proven in open court by the oaths of Isaac Bullard and William Blackwood admitted to Record and ordered to be Registered

(p 44) Monday Feby. 14th 1820

A Deed of conveyance from William Condrey to Peter Parkey for Six hundred and forty acres Land was duly acknowledged in open court by the maker thereof admitted to record and ordered to be Registered

---

A Deed of conveyance from Jacob Dobkins to John Whiteker for twenty acres of Land was proven by the oaths of Solomon Dobkins and George Campbell two Subscribing witnesses admitted to record and ordered to be Registered

---

A Deed of conveyance from Thomas Johnston by his attorney in fact Ashal Johnston to Alexander Campbell for thirty five acres of Land was duly acknowledged in open court was therefore admitted to record and ordered to be registered.

A Deed of conveyance from Isaac Cloud to William Condray for Sixty seven and one half acres of land was duly proven in open court by the oaths of Dennis Condray and Joseph McClary subscribing witnesses thereto was therefore admitted to record and was ordered to be Registered

(p 45) Monday February 14th 1820

A Deed of conveyance from George Snuffer Sheriff to John Casey for one hundred acres of land was duly proven in open court by the oaths of Dennis Condray and Reuben Rose was admitted to record and ordered to be Registered

---

A Deed of conveyance from Dennis Condray sheriff to Reubin Moss for one thousand acres of land was duly acknowledged in open court by the maker thereof was admited to record and ordered to be registered

---

A power of attorney from William Baley to William Condray was duly proven in open court by the oaths of John Condray and John Bartlet and was therefore admitted to Record and ordered to be certified for registration

---

A Bill of sale from John Wallen to Arthur L. Campbell for four negroes was duly proven in open court by the oath of John H. Lee the Subscribing witness thereto was therefore admitted to record and ordered to be certified for Registration

---

the assignment of a plat and certificate from Isaac Hobbs to Alexander Ritchie for eleven acres of land was proven in open court by the oaths of James Overton and John Condray two subscribing witnesses thereto and ordered to be certified to the surveyor General

(p 46) Monday February 14th 1820

Articles of agreement between Richard Maze and Miles Hodges was proven in open court by the oaths Joab Hill and William Hodges two subscribing witnesses thereto and ordered to be recorded at length and certified with the county seal anexed

---

Ordered by the court that the Sheriff of the county take into his custody Muslene a bastard child of which Susana Muslene has been delivered where with Joseph Jennings stand charged as the reputed father and bring the child into court on the first day of next Term to be bound out as apprentice as the law directs Isd.

---

Ordered by the court that Nelson Monday be bound an apprentice to William

Mundy attains the age of twenty one years whereupon John Evans Chairman of court of pleas and quarter sessions for said county and William Mundy interchangeably entered into Indentures according to Law

---

Ordered by the court that notice issue to Armstead Brown to Bring into court on the first day of next term Samuel Monday to be bound an apprentice as the law directs
Isd.

(p 47) Monday February 14th 1820

Court met according to adjournment

John Brock
John Neil
Wm. Savage
Josiah Ramsey
George Brock

Tuesday February the 15 1820

Court met according to adjournment Justices present in court

John Evans
John Neil
William Graham
John Huddleston
John Hurst
John Brock
William Savage
George Brock
John Lynch
John H. Lee
John Wallan
Archibald Bales
Josiah Ramsey
Alexander Campbell
Robert W. McClary
Mercurues Cook
Christopher Robinson
Luke Boyers

John Hunt Deputy Sheriff returned the venire faceas Executed on the following named Lewis Rise Robert Mann Levi Jones John Condray Francis Patterson

(p 49) Tuesday February 15 - 1820

Jeremiah Henderson
Elisha Buice
William Ritter
James Williams
Isaac Bullard
Thomas Whitehead
John Hodges
Joseph Hurst
James Dobbs
John Bunch
George Shoults
John Bowman
John Carr
Martin Sharp
Mann Maddy
Enamel Sowder
Elijah Harp

out of which venire facias the following named person was Balloted a Grand Jury to the present Term of this court who was sworn as the Law derícts and renewed their charged from the Solicitor general

X Francis Patterson F.
X John Hodges
John Harris
John Carr
X Thos. Whitehead
X Elisha Bice
X John Bowman
X Jos Hurst

John Condry X Jas Williams
Geo. Shults X Jas Dobbs
Jermy. Henderson
Isd. Feby. 24th 1820

(p 50) Tuesday February 15th 1820

After making proclamation the court proceeded to the Election of a sheriff for this county and after counting and compairing the votes it appeared that John Hunt Esquire had a majority of votes and thereupon was declared to be duly and constitutionally Elected Sheriff of this county for the Ensuing two years and entered into Bond and Security to the Satisfation of the court

——
——

After making proclamation the court proceeded to the Election of a Trustee and after counting and compairing the votes It appeared that Elias Harrison had a majority of the votes and thereupon was declared to be duly and constitutionally Elected

——
——

After makeing proclamation the court proceeded to the Election of constable in Captain Marcum Company and after counting and compairing the votes it appeared that Abraham Murphy had a majority of votes and thereupon was declared to be duly and constitutionally Elected

——
——

the court appointed Elijah Jones constable in Captain Armsted Browns Company

(p 51) Tuesday February 15th 1820

After making proclamation the court proceeded to the Election of a constable in Captain Thomas McCarty Company and after counting and compairing the votes it appeared that Absolem Hurst had a majority and thereupon was declared to be duly and constitutionally Elected -

——
——

Abner Lea a constable in Captain Browns Company Tenders his resignation which was recived and ordered to be filed

——
——

Ordered by the court that Thomas Shearmon be appointed overseer of the Road from John Hurst to the top of the ridge against David Huddleston in room and stead Briant Breeding and have the same hands and bounds of hands that said Breeding had -

——
——

Ordered by the court that Thomas Rogers be appointed overseer of the road Leeding from Tazewell to Knoxville/in room and stead of Thomas Stone and have the same part of said Road that

said Stone had from the Town to the two mile post and have the same bounds of hands said Stone had
Isd.

(p 52) Tuesday February 15th 1820

Ordered by the court that Reuben Day be appointed overseer of the road in the room and Stead of John Simmons and have the same hands and bounds of hands said Simmons had

---

Ordered by the court that John Overton be appointed overseer of the road in room and stead of Enos Hobbs and have the same hands and bounds of hands said Hobbs had

---

Ordered by the court that Peter Huffaker be appointed overseer of the road from the vally road to the Kentucky road on the top of the river hill and have for hands Lewis Huffaker William Ely and Joel Jones

---

Ordered by the court that John Jones Jesse Hurst Thomas McCarty James Poe & Peter Cotton be appointed Jury of view to veiw and Lay out a road through the lands of Absalom Hurst and make report to the next term of this court

---

Ordered by the court that Jacob Pike be appointed overseer of the State road from Powels river to Powels vally road in room and Stead of William Turner and have the same hands and bounds of hands said Turner had

(p 53) Tuesday February 15th 1820

Ordered by the court that Jesse Hurst Absalom Hurst Robert W. McClary Peter Cotton and John Cotton be appointed a Jury of view to veiw and Lay out a piece of a road Leading through Thomas McCarty land and make report to the next term of this court -

---

A Deed of conveyance Samuel Jones to Elisha Clark for forty acres of Land was duly proven in open court by the oath of Christian Plank and John Skidmore admitted to record and ordered to be registered -

---

A Deed of conveyance Dennis Condray Sheriff to Henry Sharp for one hundred and thirty five acres of land was duly acknowledged in open court was admitted to record and ordered to be registered

---

A Deed of conveyance from Abraham Hurst for thirty five acres of Land was duly proven by the oaths of Elijah Hurst and John Hurst two Subscribing witnesses thereto was admitted to record and ordered to be registered

(p 54) Tuesday February 15th 1820

A Deed of conveyance from David James to John Lynch for five hundred and fifty acres of land was proven by the oath of Jesse Daver and filed for further probate

---

A Deed of conveyance from Thomas Johnson by his attorney in fact Ashal Johnson was duly acknowledged in open court and was admitted to record and ordered to be registered

---

A deed of conveyance from John Casey and Walter Evans to Ryal Jennings for twelve acres of land was duly proven in open court by the oaths of John Bullard and Isham Jennings two Subscribing witnesses thereto was therefore admitted to record and ordered to be registered

---

A deed of conveyance from Abraham Hurst to Reuben Harper for fifteen acres of land was duly proven in open court by Elijah Hurst and John Hurst two subscribing witnesses thereto and was admitted to record and ordered to be registered.

---

A deed of conveyance from David Lynch to John Lynch one hundred and twenty four acres proven by John Bowman and filed

(p 55) Tuesday 15th Feby. 1820

A deed of conveyance from William Lane by his attorney in fact Aaron Davis to John Wallen and Elisha Wallen for four hundred and Eighteen acres of land was duly acknowledged in open court and was admitted to record and ordered to be registered

---

A deed of conveyance from James Casey to Nathan Perry for one hundred acres of land was duly proven in open by the oaths of Thomas Hill and Jesse Neil two subscribing witnesses was admitted to record and ordered to registered

---

A deed of conveyance from John Lathin to John Archer for one hundred and Eighty acres of land was duly proven in open court was admitted to record and ordered to be registered -

---

A deed of conveyance from James Casey to Benjamin Davis for fifty acres of land was duly proven by the oath of Thomas Hill and Jesse Neil two subscribing witnesses was admitted to record and ordered to be registered.

(p 56) Tuesday 15 February 1820

A Deed of conveyance from William Inglebarger to George McNeil for Seventy Eight acres of land was proven in open court by the oath of Nehemiah Hopkins and filed for further probate

—
—

A Deed of conveyance Nathaniel Davis to Daniel Coffelt was proven by the oath of John Bowman and filed

—
—

A Deed of conveyance from Elisha Clark to Jabas Hopkins fofty acres of Land was duly proven in open court by the oaths of Christian Flank and John Skidmore was admitted to record and ordered to be registered

—
—

Ordered by the court that John Sharp be appointed overseer of the Hodges ferry road in room and stead of John Hodges and have the same hands and bounds said Hodges had.

—
—

Ordered by the court that Henry Moyers be appointed overseer of the road in room and stead of George Miller and have the same hand and bounds of hands said Miller had

(p 57) Tuesday February 15th 1820

Ordered by the court that William Dokerty Alexander Ritchie Jesse Hurst Thomas McCarty and Andrew Crockett be appointed a Jury to veiw and Lay off a road from near William Dokerty to Crocketts Iron works and Cumberland Gap and make report to next court

—
—

A power of attorney from John Barnett and Polly Barnett his wife late Polly Gressum and Samuel Dodson and Elener his wife late Elener Gressum heirs and Devises of William Grissum late of Claiborne County Decd. to Dennis Condry to conevey to Robert Grissum their undived part of Six hundred acres of land whereon the said William Grissum decd. seized and possesed was acknowledged in open court by John Barnett Samuel Dodson whereupon motion of the court appointed Josiah Ramsey and John Wallen Esquires to take the private Examination of the said Polly and Elener as to their Exceeding the same freely and of their own accord who reports to court that the said Polly and Elener Execeeding the same for the purpose therein contained and without the constraint of their husband freely and of their own accord proven of atto. and report was admitted to record and ordered to be registered.

(p 58) February Tuesday 15 1820

On the petition of Robert Parks and Abel Lanham it is ordered by the court that notice issue to Mary McVey formerly now Mary Bray and Thomas Bray administrators of the estate of of Thomas McVey Deceased to appear at the next term of this court and give Security as the law directs in discharge of the said Robert Parks and Abel Langam or surrender the estate of the said Thomas McVey Dec. Isd.

---

Ordered by the court that Isaac Lane be allowed the sum of one dollar it appearing to the Satisfaction of the court that he has been overcharged therefore for the year 1819 and that the sheriff or county trustee pay the same a majority of the Justices being present Isd.

---

Ordered by the court a majority of the acting Justices being present that John Hunt be allowed four dollars and eight cents it appearing to the Satisfaction of the court that he had paid the above Same for persons who was overcharged on the tax list for the year 1819 and that the county trustee pay the same. Isd.

---

Ordered by the court that William Cary Guardian over the person and estate of Sally Nancy Daniel William and Henry Cary minor heirs of Robert Cary deceased be removed from his guardianship he having failed to render an acount to this court the said guardianship

---

A paper authorising Dennis Condray and William Hill to open and keep in repair that part of the road that passes in Virginia through the land of Martin Beaty was acknowledged,

(p 59) Tuesday February 15 1820

in open court by Martin Beaty by his attorney in fact Samuel Cogan admitted to record and ordered to be certified -

John Hodges and Elizebeth Todd adminstrators of the estate of William Todd Decd. on oath returned to court and inventory of the estate of said estate which was recived and ordered to be recorded.

John McCubbins was sworn as an officer to attend on the Grand Jury at the present term

---

Ordered by the court that Robert Suthern have leave to administer on all an Singelar the goods and chattles rights and credits of William Mason Decd. who gave bond and security and was quallefied accordingly -
Isd. Feby. 23d. 1820

---

Ordered by the court that Thomas Henderson John Hunt and Abel Langam be commissioners to allot and set apart to Matilda Mason Decd. widow and relick of William Mason Decd. so much of the crop and provesions on hands as will be suffecent to support the widow and family one year and make report to next court.

Isd.

---

Ordered by the court that the clerk Examine and ascertain what gauardian, have been appointed previous to February Session 1819 and issue a notice

(p 60) Tuesday February 15 1820

to all such guardians who have not rendered an account of their guardianship to this court and render an account of their said guardianship

---

Jesse Mullens produced to court five Justices being present the Skelp of a wolf over four months old which he proved he killed in the county of Claiborne since the year 1811 whereupon it was ordered that the sheriff burn said Skelp and that a certificate issue to the said Jesse Mullens for the sum of three being the allowance by law

Ordered by the court that John Hodges and Elizebeth Todd administrator of the estate of William Todd Deceas have leave to sell the personal estate of said estate

Isd.

---

Ordered by the court that Thomas R. McClary William Graham and John Huddleston be commissioners to lay of and allot to Elizebeth Todd widow and relick of William Todd decad so much of the crop and provisions on hand as will be suffecent to support and maintain her and the family one year and make report to next court.

Isd.

The State vs Absolom Morris } Personally appeared James Walker in open court and acknowledged himself indebted to the state of Tennessee in the sum of one hundred dollars to be levied of his goods and chattles lands and tennements but to be void on condition that the said James Walker doth make his personal appearance at the courthouse in Tazewell on

(p 61) Tuesday Feby. 1820

Wednesday after the second Monday of May next then and thereto prosecute and give evidence on behalf of the state against Absolom Morris and not depart the said court without leave acknowledged 15 February 1820

George Evans filed his petition in court praying a licence to keep an ordenary or house of public entertament at his residence in the County of Claiborne and the court being Satisfied that he is a man of good demeanor it is therefore ordered that a licence issue to him accordingly whereupon the said George Evans entered into bond with Security and was qualifed as the law directs

John Wallen
vs
John Mitchell } Attachment

The attachment having been levied on real estate and it being shewn tó the court that the defendant resides beyond the limits of this state it is ordered that said cause be continued on the docket for six months and that the defendant if convenent have notice of the Exestance of this suit.

(p 62) Court adjourned until tomorrow 9 o clock
John Evans
Isiah Ramsey
John Brock
John Neil
John Huddleston

Wednesday 16th Feby 1820

Court met according to adjournment

Anderson Whiteseds
vs
Joseph Hunt }

Rule to shew cause why the Justices proceeding Should be quashed

(p 63) Wednesday February 16th 1820

State of Tennessee

I John Bullard Ranger of Claiborne County do report to court all the money due on the stray Book up to this time as follows to wit

| | | |
|---|---|---|
| Peter Neil | X Borrow appraised | $3. |
| John Mason | 1 sow appraised to | 3. |
| John Wallis | 1 Ram appraised to | 1.50 |
| John Sanders | 1 Heifer appraised | 7.50 |
| Hardy & Campbell | 1 stear appraised to | 9.10 |
| Lewis Morris | 1 Bull appraised to | 5.10 |
| John Bartlet | 2 Barrows appraised | 4.50 |
| William Sharp | 1 Black Hog pd. to | 2.50 |

I John Bullard Ranger of Claiborne County do certifify that the above Report is true as stated

Given under my hand the 16th day of Feby. 1820

John Bullard Ranger

---

A Deed of conveyance from Thomas Grisham to Robert Grisham for fifty acres of land was duly proven in open court by the oaths of George Barnard & Pharoah Roe two subscribing witnesses thereto and was admitted to record and ordered to be registered -

(p 64) Wednesday February 16th 1820

Ordered by the court that John Bruster be appointed overseer of the Kentucky road from where the Powels vally road Intersects the same at Wallens field to the Line at Cumberland Gap in room and stead of Oliver Dodson and have the same hands and bounds of hands that said Dodson had.

Wm. Rogers
vs
Wm. Condray admr. of Alexander Southerland Decd.

On motion of the plaintiff and it appearing to the satisfaction of the court that William Rogers as the Security of Alexander Southerland paid the Sum of forty two Dollars an Execution at the Suit of Hill and McClary

It is considered by the court that said plaintiff recover of Wm. Condray administrator as aforesaid sd. sum of $42 to be levied of the goods & & of said Alexander Southerland in his hands besides the costs in this behalf Expended.

(p 65) Wednesday February 16th 1820

The State
vs
John McClary } Personally appeared in open court Mathew Bustle and acknowledged himself Indebted to the state of Tennessee in the sum of one hundred dollars to be levied of his goods and chattels lands and Tennements to be void on condition that he make his personal appearance at the courthouse in Tazewell on the first Wednesday after the second Monday in May next to prosecute and give evidense on behalf of the state against John McCrary and not depart the court without leave

---

the State
vs
John McCrary } John McCrary who was bound in Recognizance for his appearance at the present term of this court to answer the state of a charge Exhibibited against him on a bill of Indictment being Solemnly called to come into court as he was bound to do came not but wholy made default therein It was therefore considered by the court he forfeit and pay to the state that of two hundred and fifty dollars unless good cause be shewn to next term of this court

(p 66) Wednesday February 16th 1820

and that Scifa Issue

---

The State
vs
John McCrary } John Hunt who was bound as the security to bring into court the body of John McCrary being Solemnly called to bring him into court as he was bound to do wholy made default therein - It was therefore considered by the court that a forfeiture of two hundred and fifty dollars be entered up against him unless good cause be shewn to the contrary at the next Term of this court and that scifa Issue

John Wallen
vs
John Mitchell } Attach -

the attachment having been levied on Real estate and it being shewn to the court the defendant resides beyond the limits of the state it is ordered that said cause be continued on the docket for Six months and the defendant if conveniant have notice of the execution of this suit

John Deavenport
vs
David Cain } Jesse Deavers who was Security for David Cain in the above cause came into court and delivers him up in discharge of himself

(p 67) Wednesday February 16th 1820

John Deavenport
vs
David Cain } Martin Fugate and Daniel Coffelt approved in open court and undertook as Special Bail for David Cain that if he loose in this suit - they will see that he pay the condemnation money and cost or that they will pay it for him or surrender his body in person in discharge of themselves

The State
vs
Absalom Morris } Personally appeared in open open court James Walker and acknowledged Himself indebted to the state of Tennessee in the Sum of one hundred Dollars to be levied of his goods and chattels to the care of the state But void on condition he make his personal appearance on Wenesday of the next court of pleas and quarter Sessions to be holden for the County of Claiborne at the courthouse in Tazewell on the second Monday in May next then and there prosecute and give Evidence on behalf of the state on a Bill ofIndictment the state against Absalom Morris and not depart the court without leave

John Devenport
vs
Martin Fugate } David Kain and Jesse Devers appeared in open court and undertook as Special

(p 68) Wednesday February 16th 1820

Bail for the Defendants motion if he be cast in this action he will pay the condemnation money and costs or they will pay it for him or surrender his body in person in discharge of themselves as bail

George Vanbebber
vs
Wilson W. Martin } The matters in controversy in this cause and all other matters of controversy between the parties to this cause are refered to the arbitration and abatrament of and award of Marcellus Moss George Yoakum William Hagan and Moses Davis or a majority of them to be made in writing and returned to the next term of this court and when so returned their award to be made the Judgment of this court

Court adjourned until tomorrow 9 o clock

John Huddlst
John Evans
John Brock
John Neil

the State
vs
John McCrary

John Hunt appeared in open court who was bound for the defendant and Surrendered the said McCrary in discharge of himSelf - therefore it is ordered by the court that the forfeiture Set aside on payment of costs

(p 69) Thursday Feby. 16 1820

Court met according to adjournment

Thomas Boelston
vs
Wm. Acklen

Appeal

This day came the parties by their attorney and therefore came a Jury To wit -

1. Martin Sharp
2. Mann Maddy
3. Emamel Sowder
4. Lewis Morris
5. James Pitman
6. Robert Yoakum
7. Ezekel Harroll
8. Miles Hooper
9. Jesse Carpenter
10. Thos. Burges
11. Samuel Maynard
12. Andw. Hurst

who being Elected tried and sworn the truth to speak upon the matter in Despute do say they find for the plaintiff and assess his damages to Sixteen dollars and fifty cents besides costs

It was therefore considered by the court that the plaintiff recover of the defendant and John Hunt his Security said Sum of $16.50 found by the Jury besides the costs on this behalf for which Execution may Issue

(p 70) Thursday 17th Feby 1820

Samuel Dodson
vs
Thomas Grisham

Motion

On motion of Samuel Dodson and it appearing to the Satisfaction of the court that the said Samuel as the Security of said Thomas has paid an Execution at the Suit of Susannah Grisham the sum of fifty eight Dollars seventy two cts principal and sum of five Dollars seventy eight cents costs -

It was therefore considered that the said Samuel Dodson recover of Sd. Thomas Grisham said sum of fifty eight Dollars seventy two cents and the further sum of five dollars Seventy eight cents costs - and that he have execution for the Same.

Samuel Dodson
vs
Thomas Grisham

Motion

On motion of the plaintiff and it being proved to the Satisfaction of the court that the plaintiff both paid as the

(p 71) Thursday Feby. Sessions 1820

Security of the defendant of the suit of Susannah Grisham the sum of $10.10 cents principal and to be further sum of one dollar eighty seven and one half cents costs of suit

Thereupon it was considered by the court that the plaintiff on his motion recover said sum of money so paid & have Exceeded for the same -

---

William Condray administrator of the Estate Alexander Southerland deceased returned the amount of the sale of the deceased whichwas recived by the court and was ordered to be filed and recorded -

---

A Deed of conveyance from Dennis Condray sheriff of Claiborne County To William McHenry two tracts of Land was duly proven by the oaths of Hugh Graham and William Houston two Subscribing witnesses thereto and therefore was admitted to record and ordered to be registered

(p 72) Thursday February Session 1820

A Deed of conveyance from Joseph Williams by his attorney in fact Thomas L. Williams to William Condray for Six hundred acres of land was duly proven at November term by the oath of Stephen Cocke was now fully proven by the oath of Sterling Cocke the other subscribing witness and was admitted to record and ordered to be registered -

---

Abraham Murphy files his petition in court praying leave to keep an ordenary or house of public entertainment at his Residence in the Town of Tazewell and the court being Satisfied that he is a man of good demeanor it is therefore ordered that a licence issue to him accordingly thereupon the said Abraham Murphy Entered into bond with John Lynch Esqr. and Isaac Bullard his security and was qualefied as the Law derícts

---

Isaac Vanbebber and James Vanbebber Executors of the last will and testiment of John Vanbebber deceased returned into court the amount of sales of said estate which was receved by the court and ordered to be filed and recorded.

(p 73) Thursday February 17th 1820

The State
vs } Indictment
John McCrary

This day came the State by her Solecetor general Sterling Cocke and the defendant in his own proper person and being charged on the bill of indictment Submits and for plea Saith he is guilty

It was therefore considered by the court that he be fined for such his offence in the sum of two dollars and fifty cents and all costs in this behalf Expended and be in mercy & A

---

The State
vs
Robert Gibson } Indictment

Personally appeared Henry Caster and acknowledged himself indebted to the state of Tennessee in the sum of one hundred Dollars To be levied of his goods and chattels Lands and tenements but to be void on condition that he make his personal appearance at the courthouse in Tazewell on Wednesday after the 3rd Monday inApril next to prosecute and give evidence on behalf of the State against Robert Gibson on a bill of Indictment and not depart the court without leave -

(p 74) Thursday February 17th 1820

The State
vs
Robert Gibson } Indictment

Personally appeared in open court Robert Gibson and John Hunt and acknowledged themselves Indebted to the state of Tennessee in the sum of five hundred dollars that is to say the said Robert Gibson in the sum of two hundred and fifty and the said John Hunt in the sum of two hundred and fifty Dollars to be Levied of their respective goods and chattels Lands and Tenements but to be void on condition that Robert Gibson make his personal appearance at the court house in Tazewell on the first Wednesday after the 3rd Monday in April next then and there to answer the state of a charge Exhibited against him on a bill of Indictment and to a bide by and purform the Judgment of said court and not depart without leave

---

Thomas Haw assignee of Dennis Condray
vs
A. L. Campbell }

The Sheriff having returned not found on motion a Judicial attachment awarded -

(p 75) Thursday February 17th 1820

The State
vs
John Eads }

Personally appeared in open court Robert Gibson and acknowledged himself indebted to the State of Tennessee in the sum of one hundred dollars to be levied of his goods and chattels lands and Tennements But to be void on condition he make his personal appearance at the courthouse in Tazewell on the first Wednesday after the second Monday in May next to prosecute and give evidence on behalf of the State against John Eads on a charge Exhibited against him on a bill of Indictment and not depart the court without leave

The State
vs
Ezekiel Herrel } This day came the state by her Solicitor General Sterling Cocke and the Defendant in his own proper person and being charged on the bill of indictment and for plea saith he is not Guilty - and thereupon came a Jury to wit

(p 76) Thursday Feby. 1820

| | |
|---|---|
| Martin Sharp | Thomas Bridges |
| Mann Maddy | Samuel Hargraves |
| Emanuel Sowder | Andrew Hurst |
| Lewis Morris | Joseph Neil |
| James Pittman | Patrick Bray & |
| Robert Yoakum | Ralph Ford |

who being Elected tried and sworn well and truly try and the truth to speak upon the Issue of Traverse upon their oaths do say they find that the defendant Is not Guilty in manner and form as charged in the bill of Indictment

It was therfore considered by the court that the defendant go hence without day and that the county pay the costs

---

State
vs
Robert Gibson

The court in this case having sustained the Demurrer to the Bill of Indictment the state by Sterling Cocke Esquire her attorney General prays an appeal in the nature of a writ of Error to the next Cercuit Court for Claiborne County to be holden at Tazewell on the 3d Monday in April next makes his assignment of Errors whereupon said appeal is granted by the court

(p 77) Thursday February 17th 1820

Archibald Eades
vs
George Treece

this day came the defendant and filed his petition in open court praying writs of certiorari & Supersedas and the court being Satisfied therewith it is ordered that writs of certiorari Supersedas be issued whereupon the defendant gave bond and security as the law directs -

Ordered by the court that Peter Marcum be appointed commissioner to Settle with the Sheriff and trustee of this county who in the room of William Savage who gave bond Security as is by law required

Court adjourned till tomorrow 9 o clock

John Neil
John Brock
John Evans
John Huddleston

The State
vs
John Lebow
Mary Lebow

this day came the state by her Solicitor Sterling Cocke Esquire and and the defendant John Lebow and being charged on the bill of Indictment pleaded thereto guilty and confessed Judgment for himself and wife

It was therefore considered by the court that they be fined two dollars and fifty cents Each and costs

(p 78) Friday February 18th 1820

Reuben Rose
vs
William Dobbs

This day came the parties by their attornies and thereupon came a Jury to wit

| | |
|---|---|
| 1. Mann Maddy | 7. Samuel Dodson |
| 2. Emamiel Sowder | 8. Robert Mitchell |
| 3. Elijah Harp | 9. Samuel Margraves |
| 4. William Henderson | 10. Bibby Hodges |
| 5. Peter Marcum | 11. William Ritter |
| 6. Rice Whitaker | 12. James Pittman |

who upon their oaths do say They find the defendant guilty of ~~uttering~~ and publishing the word charged to have been spoken in plaintiff declaration and assess the plaintiff damages to twenty five cents therefore it was considered by the court that the plaintiff recover the damages aforesaid by the assessed and the like sum in costs and that the plaintiff pay the cost in this behalf Expended from which Judgment the plaintiff prays and appeal to the next Cercuit Court

Solomon Sailorfor Britains use
vs
Wm. Norvelle

the second plea of the Defendant with drawn by consent and the cause contimmed an affidavit of sd. defendant

(p 79) Vanbebber
vs
Vanbebber

by consent in this cause the testimoney of Charles F. Keith Esqr. is to be taken without a commission before any Justice of the peace for Jefferson County on five days notice be given to Jacob Peck Esqr. the plaintiff atto.

Ruben Rose
vs
William Dobbs

In this case the plaintiff prays an appeal to the next Cercuit Courthouse in Tazewell on the third Monday of April next files reasons gives bond & Security and the appeal is Granted

Wesley Nations
vs
George Jennings

this day came the defendant by his attorney Stephen Cocke the plaintiff being Solemly called to appear and prosecute his Suit came not but wholy made default therefore it was considered by the court the plaintiff non Suited and that the defendant recover of the plaintiff the cost in this Suit Expended for which Execution may issue

(p 80) Friday February 18th 1820

Ordered by the court that Lewis Huffacre be appointed overseer of the road from the Kentucky road to Gap Creek and to have the Same bounds for hands that the former overseer had on said Road

Ordered by the court that James Hoskins be appointed overseer of the road from Gap Creek to the ford of old town creek and to have the same bounds for hands that the former overseer had.

Preston
vs
Davis

The parties by thier attornies appearing the rule heretofore intered in this cause to quash the proceedings before the Justice and cannot being heared and the matter being fully considered and duly understood by the court the same is discharged and the rule in the above cause to dismiss the appeal is discharged by constent

(p 81) Friday February 17th 1820

The Grand and pettet Jury is discharged from further at the present Term of this court

---

A Deed of conveyance from William McConnell to Benjamin Cloud for one Lot in the Town of Tazewell of Number Sixth was duly proven in open court by the oaths of Thomas R. McClary and Anderson Barton the subscribing witnesses thereto was therefore admitted to record and ordered to be registered

---

Anderson & Whitehead
vs
Joseph Hurst

Rule to quash the Justices proceeding and now at this day the parties appeared and on argument the court were of the opinion that the proceedings of the Justices be quashed and for nothing held, and it was considered that the defendant recover of the plaintiff the costs in this behalf Expended for which Execution may issue -

(p 82) Friday Feby 17th. 1820

Stephen Hopkins
vs
John Hunt

The defendant on affidavit produced moved the court to set aside the Judgment by default entered in this case - which was opposed by the defendant attorney. But the court was of openion that that the Judgment by default should be set aside on the defendant paying the cost of this entry -

---

Ordered by the court that the following named Justices of the peace be appointed commissioners to take a list of poles and taxable property for the present year

In Captain Benjamin Davis Company John Hurst Esquire in Captain Henry Moyers Company William Savage Esqr. in Capt. Marcum Company X Wm Graham Esqr. In Captain Joseph Hurst Company John Evans. In Captain Brewers Company Christopher Robertson Esqr. In Captain Christian Flank Company Josiah Ramsey In Captain McCarty Company Robert W. McClary Esqr. In Captain A. Brown Company John Wallen Esqr.

Issued Feby. 29th 1820

(p 83) Friday February 17th 1820

In Captain Moses Davis Company John H. Lee Esquire In Captain John Rogers Company John Lynch Esquire

Ordered by the court that the following named persons be appointed Jurors to the next term of this court is as follows to wit

1. William Ely
2. William Lea
3. James Menday
4. William Hagan
5. Jesse Powers
6. Moses Willis
7. James Brasfield
8. Jacob Shoults Sen.
9. Thomas Whitmore
10. Bluford Woodall
11. William Cooper
12. Tidance Lane Junr.
13. David Huddleston
14. Dennis Condray
15. Jesse Neil
16. George Campbell
17. John Brasfield
18. Elijah Venoy
19. John Stakely
20. John Howell
21. Samuel Wilson
22. Isaac Vanbebber
23. John Rogers
24. William McNew
25. William Bowman
26. Henry Ausmus

Isd. Feb. 24 1820

The Sheriff returned to court that he let out the courthouse to the case of Abraham Murphy for the term of one year for the sum of ten dollars he being the Lowest bidder and he is bound to Keep the doors Locked and will scower the floors twice in the year and to sweep the house the first morning of each court
Isd. Feby. 28 1821

(p 84) Court adjourned untill tomorrow 10 oclock

X

John Evans
John Brock
John Huddleston
John Neil

Saturday February 17th 1820

Court met according to adjournment

A Deed of conveyance from William Rogers to Hugh Graham for one hundred acres of Land was duly proven in open court by the oaths of William Houston Abraham Murphy and Robert Mitchell the subscribing witnesses thereto and was therefore admitted to record and ordered Registered

A Deed of conveyance from John Evans to Hugh Graham for one hundred acres of Land was duly acknowledged in open court by the Bargainor was therefore admitted to record and ordered to be registered

Court adjourned to court in course

John Evans
John Huddleston
John Brock
John Neil

(p 85) Monday May 8th 1820

At a court of pleas and quarter begun and held for the County of Claiborne

at the courthouse in Tazewell on the Second Monday May 1820
Present the worshipfull

| | |
|---|---|
| John Evans | Aaron Davis |
| John Neil | Marcureus Cook |
| John Huddleston | Archibald Bales |
| John Brock | Alexander Campbell |
| John Lynch | George Brock |
| John Hurst | Christopher Robertson Esquires |

A Bill of sale from Susanah Posey and William Maddy to William Bullard for a negro girl was duly proven in in open court by the oath of Dennis Condray and William Henderson the subscribing witnesses thereto and was admitted to record and to be certified for regestration

---

Deed of conveyance from Dennis Condray to Benjamin Barney for two hundred and fifty acres of Land was duly acknowledged in open court by the bargainor and was admitted to record and ordered to be registered

(p 86) Monday May the 8 1820

Deed of conveyance from Peter Vanbebber to William Lynch for twenty seven acres of Land was duly proven in open court by the oaths of John Lynch and Jacob Vanbebber the Subscribing witnesses thereto and was admitted to record and ordered to be registered -

---

Deed of conveyance from William Lynch to Jacob Vanbebber for twenty seven acres of land was duly acknowledged in open court by the maker and was admitted to record and ordered to be Registered

---

Deed of conveyance from Hardy Hughs to Peter Lower for three hundred and fifty acres of land was duly acknowledged in open court by the maker thereof and was admitted to record and ordered to be registered

---

Deed of Relinquishment from Hardy Hughs to Peter Lower was duly acknowledged in open court by the maker thereof and was admitted to record and ordered to be registered

(p 87) Monday May 8th 1820

Deed of conveyance from Benjamin Cloud to Joseph W. Smith for thirty acres of land was duly acknowledged in open court by the maker thereof and was admitted to record and ordered to be registered

---

Deed of conveyance from William Condray to John Hurst for one hundred and thirty seven acres of Land was duly acknowledged in open court by the maker thereof and was admitted to record and ordered to be registered.

Deed of conveyance from John Casey to Jacob Cloud for three hundred acres of land was duly proven in open court by the oaths of William Wallis and John Wallis the subscribing witnesses thereto and was admitted to record and ordered to be registered

---

Deed of conveyance from Nathanel Davis to Dannel Coffett for three hundred acres of land was proven at February term by the oath of John Bowman and filed-

(p 88) Monday May 8th 1820

was at this term in full by the oath of Frederick Bowlinger and was admitted to record and ordered to be registered

---

Deed of conveyance from Thomas Atkins to Frederick Bowlinger for one hundred acres of land was duly proven in open court by the oaths of Henry Hunter and Frederick Bowlinger the subscribing witnesses thereto and was admitted to record and ordered to be registered

---

Deed of conveyance from Nethanil Davis to Frederick Bowlinger for three hundred acres of land was proven by the oath of Frederick Bowlinger and filed for further probate

---

Deed of conveyance from Frederick Bowlinger Senior to Frederick Bowlinger Junior for fifty acres of Land was duly acknowledged in open court by the maker thereof and was admitted to record and ordered to be registered

(p 89) Monday May the 8th 1820

Ordered by the court a majority of the acting Justices presant that Reuben Ford be allowed twenty dollars for Keeping Catharene Ford twelve months from the present time she being one of the poor of this county Isd.

---

Ordered by the court a majority of the Justices present that Abraham Murphy be allowed two dollars for his Services in repairing the Jail of said county Isd.

---

Ordered by the court a majority of the Justices present that Alexander Campbell Abraham Devault Michael Pearson William Russel and Thomas Hill be appointed a Jury to view and mark a Road the best and nearest way from Tazewell to the county line or greasy Rock Creek to the end of the Hawkins road and make report to the next term of this court
Isd.

(p 90) Monday May 8th 1820

Ordered by the court a majority of the Justices present that Daniel Hopson and Ann Hopson be allowed thirty one dollars for supporting Dianni Harp one of the poor of this county for the term of one year -

Isd.

---

Ordered by the court that Jubal Lee be appointed overseer of the road from Town creek to Wyatts Mill by Thomas Lees in room and stead of William Wilson and have the same hands and bounds of hands that said Wilson had.

Isd.

---

We the commissioners appointed by court to lay out and Set apart so much of the stock and provesions of the Estate of William Mason decd. as will be Sufficient to support the widow for the term of one year do report that she be allowed fifteen bushels of corn and one hundred pounds of pork 25 pounds of salt given under our hands this 29th day February 1820

John Hunt Abel Lanham
Thos. Henderson

(p 91) Monday May the 8th 1820

John Hunt Sheriff of Claiborne County returned into court the list of the time of handing out Road orderes as follows to wit

to John Overton March the 20th 1820
to Henry Moyers March 23rd 1820
to Thomas Shearmen March 22nd 1820
to Reuben Day March 4th 1820
to Ralph Shelton March 4th 1820
to Miles Hodge March 4th 1820

---

Ordered by the court that Joseph Webb be appointed overseer of the new Road from the Island ford on powels River to a point at the forks of the hollow below George Brocks as viewed and marked in Room and Stead of Jacob Cloud and have the same hands and bounds of hands said Cloud had

---

Ordered by the court that Thomas Whitehead be appointed overseer of the Road beginning at the forks of the lonesome valley below Samuel Cloud to Williams Wallens and have for hands James Brock John Wallis William Wallis Junr. and John Ashley

(p 92) Monday May 8th 1820

We the Jury of review report that we have viewed and marked a road through Thomas McCartys land agreeable the order of February term 1820

Robert W. McClary Jesse Hurst Absolom Hurst John Cotton Peter Cotton
April 29th 1820

---

James Maddy a constable for the County of Claiborne hereby tenders to court of pleas and quarter sessions his resignation and prays them to accept thereof which was recived by the court accordingly

———

———

Ordered by the court that Silas Williams Esqr. Henry Hunter and William Bowman be appointed commissioners to settle with William Cary Executor of Robert Carey deceased any two of whom may act and report to next court Isd.

———

———

On motion Joab Brewer was appointed constable in Captain Brewers Company who gave bond and Security as the Law dericts and was qulified accordingly

(p 93) Monday May 8th 1820

Ordered by the court a majority of the Justices present that Tidance Lane be allowed the sum of twelve dollars for Keeping in the common Jail of said county William Boyde and Bennett Arnold heretofore commited by sentance of the County Court and that a certificate Issue for the same Isd.

———

———

John Turner produced in open court the Scalps of two wolves and was sworn that he Killed said wolves within the confirms of Claiborne County Since the Year 1811 and that the said wolves was over four months old

It is therefore ordered by the court five Justices present that he be allowed to recive of the Treasure of East Tennessee three dollars per each sculp
Isd.

———

———

Joseph Turner produced in open court the scalp of a wolf and was sworn that he killed said wolf within the confirms of Claiborne County Since the year 1811 and that the said wolf was over four months old

It is therefore ordered by the court five Justices present that he be allowed to recived of the Treasurer of East Tennessee three dollars
Isd.

(p 94) Monday May 8th 1820

John Hurst John H. Lee Robert W. McClary and Christopher Robinson Esquires who was appointed commissioners at the last term of this court to take lists of the Taxable property and poles in Claiborne County returned their Lists which was recived by the court and ordered to be filed and recorded in tax bok.

———

———

John Hodges administrater and Elizebeth Todd administratrix of the Estate of William Todd Deceased returned into court the amount of sales of said estate which was recived by the court and ordered to be filed and recorded

———

———

Ordered by the court that the order made at the last term of this court

Ordered by the court a majority of the acting Justices present that a Boy child by the name of Malin Fields about two years old be bound an apprentice to Elisha Collens until he attain to the age of twenty one years to which Indentures was Entered into accordingly

---

Ordered by the court that the order made at the last term of this court for the sheriff this county to bring into court Musteen a feemale bastard child of which Susanna Musteen has been delivered where with Joseph Jennings Stands charged as the reputed father be renewed and that a capias Issue returnable to the next term of this court

(p 95) Monday May 8th 1820

Ordered by the court a majority of the acting Justices present that John Evans John Huddleston and Aaron Davis be appointed commissioners of the poor of this county

---

John Scrichfield
vs } certiorari
James Maddy

This day came James Maddy and presented his petition to court praying writs of certiorari and Superodeas where upon it is considered by the court that said writs issue accordingly to the prayer of said petition upon the defendants giving bond and security as the law directs which is done accordingly

---

Ordered by the court a majority of the Jystices present that the prayer of Sundry citizens of Claiborne County praying for an altration in the Lea Road be granted and that the said road be altered and estableshed as follows vis - leaving the old road at a tree marked R. and a small peace of new ground belonging to Robert Southern passing round said new ground and interesecting the old road at a tree marked S - and that the same henceforth be considered as the public road of said county

(p 96) Monday May 8th 1820

Court adjourned until tomorrow morning 9 oclock

John Evans
John Huddleston
John Neil
John Brock

Tuesday May 9th 1820

Court met according to adjournment

John Wallen
vs } Original attachment
Hugh White

This day came the defendant and by his attorney presented his petition praying the court to grant him writs of certiorari and Supersedeas in this cause which is granted by the court on the defendant giving bond and Security as the law directs which is done accordingly and the property levied on by said attachment is replevied -

(p 97) Tuesday May 9th 1820

William Norvelle
vs } Original attachment
William Owens

Roger Ferrell who was Summoned as a Guarnishee in this cause first being duly sworn, on oath makes the following Statement to wit

That he owes the Defendant one hundred bushels of corn at two Shillings pr busshel due on the first day of May one thousand eight hundred twenty

He further States that there is in the hands of Isaac Sharp of Knox County Kentucky Ten dollars and fifty cents as he belives

Further that there is in the hands of Mathew Owens Same amount But he does not know what and that Boston Graves owes the defendant by note about three hundred dollars as he has understood and further saith not

(p 98) Tuesday May 9th 1820

Solomon Sailor
George Brittain
vs } Debt & Damage
William Norvell

this day came the parties by their attorneys and thereupon came a Jury to wit - John Rogers, William McNew, John Lyford, Robert Grisham, James Hill, William Hill, William Renfro, Rice Whitaker, John Whitaker, Ezekiel Mink, Pearson Barney and Henry Ozmus who being elected, tried and sworn well and truly to try the issue joined upon their oaths do say they find that the defendant hath not paid the debt in the declaration, and assess the plaintiffs damage by reason of the detention thereof to seventy seven dollars and thirty two cents - wherefore it is considered by the court that the plaintiff recover of the defendant the sum of two hundred and thirty two dollars the debt in the declaration mentioned, and also the sum of seventy seven dollars the damages by the Jury assessed as aforesaid and also his costs by him about his Suit in this behalf Expended and the defendant in mercy & & From which Judgment defendant prays an appeal

(p 99) Tuesday May 9th 1820

Ordered by the court that Jacob Branson be appointed overseer of the road leading from Bullards upper ferry to Tazewell from the ferry to the old garrison in room and stead William McBee and have the Same hands and bounds of hands said McBee had

---

Whereas an order of review was granted at February Term 1820 and a Jury appointed to lay of a road from near William Dohertys on Mulberry to Crocketts Iron works and Cumberland Gap and it appearing that said Jury did not attend therefore it is ordered by the court that Alexander Ritchie Gidian Faris, Philip Chance Andrew McClary Jesse Hurst Absalom Hurst Andrew Crocket Thomas Martin and John Jones be appointed a Jury of veiw to mark and lay of said road make report to the next term of this court

---

A power of attorney from Christian Plank to Dennis Condray was duly acknowledged in open court by the maker thereof and was admitted to record and ordered to be certified for registration

(p 100) Tuesday May 9th 1820

The court after making proclamation proceeded to the election of a constable in the bounds of Captain Moses Davis Company and after counting and compairing the votes it appeared that John Carr was duly and constionally elected who entered into Bond and security, and was sworn as the law derects -

---

Personally appeared in open court William Cary minor heir and orphan of Robert Cary Deceased and being of the age of fourteen years was admitted to choose his guardian and thereupon choose Harden Cary who entered into bond and Security to the Satisfaction of the court

---

On motion James Walker was appointed guardian to Nancy Cary minor heir and orphan of Robert Cary Deceased who entered into Bond and Security to the Satisfaction of the court

---

A Deed of Relinquishment from Barton Ely and Solomon Ely for their undevided part of a Tract of land was duly acknowledged in open court by the Bargainor and admitted to record and ordered to be registered

(p 101) Tuesday May 9th 1820

A Deed of conveyance from thomas McCarty to James Walker was duly acknowledged in open court by the maker thereof and was admitted to record and ordered to be registered

---

Agreeable to an order of February Session 1820 - We the Jury have met and lade out a road through Absalom Hursts land agreeable to the above mentioned ordered April the 29th 1820

Jesse Hurst — John Evans
James Poe — Absalom Hurst
Peter Cotton

---

It is ordered by the court that the above report be confirmed

---

In obediance to an order of court made at February Session 1820 directing us to review and mark a part of the Lee road agreeable to the petition of Hugh Montgomery

We the under Signers do report that we find a road agreeable to the petition given under our hand this 28th day of April 1820

John Riley — Enos Hobbs
Henly Fugatt — Report confirmed — John Overton

(p 102) Tuesday May 9th 1820

Robert Southern administrator of William Mason Deceased returned into court and ordered to be filed and recorded

---

John Hunt Sheriff of Claiborne County returned in court the venire facias Executed on the following named persons to wit

| | |
|---|---|
| William Ely | Dennis Corndry |
| William Lea | Jesse Neil |
| James Munday | George Campbell |
| William Hagan | John Brassfield |
| Jesse Powers | Elijah Vency |
| Moses Willis | John Stokley |
| Jacob Sheults Senr. | John Howell |
| Thomas Whitmore | Samuel Wilson |
| Bleuford Woodall | Isaac Vanbebber |
| William Cooper | John Rogers |
| Tidance Lain Jr. | William McNew |
| David Huddleston | William Bowman |
| | Henry Osmus |

out of which venire the following named persons were balloted a grand Jury -

| | |
|---|---|
| X 1. William Bowman foreman | 7. X Bleuford Woodall |
| X 2. Jesse Neil X | 8. X Jacob Shoults |
| X 3. William Lee | 9. X Samuel Wilson |
| X 4. John Brassfield | 10. X John Howell |
| X 5. Tidance lane Jr. X | 11. X Thomas Whitmore |
| X 6. Isaac Vanbebber | 12. X William Ely & |
| | 13. X David Huddleston |

who were severally sworn recived their charge and retired -

(p 103) Tuesday 9th May 1820

Ordered by the court that Stephen Cocke Esqr. be appointed Solicitor Genl. protem for Claiborne County for May Session 1820 the solicitor Genl. being absent

John M. Preston
vs
Aaron Davis } this day came the parties by by their attornies and thereupon also came a Jury to wit John Rogers, William McNew, John Lyford, Robert Grisham, James Hill, William Hill, William Renfro, Rice Whitaker John Whitaker Ezekel Morris Pearson Barney and Eli McVey who being elected tried and sworn well and truly to try and the truth to speak on the matter in controversy between the parties upon their oaths do say they find for the plaintiff ten dollars besides his cost.

Therefore it is considered by the court that the plaintiff recover of the defendant the sum of ten dollars in form aforesaid by the Jury assed together with his cost in this behalf Expended and the defendant in mercy & & from which Judgment the defendant prays an appeal to the next cercuit court to be holden for the County of Claiborne County at the courthouse in tazewell on the third Monday of October next files reasons

Henry Carter
vs
Robert Gipson } on motion of the plaintiff by

his attorney a rule is Granted him to shew cause why the writs of certiorari and Supersedeas should be dismissed

(p 104) Tuesday 9 May 1820

David Chadwell vs William Hunt } This day came the plaintiff in open court and dismissed his Suit Therefore it is considered by the court that the defendant go hence and recover of the plaintiff his cost in this behalf Expended and the plaintiff in mercy & &

John Wallen & & vs Isaac Sharp appl. } this day came the plaintiff in open court and by his attorney dismisses his suit Therefore it is considered by the court that the defendant go hence and recover of the plaintiff his cost in this behalf expended and the plaintiffin mercy & &

John Lyford vs Jacob Vanbebber and wife } This cause comeing on to be heared the rule to quash the proceeding before the Justices in this cause and argument of counsil being heard as well in Support of said rule as against it and the matter and things therein contained being duly considered and fully understood by the court it is considered by the court that said rule be Sustaned that the preceeding in this cause before the Justice be quashed and that the plaintiffs recover of the defendant their cost in this suit by them Expended and the defendant in mercy & &

William Sparks vs Jesse Powers } this day came the plaintiff in his proper person in open court and dismisses his Suit Therefore it is considered by the court that the defendant go hence and recover of the plaintiff his cost in this Suit Expended and the plaintiff in mercy & &

(p 105) Tuesday May 9th 1820

John Deavenport vs Martin Fugate } This day came the parties by their attornes and thereupon came a Jury to wit George Campbell, Andrew Jenning Squree Hunter, Daniel Coffett, William Barnwell, Jacob Vanbebber, John Whitacre Joseph Cloud, John Rice, William Ritter George Vanbebber and Jesse Hurst who being elected tried and sworn well and truly to try and the truth to speak on the matter of constrovary between the parties upon their oaths do say they find for the plaintiff one dollar and twenty five cents

Jonas Longhmiller vs Burrel Sullevant } Motion

This day came the plaintiff by Stephen Cocke Esqr. his attorney and Joab Brewer one of the constables of Claiborne County having made his return to court that he had levied on ten acres of land belonging to the defendant lying in the Mulberry Gap on Powels Mountain adjoining Levy Long and George Gipson & & to Satisfy a Judgment of thirty one dollars and Sixty two and one half cents and seventy five cents cost which the said Jonas Longhmiller recovered against the said Burrel Sullevants before Alexander Campbell Esqr. one of the acting Justices of the peace for Claiborne County and on motion and for reasions appearing to the Satisfaction of the court it is ordered by the court that an order of sale issue to the Sheriff commanding him to Expose to sale and sell the land levied on to satisfy the said Jonas his Debt and cost aforesaid and it is further considered by the court that the said Jonas Longhmiller recover of the

(p 106) Tuesday May 9 1820

Said Durrel Bullemants the cost of this motion & &

John Devanport )
vs certoa. ) it is considered by the court
Martin Fugate ) that the plaintiff in this cause
recover of the defendant and John Cary his security the sum of one dollar and twenty five cent in manner and form by the Jury assessed for which execution may issue together with the costs in this behalf expended

John Devenport ) On motion of the Debt by his
vs ) attorney it is considered by the
David Cain ) court that the plaintiff give
other and sufficent security for the prosecution of this Suit at the present term of this court or that this suit Stand dismissed -

Court adjourned until tomorrow morning 9 oclock John Huddleston
John Evans
John Neil
Josiah Ramsey
John Brock

With leave of the court Sarah Claxton was admitted to administer on all and Singular the goods and chattels rights and credits of William Hullons Deceased who Entered into bond with Josiah Ramsey for her security and was qualified as the Law directs.

(p 107) Wednesday May 10th 1820

Court met according to adjournment

A majority of the acting Justices of the peace being present it is ordered by the court that Pearson Barney be allowed the sum of fifteen dollars and fifty cents for keeping and supporting Elizebeth Franklin Six months immediately proceeding the present time she having been one of the poor of the county.
Isd.

A majotity of the acting Justices being present it is considered and ordered by the court that Pearson Barney be allowed the sum of thirty one dollars for keeping and supporting Elizebeth Franklin twelve months from the present date, she being one of the poor of Claiborne County
Isd. 6th June 1820

John Anthony )
vs ) Original attachment
Arthur L. Campbell )
Ordered by the court that all further proceedings in this cause be

stayed for the Term of Six months.

(p 108) Wednesday May 10 1820

The Excutors of the last will and Testement of Obedeah Martin Deceased Returned into court an Inventory of said Estate which was recived by the court and filed and ordered to be recorded

---

Susannah Posey presented to court a petition praying leave to Keep an ordinary or house of public Intertainment in said county who intered into Bond and security to the Satisfaction of the court and was sworn as the Law directs

(p 109) Wednesday May 10th 1820

Ordered by the court John Neil Joab Hill and John Simmons be appointed commissioners to make a final Settlement with the administrators of Martin B Bunch deceased and make report to the next term of this court -

---

William Savage who was appointed a commissioner to take a list of Taxable property and poles in the bounds of Captain Moyers Company for the year 1820 returned his list which was recived by the court and filed

---

Elijah Jones a constable for Claiborne County tenders to court his resignation on which was recived by the court and ordered to be filed

---

And on motion the court appointed William Fly a constable in the bounds Armsted Browns Company who gave Bond and security to the Satisfaction of the court and was qualiefed.

---

Ordered by the court that John Bowman be appointed overseer of the road leading up and down powels valley begining at the ford of the branch below James Rogers and from that up to the haw branch and have the hands that Solomon Lewis when overseer of said road

(p 110) Wednesday May 10th 1820

William Graham who was appointed commissioner to take lists of Taxable property and poles in Captain Marcums Company returned his list which was Recived by the court and ordered to be filed

---

Deed of Conveyance from William Ritter to Isaac Sanders for fifty acres of land was duly acknowledged in open court by the make thereof and was admitted to record and ordered to be registered -

State vs Absalom Morris — Personally appeared in open court Absalom Morris and Thomas Lee and acknowledged themselves indebted to the state of Tennessee in the sum of two hundred and fifty Dollars to the use of the state to be levied of their respective goods and chattels land and tenements that is to say one hundred and twenty five Each to be void on condition that Absalom Morris make his personal appearance at the courthouse

(p 111) Wednesday May 10th 1820

in Tazewell on the wednesday after the second Monday of August next then and thereto abide by and purform the sentance of the court and not depart without leave

---

State vs Absalom Morris — Personally appeared in open court James Walker and acknowledged himself indebted to the State of Tennessee in the sum of one hundred and twenty five dollars for the use of the State to be levied of his respective goods and chattels lands and tenements to be void on condition that he make his personal at the courthouse in Tazewell on the first Wednesday after the second Monday of August next then and there to prosecute and give evidence on behalf of the State against Absalom Morris and not depart the court without leave

(p 112) Wednesday May 10th 1820

Susannah Posey admr. & & vs Brice M. Mayfield & others

Ordered by the court that a capias to Issue to Giles County for Brice M. Mayfield

State vs Elijah Claiton Thomas Collens — the defendant in this cause being Solemenly called to come into court as they was bound to do came not but wholy made default therein therefore it is considered by the court that they forfeit and pay the sum of five hundred dollars unless they Shew suffecent cause to the contrary by the next term of this court and that Secirifacias Issue for them to shew cause & &

State vs Robert Gibson — this day came the state by the Solecetor genl. and the defendant in his proper person and being charged on the Bill of indictment pleads thereto not guilty and puts himself on the county and the Solicitor doth the like whereupon came a Jury to wit John Rogers, Nethemiah Hopkins Rice Whitacre, James William Almon Johnson, Lewis Rice Squire Hunter, Martin Fugett John Bundon, Andrew Johnson, Mitchell Hendricks & Ransom Day who being elected tried and sworn well and truly to try the issue of Traverse upon their oaths do say the find the defendant guilty in manner and form as charged on the bill of indictment therefore it is therefore considered by the court that the defendant for this his offence be fined fifty cents and that he pay the cost in this cause Expended for which execution may issue (p 113) Wednesday May 10th 1820

The State
vs
John Clayton

This day came the state by her solicitor and the defendant Solomly called to bring into court the bodies of Elijah Clayton and Thomas Collens as he was bound to do this day brought them in not but wholy made default Therefore it is considered by the court that the said defendant forfeit and pay to the state the sum of five hundred dollars his recognizance unless he shews suffecent cause to the contrary by the term of this court and that Scirefacias issue -

A paper porporting to be the last will and testament of Obediah Martin deceased was duly proven in open court by the oaths of Thomas McCarty Jesse Hurst and John Colner the subscribing witnesses thereto who swore that they saw the said Obediah Martin Sign Seal publish and declare the same to be his last will an testament that the will was executed the time it bears date that they were called upon by the said Obediah Martin and his presence did witness the same and that the said Obediah Martin was of Sound mind and desposing memory at the time of executing the same

Elizebeth Martin Maron Martin and John Martin the executors appointed by the last will and testament of Obediah Martin decd. came into court and took up on themselves the execution of said will gave bond and security and qullefid as the law directs.

(p 114) Wednesday May 10th 1820

The State
vs
Jacob Shoults

This day came the state by the solicitor and the defendant in his proper person and the Solicitor entered a noleprosequi and the defendant confesses Judgment for the cost in this behalf expended -

therefore it is considered by the court that the defendant be discharged from his recognizance and that the state recover of the defendant the cost in this behalf expended in manner and form aforesaid confessed for which execution may issue

The State
vs
Pearson Barney

this day came the state by her solicetor and the defendant in his proper person and on motion of the defendant by his attorney it is considered by the court that the defendant be henceforth discharged from his recognizance and it is also considered by the court that William McNew the prosecutor be taxed with the cost in this behalf expended for which execution may issue -

The State
vs Indictment
Pearson Barney

This day came the state by her Solictor and the defendant in his proper person and the defendant being charged on the bill of indictment pleads thereto not guilty and puts himself on the county and the Solicitor doth the like and thereupon came a Jury to wit Elijah Hurst, Martin Fugate, Ralph ford, Jacob Vanbebber Coventon Collensworth, Reuben Harper Armsted Brown Thomas Norvell James Ellison, Caleb Dobbs, William Hunt Henry Caster who being elected tried and sworn well and truly try and the truth to speak on the issue of traverse upon their oaths do say they find the defendant not guilty in manner and form as charged in the bill of indictment Therefore it is considered by the court that the defendant forever be henceforth discharged from this prosecution and on motion it is considered by the court that William McNew the prosecutor pay the cost in this behalf expended for which execution may issue

(p 115) Wednesday 10th May 1820

State
vs
John Eades

Pearsonally appeared in open court Robert Gibson and acknowledged himself indebted to the state of Tennessee in the sum of one hundred and twenty five dollars for the use of the state to be levied of his respective goods and chattels lands and tennements but to be void on condition that he make his personal appearance before the Justices of our court of pleas and quarter Sessions to be holden for the county of Claiborne at the courthouse in Tazewell on the Wednesday after the Second Monday of August next then and there to prosecute and give evidence on be half of the state against John Eades and not the court without leave -

William Norvell
vs
William Owens

Boston Graves a Garnishee in this States that that the fall of 1818 he gave his note to William Owens for three hundred dollars to be paid in current bank notes due on the first of May 1820 he knows not who now has the possission of said note that he has not paid any part thereof he also states that when said Owens went awah he agreed with him to pay him Owens for any of his hogs that might return such twice as they might be valued at by any two good men that three of said hogs did return and were valued by Isaac Yoakum and Roger Ferrel to ten Dollars and fifty cents which five other pigs a three shillings and Six pence each which moved to

(p 116) Wednesday May 10,1820

Owens or Charles Royal who had made a Kind of contract with Owens for the hoggs before he Owens moved away

Roger Ferrell got some corn which is not yet paid for or as beleved and Mathew Owens he thinks got some corn whether paid for or not he does not know-

The State
vs
William Maddy
Benjamin Lankford

This day came the state by the Solicitor and the defendants in their proper person and being charged on the bill of indictment plead thereto guilty and submits to the court whereupon it is considered by the court that the defendants for this their offence be fined the sum of two dollars and fifty cents each and it is further considered by the court that the State recover of the defendants the cost in this behalf expended and the defendants in mercy & &

The State
vs
William Maddy
Joseph Cloud

this day came the state by her Solecitor and the defendants in their proper person and sever in their pleading and insist on being tried Separately - therefore it is considered by the court that the defendants be permitted to plead Separately and that they be tried tried separately

The State

vs ) this day came the state by her
William Maddy ) Solecitor and the defendant as his Separate plea in the cause of the state against William Maddy and Joseph Cloud for plea to the Bill of indictment pleads guilty and Submits to the court

Therefore it is considered by the court that for this his offence the defendant be fined the sum of two dollars and fifty cents - and that the pay the cost in this behalf expended to be in mercy & &

(p 117) Wednesday May 10 1820

The State
vs
Joseph Cloud

This day came the state by her solecitor and the defendant in his proper person for his Separate plea to the bill of Indictment against William Maddy and Joseph Cloud pleads thereto not guilty and puts himself on county and the Solecitor Genl. doth the like and thereupon came a Jury to wit William McNew, Elisha Buice, William Henderson, Lewis Bice, John Whitacre, Joseph Bullard, John Bice Timothy Filpot, Mitchell Hendrick, William Ritter, Joshua Foster, Christian Plank who be lectred and sworn well and truly to try the issue of traverse the examination of this cause not being concluded the Jurors are respited until tomorrow

The State
vs
David Cain

Personally appeared in open court David Cain, Timothy Filpot and Jesse Devers and severally acknowledged themselves indebted to the state of Tennessee in the sum of four hundred dollars for the use of the state to be levied of their respective goods and chattels land and tenements that is to say David Cain in the sum of two hundred dollars and Timothy filpot and Jesse Devers in the sum of one hundred dollars each to be void on condition that David Cain make his personal appearance at the courthouse in Tazewell on the Wednesday after the second Monday of August next and then there to abide by and purform the sentance of the court and not depart the court without leave

(p 118) Wednesday ~~10th~~ May 10th 1820

The State
vs
David Cain

Personally appeared in open court John Deaveport and acknowledged himself indebted to the state of Tennessee in the sum of one hundred dollars to the use of the state to be levied of his goods and chattles lands and tennements to be void on condition that he make his personal appearance at the courthouse in Tazewell on the Wednesday after the second Monday of August next then and there to prosecute and give Evidence on behalf of the state against David Cain and not depart the court the court without leave

The State
vs
David Cain

personally appeared in open court John Deavenport and acknowledged himself indebted to the state of Tennessee in the sum of one hundred dollars to the use of the state to be levied of his respective goods and chattels Land and tennements but to be void on condition that Isom Devenport make his personal appearance at the courthouse in Tazewell on the second Monday of August next then and there to give evidence on behalf of the state against David Cain on a bill of indictment and not depart the court without leave

(p 119) Wednesday May 10th 1820

The State
vs
David Cain
) This cause is considered as on the affidavit of the Defendant until the next term of this court and the Defendant being charged on the bill of Indictment pleads not guilty

The State
vs
Jesse Devor
) This day came the state by the Solicitor and the defendant in his proper person and being charged on the bill of indictment pleads thereto not guilty and puts himself on the county and the Solicitor doth the like and for reasons appearing to the Satisfaction of the court on the affidavit of the defendant this cause is continued until the next term of this court

Court adjourned until tomorrow morning 9 oclock John Neil
John Brock
John Evans
John Huddleston
JosiahRamsey

(p 120) Thursday May 11th 1820

Court met according to adjournment present the Worshipful John Evans John Huddleston, John Neil, John Brock, Josiah Ramsey,

The State
vs
Joseph Cloud
) this day came the state by her Solecitor genl. and the defendant in his proper person and there upon came the same Jury who was respited from rendering their verdict on yesterday and upon their verdict on yesterday and upon their oaths do say they find the defendant not guilty in manner and form as charged in the bill of Indictment

Therefore it is considered by the court that the defendant go hence discharged on motion a rule is Granted to shew cause why the defendant should be taxed with the cost and on argument of council it is considered by the court that said rule be discharged and that the County of Claiborne pay the cost in this prosecution expended for which tickets may issue -

The State
vs
Philip Coffelt
) This day came the state by her Solecitor and the defendant being Solemly called to come into court and answer a charge the state has Exhibited against him came not but wholy made default therefore it is considered by the court that the said defendant forfiet and pay the state of tennessee the sume of two hundred dollars unless he shew suffecent cause to the contrary by the next term of this court and that scirefaceas issue

(p 121) Thursday May 11th 1820

The state
vs
Daniel Coffelt
) This day came the state by the solecitor and the defendant being called to bring into court the body of Philip Coffelt as he was bound to do this day brought him not but wholy

made default therefore it is considered by the court that the defendant forfeet and pay to the state of Tennessee the sum of two hundred dollars his forfeeted recognizance unless he shew cause to the contrary by the next term of this court and that Scirefaceas issue

Isd.

The State } This day came the State by her
vs } Solicitor and the defendant
Jacob Coffelt } being Solemly called to come into court and answer a charge the state had exhibited against him came not but wholy made default therefore it is considered by the court that the state recover of the defendant the sum of two hundred dollars his forfeeted recogniance unless he shew suffecient cause to the contrary by the next term of this court and that a Scirefacias issue

Isd.

The state } This day came the state by her
vs } solecitor and the defendant
Daniel Coffelt } being solemly called to bring into court the body of Jacob Coffelt as he was bound to do this day brought him not but wholy made default therefore it is considered by the court that the said defendant forfeet and pay two hundred dollars his forfeeted recognisence unless he shew suffecent cause to the contrary by the next term of this court and that scirefaceas issue

Isd.

(p 122) Tuesday May 11th 1820

The state } This day came the state by her
vs } solecitor and the defendant being
John Cary } solemly called to come into court and answer a charge the state had exhibited against him came not but wholy made default therefore it is considered by the court that the defendant forfeet and pay the sum of two hundred dollars his forfeeted recognizance unless he shew sufficent cause to the contrary by the next term of this court and that Scirefacias issue

Isd.

The state } This day came the state by
vs } her solecitor and the defendant
Rubin B. Rogers } being solemly called to bring into court the body of of John Cary as he was bound to do this day brought him not but wholy made default - Therefore it is considered by the court that the said Defendant forfeet and pay to the state the sum of two hundred dollars his forfeeted recognizance unless he shew Suffecent cause to the contrary by the next term of this court and that a Scirefacias issue -

Isd.

The State } Personally appeared in open
vs } court Jesse Devor and Martin
Jesse Devor } Fugate and acknowledged themselves indebted to the state of Tennessee in the sum of one hundred dollars each to be to be levied of their respective goods and chattles lands and and tennements but to be void on condition that the said Jesse Devor make his personal appearance at the courthouse in Tazewell on the Wednesday after the

second Monday of August next then and thereto answer a charge the state has exhibited against him and not depart the court without leave -

(p 123) Thursday May 11th 1820

The State
vs
Jesse Devor

Personally appeared in open court John Devenport and acknowledged himself indebted to the state of Tennessee in the sum of one hundred dollars to be levied of his goods and chattles lands and tennements but to be void on condition that the said John Devenport shall make his personal appearance before the Justices of our court of pleas and quarter sessions to be holden for the County of Claiborne at the courthouse in Tazewell on the Wednesday after the second Monday of August next then and there to prosecute and give evidence on behalf of the state against Jesse Devor and not depart the court without leave

Henderson Beaty & Hagan & &
vs
Armsted Brown

John Hunt came into court and broght the body of the defendant in discharge of himself whereupon it is considered by the court that the defendant be in the custody of the Sheriff

(p 124) Thursday May 11th 1820

Ordered by the court that the following named persons be appointed Jurors to the next Circuit Court wo wit

1 Fielding Lewis
2 William Stallings
3 Thomas Gowing
4 Alexander Bales
5 Archibald Bales
6 Lipscomb Parrott
7 Martin Miller
8 Hardy Hughs
9 Elijah Hurst
10 John Neil
11 William McCullough
12 John H. Lee
13 Joab Hill
14 Aaron Davis
15 Edward Rily
16 John Bruster
17 Jacob Pike
18 John Berry
19 George Sharp Jnr.
20 Jesse Devors
21 John Dokerty
22 Jacob Cloud
23 Thomas Berry
24 James Brock
25 John McCarty
26 Edward Jennings

(p 125) Thursday May 11th 1820

Ordered by the court that the following named persons be appointed Jurors to next term of this court to wit

1 Willis Harper
2 Joseph Lanham
3 Charles Shearmon
4 Alexander Bales
5 Archibald Bales
6 Lipscomb Parrott
7 Martin Miller
8 Hardy Hughs
9 Elijah Hurst
10 John Neil
11 William McCullough
14 Samuel Rogers
15 James Lemar
16 John Bruster
17 Jacob Pike
18 John Berry
19 George Sharp Jnr.
20 Jesse Devors
21 John Dokerty
22 Jacob Cloud
23 Thomas Berry
24 James Brock

12 John H. Lee
13 Joah Hill
25 John McCarty
26 Edward Jennings

(p 125) Thursday May 11th 1820

Ordered by the court that the following named persons be appointed Jurors to next term of this court to wit

1 Willis Harper
2 Joseph Lanham
3 Charles Shearmon
4 John Thompson
5 Uriah Gowing
6 Elijah Hurst
7 Bryant Breeding
8 Nehemiah Hopkins
9 Martin Conner
10 Archibald Cooper
11 Thomas Givens
12 Ralph Hatfield
13 John McCollom
14 Samuel Rogers
15 James Lemar
16 Benjamin Pike
17 Andrew Smith
18 William Jackson
19 William Jinkins
20 Christopher Huffaker
21 Solomon Fly
22 James Cadle Jnr.
23 Drury Herrell
24 Ralph Shelton
25 James Hopson
26 John Condray

---

Stephen Hopkins vs John Hunt } This day came the parties by their attorney and thereupon also came a Jury to wit George Campbell Abel Lanham, William Maddy, James Bunch, Edward Harper, Robert Mitchell, Elijah Hurst Jacob Shoults, Alfred Lynch Timothy Philpot, Joshua Foster & Kenny Grady, who being elected tried and sworn well and truly to try the issue joined upon their oaths do say they find the

(p 126) Thursday May 11th 1820

defendant not guilty whereupon it is considered by the court that the defendant go hence without day and recover of the plaintiff his costs about his suit in this behalf expended and the plaintiff in mercy - From which Judgment the plaintiff prayed an appeal to the next Cercuit Court filed reasons and gave bond with security as the law deriets and the appeal is granted -

This day came Eleanor Vanbebber into court and presented his petition praying that Dower may be assigned her if the real estate of her deceased husband Peter Vanbebber and the court being satisfied that the parties interested in the primises had notice accofding to law by their acknowledgments made in open court it is considered and ordered by the court that Dower of the real estate of said Peter Vanbebber deceased be allotted and assigned to Eleanor Vanbebber his widow according to the prayer of her petition an as the Law derects and that Robert Gibson, Thomas Lea, Marcellus Moss

Isd.

(p 127) Thursday May 11th 1820

Reuben Moss, Adam Sowder Daniel Root, Salathiel Martin Harmon Davis, Moses Davis William Norvell, Thomas Hoskins and William Wilson be appointed a Jury to lay out the said Dower accordingly -

Robert W. McCleary ) Treespass on the case
vs )
John Dundron ) This day came the plaintiff by his attorney and the defendant being Solemnly called to come and defend his suit came not but made default whereupon as the court is not advised what Judgment to render it is considered that a writ of inquiry be awarded to acertin damage in this cause as the law deriots

A marjority of the acting Justices being present it is ordered by the court that the state and county Taxes be the same this year in every respect as they was last year -

Solomon Sailor & Geo Britain )
vs )
William Worvell )

The defendant gave bond and Security for his appeal reasons or filed and the appeal is granted -

(p 128) Thursday May 11th 1820

On reasons appearing to the Satisfaction of the court it is considered that John Brassfield, William Ely, Bluford Woodall William McNew, William Bowman William Lea, and John Rogers be discharged from further attendance as Jurors at the present term -

Jeremiah Cloud who was formnly appointed Deputy Clerk of the court is discontinmed in that appointment by Benjamin C loud the principal clerk

John Wallen and Company ) trespass on the case
vs )
James C. Martin )

The defendant who was attached by his land to answer the suit brought against him by the plaintiffs being Solemnly called to come into court and replevy the same and defend the said suit came not, but made default wherefore it is considered by the court that the plaintiffs recover against the defendant their demages together with their costs about the prosecution of their suit in this behalf expended But the court being advised of what claimes the plaintiffs have sustained therefore let a Jury come at the next court of pleas and quarter sessions to be held for Claiborne on the second Monday of August next to enquire thereof and assess the same

(p 129) Thursday May 11th 1820

William Maddy ) The plaintiff by attorney
vs ) came into court and dismisses
Armsted Brown ) his Suit therfore it is considered by the court that the defendants recover against the plaintiff his writs by him about his defence in this behalf expended for which execution may issue

Benjamin Cloud ) The plaintiff in his proper person
vs ) comes into court and dismisses
David Kesterson ) his suit therefore it is considered by the court that the defendant go without day and recover of the plaintiffs his costs by him about his defence in this behalf expended for which execution may issue -

Court adjourned till tomorrow 9 oclock

John Brock
Josiah Ramsey
John Neil
John Huddleston
John Evans

(p 130) Friday May 12 1820

Court met according to adjournment present John Brock, Josiah Ramsey, John Neil, John Huddleston John Evans Esqrs.

The state vs John Cary ) The state vs Philip Coffelt ) The state vs J. A. Coffelt

Personally appeared Martin Fugatt in open court and acknowledged himself indebted to the State of Tennessee in the sum of two hundred dollars to be levied of his goods and chattles land and tennements but to be void on condition that they make his personal appearance before the Justices of our court of pleas and quarter sessions to be holden for the County of Claiborne at the courthouse in Tazewell on the Wednesday after the second Monday of August next then and thereto prosecute and give evidence on behalf of the state against the defendant in the above cause and not depart the court without leave

Richard Bundron vs Martin Webb ) Case

The plaintiff comes into Court and dismisses his suit; therefore it is by the court that the defendant go hence without day and recover of the plaintiff his costs by him about his defence in this behalf expended for which execution may issue

John Dobkins vs Drury Gibson ) Court

The plaintiff comes into court and dismisses his Suit therefore it is considered by the court that the defendant go hence without day and recover of the plaintiff his cost by him about his defence in this behalf expended for which execution may issue

(p 131) Friday May 12 1820

The State vs Benjamin Lankford ) William Maddy came into court and took upon himself that the defendant shall pay the fine and cost in this suit or that he will pay pay for him

The State vs William Maddy ) Personally came Benjamin Lankford in open court and took upon himself that the defendant shall pay the fine and cost in this suit or that he will pay it for him

The state vs William Maddy ) Personally appointed in open court Benjamin Lankford and took upon himself that the defendant shall pay the fine and cost in this Suit or that he will pay it for him

The State ) Personally appeared in open court

vs ) Jeper Ward and acknowledged
John Bundon ) himself indebted to the state
of Tennessee in the sum of one hundred dollars to be void on condition that he make his personal appearance in open court on the Wednesday after the second Monday of August next then and there to prosecute and give evidence on behalf of the state against John Bundon and not depart the court without leave leave -

William Maddy for ) the plaintiff comes into court
Dennis Condry & & ) and dismisses his suit Therefore
vs ) it is considered by the court
Susanah Posey ad. ) the defendant recover of plaintiff
the cost in this behalf expended.

(p 132) Friday May 12 1820

John Devenport ) Ordered by the court that the
vs ) plaintiff have until Wednesday
David Cain ) of next court to give Security
for the prosecution of this suit -

Ordered by the court that the Sheriff be instructed to employ some Suitable person to Keep and support the infant children of Edmon Males until next court and that they be brought here at next court -
Isd.

John Campbell ) Original attachment
vs )
Arthur L. Campbell )

This day came the plaintiff by his attorney, and the defendant being Solemnly called to come into court and replevy the property attached in this cause and defend his suit, came not but made default whereupon it is considered by the court that the plaintiff recover of the defendant the sum of Six hundred dollars the debt in the declaration mentioned, and the further sum of forty three dollars and fifty cents interest and damages for the detintion of the debt aforesaid, togetherwith all costs by him about his suit in this behalf expended and the defendant in mercy & & and it is further considered that the plaintiff have an order of sale to sell the land attached in this case
Isd.

(p 133) Friday 12 May 1820

William Cincaid for the use )
of Absolom Morris )
vs )
William Maddy )

In this cause the plaintiff being Solemnly called to come into court and prosecute the suit brought by him against the defendant came not but made default therefore it is considered by the court that the plaintiff Suffer a non suit, that the defendant go hence without day and recover of the plaintiff his costs by him about his defence in this behalf expended for which execution may issue -

Archibald Eades ) certoria
vs )
George Treas )

In this cause the plaintiff being Solemnly called to come into court and prosecute his suit came not but made default Therefore it is considered by the court that plaintiff suffer a non suit, that the defendant go hence without day and recover of the plaintiff his costs by him about his defence in this behalf expended for which execution -

Thomas Johnson
vs
Ransom Hays
} Stephen Cocke and Dennis Condry came into court and replevied the goods attached in this cause and took upon themselves

(p 134) Friday May 12th 1820

that of the defendant in this action be cast that he shall pay the condemnation money & cost or surrender himself in prison in discharge of the same or that they will pay them for him and time given to plead or demur so as not do delay the grand & petit Jurors is discharged from further attendance at the present all causes not disposed of are contimued until the next term of this court -

Court adjourned until court in course

John Huddleston
Josiah Ramsey
John Neil
John Evans
John Brock

(p 135) Monday August 14th 1820

At a court of pleas and Quarter sessions began and held for the county of Claiborne at the courthouse in Tazewell on the second Monday of August 1820

Present the Worshipful

John Evans, John Neil, John Brock, John Wallen, Archibald Bales, Mercureus Cook, Aaron Davis, John Hurst, William Savage, John Huddleston, George Brock Silas Williams, Robert W. McClary, Alexander Campbell and Christopher Robinson Esquires -

---

A Deed of conveyance from John Crowly and thomas McLane for two hundred and twenty one acres of land was proven in open court by the oath of Henry Long a subscribing witness and filed for further probate

---

A Deed of conveyance from William Mayes to Isaac Cup for twenty acres of Land was duly proven in open court by the oaths of John Dobbs and Wylie Mayes the subscribing witnesses thereto and was therefore admited to Record and ordered to be Registered

---

A Deed of conveyance from Alexander Ritchie to James Overton for one hundred acres of Land was duly acknowledged in open court by the maker and was admited to Record and ordered to be Registered

(p 136) Monday August 14th 1820

A Deed of conveyance from Edward Turner to William Ely was proven at August Term 1818 by the oath of William Chrichfield and filed is now proven in full by the oath of William Turner the other subscribing witness and admited to record and ordered to be Registered

---

A Deed of conveyance from John Simmons to Ransom Day for twenty five acres of Land was duly acknowledged in open court by the maker and was admited to Record and ordered to be registered

---

A Deed of conveyance from Edward Dodson to Langly Welch for thirty acres of Land was duly acknowledged in open court by the maker thereof and was admitted to record and ordered to be Registered -

---

A Deed of conveyance from Jesse Lay to thomas Anderson for fifty acres of Land was duly proven in open court by the oaths of Joshua Anderson & Edward Burk the subscribing witnesses thereto and was admitted to Record and ordered to be registered

(p 137) Monday August 14th 1820

A Deed of conveyance from Thomas Anderson to Hardy Hughs for fifty acres of Land was duly proven in open court by the oaths of David Lay and William Streble the subscribing witnesses thereto and was admited to record and ordered to be Registered

---

A Deed of conveyance from James Glassgow by his attorney John Adair to Joshua Anderson for Eighty four acres of Land was duly proven in open court by the oaths of Thomas Anderson and William Streole the subscribing witnesses thereto and was admited to Record and ordered to be registered

---

A Deed of conveyance from Daniel Rice to Edward Walker for fifty acres of Land was duly acknowledged in open court by the maker thereof and was admited to record and ordered to be Registered

---

A Deed of conveyance from Eli Griffet to Mark Cadle for one hundred acres of Land was duly proven in open court by the oaths of William Critchfield and Zachariah Cadle the subscribing witnesses thereto and was admited to Record and ordered to be Registered

(p 138) Monday August 14th 1820

A Deed of conveyance from Daniel Foster to Daniel Rice for fifty acres of Land was proven in open court by the oath of Henry Rice and filed for further probate -

A Deed of conveyance from Theophilus Miller to Mathew Owens for one hundred acres of Land was duly proven in open court by the oaths of Jacob Sowder and Emarmel Sowder the Subscribing witnesses thereto and was admited to Record and ordered to be registered

---

A Deed of conveyance from Isaac Vanbebber to Man H. Maddy for fifteen acres Land was duly acknowledged in open court by the maker thereof and was admited to record and ordered to be registered

---

Ordered by the court a majority of the acting Justices present that Peter Huffaker, Aaron Davis, William Norvell, Lewis Huffaker, John Roddy, James Munday, William Lea & William Critchfield or a majority of them view and mark out that part of the road Leading from Isaac Vanbebbers
Isd. Augt. 24th 1820

(p 139) Monday August 14th 1820

to intersect the Kentucky road in a derection to Lee County then to the state line near John Hardies best was to injure farm as little as may be and make report to the next Term of this court -
Isd.

---

Ordered by the court that William Russel be appointed overseer of the road from greasy rock creek through Troublesome and have the hands in the bounds as follows from the Hawkins line down the river to Robert Grishams and from that to Hards old quarter from thence to the top of Powels Mountain thence along said Mountain to Mulberry Gap
Isd. Augt. 24

---

Ordered by the court that Micheal Pearson be appointed overseer of the Road from a branch called troublesome to the Kentucky road from Russels Lain down the river and Mountain to the Kentucky road and have all the hands between Powels Mountain and Clynch river -
Isd. August 24th

---

Ordered by the court that Isham Jennings be appointed overseer of the upper Bullard ferry road from the old garrison to the forks of said road at William Grahams fence and have the same hands and bounds for hands aloted to said road.
Isd. August 24

(p 140) Monday August term 1820

Ordered by the court of 9 Justices being present that Absolam Hurst be allowed of twenty five dollars for supporting two orphant childern to wit thomes Maples to selela Maples from May term 1820 up to the present time
Isd. August 24

Ordered by the court that Bibby Hodges be appointing overseer of the Kentucky road in the room of Thomas Hill resigned & have the same bounds for hands that said Hill had
Isd. August 24

---

Ordered by the court that William Stillings be appointed overseer of the road in the room of Andrew Davis resigned & have the same bounds for hands that said Davis had
Isd. August 25

---

Ordered by the court that David C. Posey be appointed overseer of the road in the room of William Cooper resigned & have the same bounds for hands said Cooper had
Isd. August 25

---

With licence of the court James Jenkins administrat on all & singular the goods & chattles rights & credits of Timothy Jenkens deceased who gave bond & was qualified

---

Thomas McCarty & Thomas Henderson presented to court a paper supposing to be the last will and testement of John McCarty decd. & prayed the same

(p 141) Monday August term 1820

may be admitted to record whereupon John Hunt & Jeremiah Henderson the only subscribing witnesses thereto came into court & made oath that he saw John McCarty the deceased sign seal publish & declair the same to be his last will & testement & at the time of executing the same he was of sound & disposeing mind & memory it is therefore ordered by the court that said paper be admitted to record & the said thomas McCarty & thomas Henderson the Executors in said will named came into court & took upon themselves the execution of said will gave bond & was qualefied

---

Hugh W. Dunlap presented to court a licence authorising him to prosecute law in the several court of this state who took & oath to support the constitution of the United states & of this state & also the oath of an attorney & is admitted to prosecute law in this court

---

Alexander B. Bradford presented to court a licence authorrising him to prosecute law in the several courts in this state who took an oath to support the constitution of the United States & of this state and also the oath of an attorny & is admitted to prosecute law in this court.

(p 142) Monday August term 1820

Ordered by the court 9 Justices being present that Nathan Perry constable be allowed the sum of four Dollars for his Services in attending on the court four days at the last term of the court
Isd. August 25

---

Ordered by the court 9 Justices being present that Tidance Lain Senr. be allowed the sum of twelve dollars & fifty cents for supporting William Boyde & Bennet Arnold who were comitted to the jail of this county
Isd. August 25

---

George Yoakum who was commissioned by his Execellings the Governor of the state a Justice of the peace in & for Claiborne County came into court & was qualefied

---

With leave of the court John Wallen Esqr. returns to court his list of taxable property & poles for the year 1820 by him taken in the bounds of Captain Browns Company

---

A bill of sale from Jacob Sharp to James McBroom for a negro boy named Lewis was proven in open court by William Lay one Subscribing witness & ordered to be filed for further probate

---

A power of attorney from William J. Alvis to Marcellus Moss was proven in open court by John Gross one Subscribing witness & ordered to be filed for further probate

William Ely presented to court his resignation as one of constables in Captain Browns Company which was excepted by the court

(p 143) Monday August term 1820

James Severs records the ear mark of his stock to wit a swallow fork in the right ear & underhalf crop in the left ear

---

John Simmons records the ear mark of his stock to wit a Smoth crop off the left ear

---

Oliver dodson exhibeted to court 9 Justices being present the scalp of one wolf over Six months old & proved he killed said wolf in the county of Claiborne & in the year 1819 the court being satisfied therewith It is ordered that the sheriff burn said sculp & that the said Oliver Dodson recive from the tresurer of East Tennessee the sum allowed by law
Isd. 30th Jany. 1821

Joel Jones exhibited to court 9 Justices being present the sculps of two wolfs over six months old & proved he killed said wolf in the County of Claiborne in the year of 1820 & the court being Satisfied therewith It is ordered that the sheriff burn said sculps & that the said Joel Jones recive from the treasure of East tennessee the sum allowed by law

---

Andrew Crockett, Jesse Hurst Andrew McClary Alexander Richy Philip Nants & thomas Martin who were appointed a Jury to veiw and lay out a road from William Doherty on Mulberry Creek to Crocketts Iron works & Cumberland Gap made their report in the following wards & figures to wit agreeable to an
Isd. 30th Jany. 1821

(p 144) Monday August term 1820

order of the honorable court of Claiborne County we your jurors have laid out & marked the road agreeable to your order Begining at a nine mile post near William Dohertys on Mulberry there to at McClary Mill on hoop creek then down said creek to the mouth crossing powels river at Jesse Hunts then down the river between sd. Hunts field & the river leaveing said river between Hursts field and John Jones field cuting off about twelve pannels of said Jones _____ at upper corner of said field from thereto Crocketts Iron Works & from there to intersect the powells vally road at the end of John Hardys lane on the state line

Andrew Crockett
Jesse Hurst
Andrew McClary
Alexander Richey
Philip Nants
thomas Martin

which report being inspected by the the Court a majority of Justices being present It is ordered that the road as laid out by the Jury aforesaid be estableshed & made a public road

---

Alexander Campbell, Abraham Devault, Micheal Pearson William Russell, & thomas Hill who were appointed a Jury to view & lay out a road the nearest & best way from tazewell to the county line on greasy rock creek to the end of the Hawkins road made their report to wit We the Jury have viewed & marked a road

(p 145) Monday August term 1820

agreeable to the order & we consider it a road given under our hands this 12th day of August 1820

Alexander Campbell
Abraham Devault
Michael Pearson
William Russell
Thomas Hill

which report being inspected by the court a majority of the Justices being present It is ordered by the court that the road as laid out by the Jury aforesaid be established & made a public road - Isd. August 25

---

Ordered by the court that Barton Ely be appointed overseer of the road in the room of John Rody resigned & have the same bounds for hands that said

Rody had
Isd. August 25

---

Ordered by the court that Henry Moyers be appointed overseer of the road in the room of Nathan Moore resigned & have the same bounds for hands that said More had.
Isd. August 25

---

Ordered by the court that Jacob Coal be appointed overseer of the road in the room of Jesse Hopper resigned & that he have the same bounds for hands that said Hopper had.
Isd. August 25

---

Ordered by the court a majority of the Justices being present that Richard Harper Bryant Breeden, thomas Shearmon John Hurst Esqr. (p146) & Elijah Hurst Jnr. be appointed a Jury to view & lay out a road that is now afermed round the upper side of the house & fence of the field that James Hodges lives in leaving the old road Just below the said Hodges Spring & intersecting the same against near the old school house & make report to next court

---

Court adjourned untill tomorrow 9 oclock

John Wallen
John Huddleston
Robert W. McClary
John Brock
John Evans
Aaron Davis

Tuesday August 15th 1820

Court met according to adjournment present John Evans, John Neil, John Huddleston, John Brock & Josiah Ramsey Esqr.

---

Deed of conveyance from John Bundron to Michael Pearson for forty acres of Land was duly acknowledged in open court by the maker there of and was therefore admitted to record and ordered to be registered

(p 147) Tuesday August 15th 1820

Deed of conveyance from John Bundron to Michael Pearson for thirty nine acres of Land was duly acknowledged in open court by the maker thereof and was admited to record and ordered to be registered

---

A Deed of conveyance from Thomas Gibbons to William Hill for one hundred and fifty acres of Land was duly proven in open court by the oath of James Hill and Joab Hill the Subscribing witnesses and was admited to record and ordered to be registered -

---

A Deed of conveyance from Thomas Gibbons to William Hill for one hundred and fifty acres of Land was duly acknowledged in open court by the maker thereof and was admited to record and ordered to be registered

---

A Deed of conveyance from William Sumpter to Thomas Baker was duly acknowledged in open court by the maker thereof and was admited to record and ordered to be registered

---

A deed of conveyance from thomas Baker to Enos Hobbs for fifteen acres of Land was duly acknowledged in open court by the maker and was admited to record and ordered to be registered

(p 148) Tuesday August 15th 1820

A Deed of conveyance from Thomas Johnson to Richard Hitson for two hundred acres of Land was duly proven in open court by the oaths of Joab Bruer and thomas Givens the subscribing witnesses thereto and was therefore admited to Record and ordered to be registered

---

A Deed of conveyance from John Casey to Sammel Cloud for three hundred and fifty acres of Land was duly proven in open court by the oath of Jacob Cloud and Polly Cloud the subscribing witnesses thereto and was admited to record and ordered to be registered

---

John Hunt Sheriff of Claiborne County Returned into court the venire Executed on the following persons to wit

1 Willis Harper
2 Joseph Lanham
3 Charles Shearmon
4 John Thompson
5 Briant Breeding
6 Uriah Gowing
7 Elijah Hurst
8 Nehemiah Hopkins
9 Martin Corner
10 Archibald Cooper
11 thomas Givens
12 Ralph Hatfield
13 John McCallom
14 Samuel Rogers
15 James Lemar
16 Benjamin Pike
17 Anderson Smith
18 William Jackson
19 Christopher Huffaker
20 Solomon Ely
21 James Cadle
22 Drury Herrel
23 Ralph Shelton
24 James Hopson
25 John Condray
26 William Jenkins

(p 149) Tuesday August 15th 1820

out of which venire the following named persons were balloted a Grand Jury to the present term

1 John Condray foreman
2 William Jackson
3 Willis Harper
4 Samuel Rogers
5 Charles Shearmon
6 Drewry Merrell
7 Thomas Givens
8 Christopher Huffaker
9 Uriah Gooing
10 Archibald Cooper
11 Joseph Lanham
12 William Jenkins
13 Ralph Shelton

who were severally sworn recived their charge & Retired to consider of their presentents

John McCubben constable was sworn to attend the Grand Jury at the present term

John Lay vs Thomas Hill } Abraham Murphy one of the constables returns to court an execution Issued by John Huddleston Esqr. for the sum of twenty six dollars & fifty cents Debt and the further sum one dollar and twelve and one half cents costs with the following returns and _______ _________ no personal property known to me therefore (p 150) levied on a tract of land lying on the north bank of Clinch river Just above Isaac Meeders not far below some large falls in the river June 20th 1820

On motion of the plaintiff by John Cocke Esqr. his attorney & for reasons appearing to the court It is considered by the court that an order of sale Issue to the sheriff of Claiborne County commanding him to expose to sale & sell said land so levied on to Satisfiy the plaintiff his debt and costs aforesaid together with the costs of this motion

---

David Wilson vs Fielding Advanld } this day came the plaintiff by John Cocke Esqr. his attorney & moved the court for Judgment against the Defendant for the sum of fifty two Dollars & twenty five cents and the court being satisfied that the plaintiff had been compelled to pay said sum as the security of said defendants It is therefore considered by the court that the plaintiff recover against the defendants the sum of fifty two dollars twenty five cents the sum aforsaid together with the costs of the motion & the defendants in mercy & &

John Devenport vs David Kain } This day came Daniel Coffelt into open court and surrendered the defendant in discharge of himself as his bail in this suit

(p 151) Tuesday August 15th 1820

whereupon the said defendant was prayed in custody of the sheriff & there upon Jesse Deavers & Martin Fugate came into open court and took upon them selves that in case the defendant David Kain should be cast in this action he shall pay the condemnation money & costs or surrender himself in person in execution for the same or they the said Jesse Deavers & Martin fugate will pay it for him

---

John Devenport vs David Kain } this day Henry Sharp came into open court and took upon himself that in case the plaintiff Should be cast in this action he shall pay the costs in this behalf expended or that he the said Henry Sharp will pay it for him

---

John Lea was Elected constable in the County of Claiborne for Captain Brewers Company who gave bond & Security & took the oaths presented by law

---

A Deed of conveyance from James Glasgow to John Casey for five hundred & fifty acres of land was proven in open court by William Blackwood & Ralph Shelton two subscribing witnesses thereto admitted to record & ordered to be registered

---

A bill of sale from Richard Hilts to Hugh Graham for a negro boy named Adam was proven in open court by thomas Givens one of the subscribing

(p 152) Tuesday August 15 1820

witnesses thereto & ordered to be filed for further probate

the state vs Jacob Campbell } this day came the state by sterling Cocke Esqr. the solecitor General who prosecutes on behalf of the state and the defendant in his proper person & pleads guilty to the charge exhibited against him It is therefore considered by the court that for his offence he pay a fine of two Dollars & fifty cents & costs

Thomas Johnson vs Ransom Hays } this day came the defendant and surrendered himself in discharge of his bail whereupon Jesse Carpenter came into court and took upon himself that in case the Defendant shall be cast in this action he shall pay the costs & condemnation or surrender himself in person in execution for the same or that he will pay it for him

Thomas Brasfield produced to court the sculp of a wolf over six months old & proved he killed the wolf in the County of Claiborne 6 Justices being present It is ordered that the sheriff burn said Sculps & that the said thomas recive from the treasurer of East Tennessee the sum presented by law

James Vanbebber & Isaac Vanbebber ) this day came the parties by

vs
Elenor Vanbebber
Jacob Vanbebber

their attornies and thereupon also came a Jury to wit

(p 153) Tuesday August 1820

| | |
|---|---|
| 1 James Cadle | 7 Harrod Hopson |
| 2 Benjamin Pike | 8 Solomon Dobkins |
| 3 Ralph Hatfield | 9 George Richardson |
| 4 James Hopkins | 10 Hezekiah Brooks |
| 5 Charles Pain | 11 George Trees |
| 6 Ambrose Briant | 12 John Harper |

who being elected tried and & sworn well and truly to try and the truth to speak on the Issue Joined upon their oaths do say they find the defendant did assum & take upon themselves in manner & form as the plaintiff in their declaration both complained within them years next before sueing out the writ in this cause and assess the plaintiff damage by reason thereof to one hundred & thirty nine Dollars & thirty nine cents besides his costs

It is therefore considered by the court that the plaintiffs recover against the defendant the damages aforesaid in form aforesaid assessed together with the costs in & about prosecuting their suit in this behalf expended & the Defendants in mercy & &

from which Judgment the defendant prayed an appeal to the next Cercuit Court to be holden for the County of Claiborne

In the progress of this cause the defendants tendered their bill of exceptions to the openion of the court which was signed & sealed & made part of the record

(p 154) Tuesday August 18 1820

Ordered by the court that John Evans and William Graham Esqrs. be appointed to settle the administration account of William Jenings administrator of William Jennings Deceased and make their report to the next term of this court

Isd. August 22

---

Ordered by the court that William Drummons be appointed overseer of the road from the Island ford on powells river to the nine mile tree & have for hands to work under him John Kick, Alford Crichfield, Jesse Crichfield, John Henly, Joseph Serrel & all the hands in said bounds.

Isd. August 27

---

Ordered by the court that Coventon Collensworth be appointed overseer of the Jenings ferry road from the top of the river ridge to John Simons in the room of Harrod Hopson & have the same bounds for hands said Hopson had

Isd. August 27

---

Ordered by the court that Christain Sharp be appointed overseer of the road from the nine mile tree to the vally road & have the following hands to work under him Thomas Jenkings, William Stinnet, David Sweet, Daniel Rute,

Isaac Parker, Daniel Sowder Boston Graves, Emanuel Sowder, Britain sowder & all the hands in said bounds
Isd. August 27

---

Ordered by the court that the Sheriff let out to the lowest bidder for their support for three months the childern of Barnard Maples who thereupon reported to court that he had in obedence to the order of the court let out said childern to Absolom Hurst for forty Dollars twenty five cents he being the lowest bidder
Isd. Augt. 27

(p 155) Tuesday August 15 1820

Henry Long, John Sharp & Joel Bays who were appointed heretofore to set apart so much of the crop & provesions on hand of the Estate of John McNew as would be suffecent for the support of the widow & family of said John for one year made their report to wit we the commissioners appointed to lay off one years provesions for the widow & orphants of John McNew Decd. according to order do allow them Sixty bushels of corn & twelve bushels of wheat & Six head of hogs & a Suffecant quantly of corn to make them completly fat & one hundred lbs. salt 30 lbs of sugar & 10 lbs of coffee 1 lb. of alspice Jinger 1 lb. pepper 1 lb. ½ also for leathering 8 lbs. of wool & 35 lbs. of cotton given under our hand this 29 day of November 1819

Henry Long
John Sharp
Joel Bays

N.B. We also allow them leather suffecsant for wearing shoes for said term

William Norvell vs William Owens } this day came the defendants in open court & sayeth he cannot gainsay the plaintiffs action for the sum of two hundred & Sixty nien Dollars but confesses Judgment for the same & costs It is therefore considered by the court that the plaintiff recover against the defendant the sum aforesaid in form aforesaid confessed together with the costs

(p 156) Tuesday August 1820

in and about prosecuting his said Suit in this behalf expended & the defendant in mercy & &

Court adjourned untill tomorrow 9 oclock

John Neil
John Evans
John Brock
Josiah Ramsey
John Huddleston

Court met according adjournment present the same Justices as of yesterday

The State vs Absolom Morris } this day came the state by Sterling Cocke Esqr. who prosecuted on behalf of the state & the defendant in his proper person & thereupon also came a Jury to wit Briant

Breedon, John McCollum, Nehemiah Hopkins, Elijah Hurst, Tidance Lain, Peter Neal, Jesse Neal, Henry Gratner, Mathew Hamilton, John Whitacre, Asa Watson & David Wilson who being Elected tried and sworn well & truly to try & the truth to Speak on the Issue of traverse do say they find the defendant guilty in manner and form as charged in the bill of Indictment It is therefore considered by the court that for this his office he pay a sum of four Dollars besides costs
Taxed

(p 157) Wednesday August 16th 1820

It is therefore considered by the court that the state recover against the Defendant the fine & costs aforsaid & be in mercy & &

---

Ordered by the court that Joab Hill & John Neal Esqr. be appointed to settle with Susannah Grisham administratix of William Grisham Deced her administrations accounts & make report at next term of this court
Isd. August 27

---

Ordered by the court that William Houston, Hugh Graham & John Huddleston be appointed to settle with Susannah Posey administratrix of Benjamin Posey Deceased her administration accounts and make report to next term of this court
Isd. August 27

---

A Deed of conveyance from James W. Glasgow to Hugh Graham for one hundred acres of Land was duly proven in open court by the oaths of William Houston and John Huddleston the subscribing witnesses thereto and was admited to record and ordered to be registered

the state
vs
Jesse Deaver } this day came the state by the Solicitor General who prosecutes on behalf of the state & the defendant in his proper person & thereupon also came a Jury to wit
Taxed

(p 158) Wednesday August 16th 1820

James Cadle, Benjamin Pike, Ralph Hatfield, James Hopson, Moses Davis, James Dobbs, William McNew, Elijah Jones, Jacob Vanbebber, Archibald Eads, John Williams & Elijah Hurst who being Elected tryed & sworn well and truly to try & the truth to speak on the Issue of traverse this cause not being determined the Jurors aforsaid for rendering their verdict are respited untill tomorrow

State of Tennessee
Claiborne County } On this 16th day of August 1820 Personally appeared in open court being a court of record for said county created as such by the Law of the state Joseph Wilson aged 75 years who being first duly sworn according to Law doth on his oath make the following declaration in order to obtain the provisions made by and act of congress of the 18th of March 1818 and 1st of May 1820 that he the said Joseph Wilson enlisted for the Term of five years

the day not remembered on or about the year 1777 in the state of North Carolina my memory will not admit of my being mose particular in the company commanded by Captain McDowel in the regement commanded by Col. Mathew Lock in the line of the state of North Carolina

(p 159) Wednesday August 16th 1820

Continental establishment that he contimued to serve in the said corps in and about five years and got his discharge from said Service on the return of peace in the state of North Carolina that was the seige of ninety Six and in a battle at the Hutors in in several on Pedee and in a battle at Monks corner and that he has no other evidence now in his power of his said Service except his own oath his discharge being lost by time or accident and in pursuance of the act of the first of May 1820 I do Solemnly swear that I was resedent citizen of the United state on the 18th day of March one thousand eight hundred & eighteen and that I have not Sence that time by gift, sale or in any other manner disposed of my property or any part thereof with intent thereby so as to deminish it as to bring myself within the provisions of an act of congress entitled an act to provide for certain persons engaged in the Land & Navel Services of the United Statest in the revolutionry war passed on the 18th day of March one thousand Eight hundred and eighteen

(p 160) Wednesday August 16th 1820

and that I have not nor has any person in trust for me any property securities contracts or debts due to me nor have I any interest other than contained in the schedule hereunto anexed & by me Subscribed

Schedule

| | |
|---|---|
| 1 mare Small & old | $10.00 |
| 1 cow | 10.00 |
| 9 head of swine | 10.00 |
| 1 pot 5 plates ½ doz knives & forks | 3.50 |
| 1 Flax wheel | 1.00 |
| 3 hoes & 1 axe | 2.00 |
| Chickens | 1.00 |
| | $37.50 |

his
Joseph X Wilson
mark

My occupation that of a farmer but of decay & Rheumatic/ pains rendered all but incapable of doing anything at it, my Family residing with me consists of Elizebeth Wilson aged 23 years able to earn her living Katherine Wilson aged 2 years 7 months

On proof advised to the court of the value of the property in said schedule It is the openion of the court that the value thereof is thirty seven Dollars & fifty cents

(p 161) Wednesday August 16th 1820

A Deed of conveyance from James Roddy to John Crechfield for two hundred acres of land was proven in open court by the oath of William Crechfield one of the subscribing witnesses and said Cricthfield made oath that he saw James Wright the other Subscribing witness sign his name thereto and that the said Wright is not an enhabitant of this state it is therefore admited to record & ordered to be registered -

---

A Deed of conveyance from John Riley to William Condray for Six hundred and forty acres of Land was proven in open court by the oath of John Cocke one of the subscribing witnesses and filed for further probate

---

Nathan Perry is appointed constable in the bounds of Captain Morris Company who gave bond and Security to the Satisfaction of the court and was qualified as the law direct

---

Ordered by the court that Alexander Ritchie be appointed overseer of the new road leading from the nine mile post at Dohertys to the Powel Valley road at John Hurst that is from the said nine mile post to Powels river
Isd. August 27

(p 162) Wednesday August 16th 1820

and have for hands the following bounds that is all Captain Thomas McCartys Company south of Wallens ridge and the following named hands on the north side of said Ridge William Herrold, John McDowell, Joseph Baker, William Baker, William Medlock, William McDowell and Robert G. Parks

---

Ordered by the court that Jesse Hurst be appointed overseer on apart of the new road leading from Dohertys to Crocketts Iron works that is from Powels river to the Top of the ridge between the forks of Coxes branch and have for hands the following bounds that is all Captain McCarteys Company north of Powels river thence south of Powels River beging at Nathan Lawsons thence to the ridge to Martins thence leading out Robert McClary and Robert G. Parks to Dunns from Dunns to Walkerses thence to Parkers thence to Kestersons thence to the river thence up said river including all in said bounds
Isd. Aug. 28

(p 163) Wednesday August 16th 1820

Ordered by the court that Henry Jenkins be appointed overseer of the road leading from Wiatts Mill Gap Creek up the Kentucky road and have for hands the following bounds that is from John Lingars to Major Leas then to William Crictchfields and the widow Cadles and Down the river to the mouth of Gap Creek then by Jesse Eads then to Shumates out plantation then to James Millers and all the hands in said bounds so to include Jesse Eads and John Shumate and leaving David Roark to Lees Company.
Isd. August 29, 1820

---

Ordered by the court that Jubal Lee have in addition to his hands Rogers Ferrel and all William Norvells and the widow Norvells hands to include George Yoakum Isaac Owens Thomas Walker, David Roark, Thomas Hoskins, George Eads, Godphrey Homes and to have all the men in the above named bounds for his hands to work the road from Town Creek to Wyitts mill on gap creek in Powels Valley -
Isd. 4 Sept. 1821

Ordered by the court that John Buck be allowed fifty Dollars for the support of himself for one year from this present term he being one of the poor of this county and that John Graves taken the money and disturbution his as need requires

Isd. 4 Sept. 1821

(p 164) Wednesday August 16th 1820

Ordered by the court that Thomas Henderson be allowed twenty Dollars for Keeping two orphant children for three months compleate court being present

Isd.

---

Ordered by the court that Samuel Cloud be appointed Guardean of the minor heirs of Daniel Cloud Deceased to Elenazar James Aaron Polly & Ann Cloud who gave bond & was qualified

Isd.

---

Wm. McNew & Sally McNew administrator of the Estate of John McNew Decd. returned to court an account of the sales of said Estate which was ordered to be recorded

---

Isaac Sawer vs John S. Hardy } for reasons appearing to the satisfaction of the court John Wallen is released from his undertaking as security for the appeal in this cause therefore John Herrel came into court & took upon himself that in case the defendant shall be cast in this action he shall pay the condemnation & cost or he will pay it for him

---

Isaac Sawyer vs John S. Hardy } On motion a rule is granted for the plaintiff at the next term to give Security for the prosecution of this suit or the same shall be dismissed

A power of attorney from Samuel Moore to Samuel Boreff was duly

(p 165) Wednesday August 1820

proven in open court by the oath of Richard Malone who also proved that he saw the other subscribing witness James Anderson Subscribe his name as a witness to said power of attorney and further proves said James Anderson is not an inhabitant of this state whereupon said power of attorney is admitted to record and ordered to be Recorded

Court adjourned untill tomorrow 9 oclock

John Evans
John Brock
John Neil
Josiah Ramsey
John Huddleston

Court met according to adjournment

Thursday August 17th 1820

State of Tennessee }
Cleiborne County }

On this 16th day of August 1820 Personally appeared in open court being a court of records created as such by the laws of the state Jonathan Barnard aged 60 years who being first Duly sworn according to Law doth on his oath make the following declaration that he served in the revolutionary war as follows in regiment commanded

(p 166) Thursday August 17th 1820

by Col. Witcome or Witcomb in a company commanded by Capt Grantham Massachusetts Line also in a regiment of artillery commanded by Col. Henry Knox in a company in a company commanded Eliphlat Norvel Massachusetts Line -

the date of his original Declaration in or about the 4th day of March 1818 the number of his pension certificate 9339 I do solemly sware that I was a resident citizen of the United States on the 18th day of March 1818 and that I have not since that time by gift sale or in any manner disposed of my property or any part thereof with intent thereby so to diminish it as to bring myself within the provisions of an act of congress entitled an act provide for certain persons employed in the land and navel Service of the United states in the revolutionary war post on the 18th day of March 1818 and that I have not nor has any person in trust for me any property Securities contracts or debts due to me nor have I any income than what is contained in the schedule hereunto annexed and by me Subscrib

Schedule

(p 167) Schedule

| | |
|---|---|
| 5 sows and no of pigs if all alive worth | $18.00 |
| 3 Books | 5.00 |
| 1 Razor | 0.50 |
| 1 pocket Knife | 0.25 |
| Debts Due to me as bad debts | 40.00 |
| 1 Do | 20.00 |
| 1 Do | 7.00 |
| 1 Do - Do | 5.00 |
| | 95.75 |

---

| | |
|---|---|
| Debts due from me | $250.00 |
| 1 Do | 175.00 |
| 1 Do | 86.00 |
| 1 Do | 106.00 |
| 1 Do | 60.00 |
| 1 Do | 30.00 |
| 1 Do | 30.00 |
| | 737.00 |
| | 95.75 |
| Balance against me | 641.25 |

Jonathan Barnard

My occupation that of a Teacher but by loss of my sight occasioned by a paiñ Disquallefied for the pursuit of that calling and by means of a fall & pain rendered of hard labour my residence is Shifting with my sons and my sons in law having no family on proff ________ it is of the openion of the court that said Debts are worth nothing & that the property in said schedule mentioned is worth twenty four dollars only

(p 168) Thursday August 17th 1820

A Deed of conveyance from David C. Jones to Andrew & Robert Crockett was proven at November Term 1819 by the oath of David Cosby one of the subscribing witnesses and filed for further probate, and at this term the said David Cosby proves that he saw Moses Ball Sign the said deed as an attesting witness and that he now lives in the state of Kentucky - it is therefore considered by the court that the same be admited to record and certified for Registration

A Bill of sale from William Graham and Benjamin Cloud Executors of the last will of Christopher Dawron Deceased to Hugh Graham for a negro girl named Cherry was duly proven in open court by the oath of Jacob Peck and John Hunt and was admited to record and ordered to be certified for registration

Ordered by the court that notice Issue to William Cook administrator of James Johnson to appear at next term of this court and settle up his administration
Isd.

(p 169) Thursday August 17th 1820

Ordered by the court that Silas Williams Henry Hunter and William Bowman be appointed to settle the Estate of Robert Cary Deceased with William Cary the Executor of Said Estate and make report to the next Term of this court
Isd.

Ordered by the court that William Graham and John Huddleston be appointed commissioners to settle the Estate of Alexander Southerland Deceased with William William Condray administrator and make report to next Term of this court
Isd.

Isaac Sayers
vs
John Hardy

Personally appeared in open court John Wallen & Took upon himself that if the plaintiff is cast in this action he will pay the costs of this suit or he will pay for him

The State
vs
Jesse Deavers

this day came the Solecetor Genl. & the defendant in his proper person and the same

Jury as of yesterday who upon their oaths do say they find the defendant Guilty in manner & form as charged in the bill of Indictment It is therefore considered by the court that for this his offence he pay a fine of
taxed

(p 170) Thursday August 1820

ten dollars besides the costs & that the state recover against the defendant & Daniel Colfelt who confesses judgment for the same fine & costs aforesaid & be in mercy & &

---

for reasons appearing to the Satisfaction to the court & the court being satisfied that in the settlement of the account of the Executiors of the Estate James Johnson there had an error advanced for the sum of five Dollars against the gardean it is ordered that said Guardean have a further credit for said sum of five Dollars

State vs Dennis Brasfield } Personally appeared in open court Dennis Brasfield John Dobbs and thomas Brasfield & John Cocke and severally acknowledged themselves indebted to the state of Tennessee in the sum of two hundred Dollars to be levied of their respective goods and chattals lands and Tenments that is to say Dennis Brasfield in the sum of two hundred Dollars and John Dobbs, John Cocke & thomas Brasfield in the sum of Sixty Six dollars 66 Each void on condition that Dennis Brasfield make his appearance from Day to Day during the Term of this court and not depart without leave

---

The State David Cain } this day came the state by the solicitor General and who prosecutes for the state and the defendant in his proper person and thereupon also came a Jury to wit
Briant Breeding, John McCollom Nehemiah Hopkins Daniel Smith Joseph Hurst, Jacob Coffelt, Joseph Bullard

(p 171) Thursday August 1820

William Henderson, Jacob Cloud, David Huddleston, Timothy Philpot, Richard Moore, who being Elected tried and sworn well and truly to try the issue of traverse the state against David Kain from rendering their verdict are respited untill tomorrow.

Thomas Johnson vs Wm. Hooper } The defendant in proper person came into court and saith he cannot gainsay the plaintiff action for Sixty nine dollars and 43 cents besides the costs but doth confess for the same - It was therefore considered by the court that the plaintiff recover of Abraham Murphy & Ruben Rose his securities of the defendant the sum of $69.43 & the costs of such and by assent of said Plaintiff Execution is hereby stayed until next February court

(p 172) Thursday August 1820

A deed of conveyance from Thomas Johnson and Jacob Peck by their atto. in fact Archel Johnson was acknowledged in open court By Jacob Peck one of the Grantors & is retain for probate or acknowledgement as to the other Grantor

Court adjourned until tomorrow 9 oclock

John Brock
John Evans
John Huddleston

Friday August 1820

Ruben B. Rogers vs Absolom Morris } On yesterday the plaintiff in their proper person came and Dismissed his Suit and confessed Judgment for the costs

It is therefore considered by the court that the Defendant go hence with out day and recover of the plaintiff his costs of the said Suit in this behalf Expended and that Execution Issue for the same

(p 173) Friday August 18th 1820

The State vs Jacob Coffelt } this day came the state by Sterling Cocke Esquire her SolicitorGeneral who prosecuters on behalf of the state and the defendant in his proper person and thereupon also came a Jury to wit

1 James Cadle
2 Benjamin Pike
3 Ralph Hatfield
4 James Hopson
5 John Dobbs
6 William Maddy
7 Robert Mitchell
8 Ransom Day
9 Andrew Davis
10 John Honey
11 William Hooper
12 John Lyford

who being elected tryed and sworn well and truly to try and the truth to speak on the Issue of traverse upon their oath do say the find the defendant guilty in manner and form as charged in the bill of Indictment It is Therefore considered by the court that for his offence he be fined one Dollar & it is further considered by the court that the state recover against the defendant the fine & costs in this behalf Expended whereupon Daniel Coffelt came into court & confessed Judgment for the fine & costs aforesaid It is therefore considered by the court that the state recover against the said David Coffelt the fine and costs aforesaid in form aforsaid confessed & be in mercy & &

Taxed

Susanah Posey administratix returns into court and account of the sales of the Estate of Benjamin Posey Decd. which is ordered to be recorded

(p 174) Friday August 18th 1820

Thomas Haws assignee of Dennis Condray vs A. L. Campbell } Debt Attachment

This day came the plaintiff by his attorney and filed his declaration and the defendant being solomnly called to come into court and replevy the estate attached came not - It was therefore considered by the court that the plaintiff recover of the defendant the debt in the declaration mentioned except the sum of fifteen dollars credited on the writing Oblyatory amounting to four hundred & eleven dollars and damages for the detention of said debt deducting said $15 - amounting to forty four dollars besides the costs in this behalf expended and that execution issue for the same

(p 175) Friday August 1820

Sammuel Wilson vs James Maddy } Appeal

On motion of the plaintiff by J. Peck atto. for Judgment against the defendant for not appearing it was considered that the Justices Judgment be in all things affermed and that execution issue therefor costs of such in this behalfs

John & Jubal Lea vs Wm. Maddy } Appeal

On motion of the plaintiff by J. Peck atto. for Judgment the defendant not having appeared

It was considered by the court that the Judgment be affermed with cost of suit and that execution issue for the same

(p 176) Friday August 18th 1820

A Deed of conveyance from John Cocke and John Hunt for two Town Lotts in the town of Tazewell to William Baker was duly acknowledged in open court by the makers thereof and was admitted to record and ordered to be Registered

---

A Deed of conveyance from Thomas Johnson and Jacob Peck to William Hooper for one hundred and thirty three acres of Land was acknowledged by Peck and filed for further probate

---

A Deed of conveyance from Thomas Johnson and Jacob Peck to John Brock for three hundred and fifty acres of Land was acknowledged by Peck and filed for further probate

State vs Jesse Deavers } On motion & It appearing to the Satisfaction of the court that there had been more witnesses Sumoned on behalf of the state that to prove ________ ________ of the defendant it is considered that said defendant be taxed with the costs of two witnesses only for their attendance whereupon Daniel Coffelt came into court

(p 177) Friday August 18th 1820

and confessed Judgment for the fine & costs in this behalf expended It is therefore considered by the court that the State recover against the said Daniel Coffelt the fine in this case imposed & the costs in form aforesaid confessed & be in mercy & &

State vs }

David Cain ) this day came the State by the solicitor General who prosecutes on behalf of the state & the defendant in his proper person & being charged on the bill of Indictment for plea says he is not guilty & puts himself on the county & the solecitor General doth the like & thereupon also came a Jury to wit

| | |
|---|---|
| Bryen Breeden | Joseph Bullard |
| John McCollom | William Henderson |
| Nehemiah Hopkins | Jacob Cloud |
| Daniel Smith | David Huddleston |
| Joseph Hurst | Timothy Philpot |
| Jacob Coffelt | Richard Moore |

who being elected tryed & sworn well & truly to try & the truth to speak on the Issue of traverse upon their oaths do say they cannot agree on their verdict with the consent of the parties & with the assent of the court Bryan Breeden one of the Jurors aforesaid is with drawn a mistral is intered & that this cause be continued untill next court

(p 178) Friday August 18th 1820

John Whitacre
vs
Andrew Johnson ) this day came the plaintiff by his attorney & files his declaration & the defendant being solemnly called to come into court & defend the suit brought against him came not It is therefore considered by the court that the plaintiff recover against the defendant his damages in case Sustained but become the court are unadvised what of but on the damage sustained by the plaintiff It is considered that a Jury came at the next term of this to inquire thereof & that this cause be continued.

---

State
vs
John Cary ) this day came the state by the solecitor Genl. & the defendant in his proper person & being charged on the bill of Indictment says he is guilty thereof It is therefore considered by the court that he pay a fine of ___________ Dollars & fifty cents the costs of this prosecution
Taxed

State
vs
George Coffelt ) this day came the state by the Solector Genl. & the defendant in his proper person & being charged on the bill of Indictment says he is guilty thereof It is therefore considered by the court that for this his offence he pay a fine of one Dollar & costs whereupon Daniel Smith came into court & confessed Judgment for the fine & costs aforesaid It is therefore considered by the court that the state recover against the said Daniel Smith the fine & costs in form aforsaid confessed and be in mercy & &
Taxed

(p 179) Friday August 18th 1820

Archabald Eads
vs
George Trese ) for reasons appearing to the court & by consent of the parties the non suit in

this case is set aside & a rule is Granted to shew cause why the certioria & supercedas should be dismissed

---

Wilson Kincade for the use of Morris vs William Maddy ) by consent of the parties the non suit in this cause is set aside and costs It is therefore considered by the court that the defendant recover against plaintiff the costs aforsaid expended

---

Abel Lanham & Robert G. Parks vs Thomas Bray & wife ) this day the plaintiff came into court and Dismisses their suit It is therefore considered by the court that the defendant go hence without day & recover against the plaintiff their costs in & about their defence in this behalf expended & &

---

Douglas Grady vs Ranson Day ) this day came the plaintiff & dismisses his suit It is therefore considered by the court that the defendant go hence & Recover against the plaintiff his costs in & about his defence expended It is agreed that no execution Issue for them month

---

John McCubbens a constable appointed & sworn to attend on the Grand Jury at this turn attended four days & is entitled to recive of the trustee of Claiborne County sum of one dollar per day

(p 180) Friday August 18th 1820

John Evans Esqr. came into court & resigns his office of Justice the peace which is Excepted & ordered to be certified to the next General Assembly

---

The Grand & petitit Jury are discharged & all causes not determined is continued.

---

Isaac & James Vanbebber vs Jacob & Elenor Vanbebber ) this day came the defendants into open court & intered into bond & security to prosecute the appeal prayed in this case files their reasons for said appeal & the appeal is granted

The State ) On motion & for reasons

vs
Dennis Brasfield } appearing to the satisfaction of the court the proceeding had before the Justices are quashed & the defendant discharge from further attendance

State
vs
John Dundan } this day came the state by the Solicitor genl. who prosecutes on behalf of the state & the defendant in His proper person & thereupon also came a Jury

John McCollom
Nehemiah Hopkins
Elijah Hurst
Thomas Bridges
William Wallen
Luke Parker
Ruben Harper
William Lewis
Nathan Moore
Edward Wooten
Richard Mays
& John Hurst

(p 181) Augt. Term 1820

who being Elected tried & sworn well & truly to try & the truth to speak on the Issue of traverse upon on their oaths do say they find the defendant guilty in manner & form as charged in the bill of Indictment It is therefore considered by the court that for his offence he pay a fine of two Dollars & fifty cents & costs

The State
vs
David Kain }

Personally appeared in open court John Davenport and acknowledged him self indebted to the state of Tennessee in the sum of one hundred dollars to be levied of his goods and chattels lands and tennements but to be void on condition that he appear at next court of pleas and quarter Sessions to be holden for the county of Claiborne on the Wednesday after the second Monday of November next there and then to prosecute and give evidence on behalf of the state on an indictment against David Kain and not depart the court with out leave -

The State
vs
David Kain }

Personally appeared in open court David Kain Martin Fugett and Jesse Devers and acknowledged themselves indebted to the state of Tennessee to wit the said David Kain in the (p 182) sum of two hundred and fifty dollars and the said Martin Fugett and Jesse Devers in the sum of one hundred each to be levied of their goods and chattels lands and tenements respectively to be void on condition that the said David Kain appear at the next court of pleas and quarter Sessions to be holden for the County of Claiborne on the Wednesday after the second Monday of November next then and there to answer a charge exhibited against him by the state by bill of Indictment and not depart the court with out leave

John Davenport
vs
Jesse Devers }

On motion of the defendant and Suffecient cause shewn to the court it is ordered by the court that a commission issue to any two Justices of Russell County in the state of Virginia to take the deposition of Rachel

Davenport to be read in evidence in this cause on giving to the plaintiff twenty days notice of the time and plan of taking the same

(p 183) Vanbebbers representatives } vs } Vanbebbers representatives }

In this cause the defendants who heretofore prayed an appeal from the Judgment rendered against them at the present term of this court and having come into court and given bond with security and filed reasons for prosecuting the same their appeal is granted them

State } vs } John Cary } Scirefacias

The forfecture in this case is set aside on the condition that the defendant pay the costs

It is therefore considered by the court that the state recover against the defendant the costs in this behalf expended and the Defendant in mercy & &

---

A Deed of conveyance from from James Glasgow to Susannah stone was duly proven in open court by the oaths of Hugh Graham and William Cowing Subscribing witnesses thereto admitted to record and ordered to be registered

(p 184) Friday August 18th 1820

State } vs } Philip Coffelt } Daniel Coffelt personally appeared in open court and acknowledged him self indebted to the state of Tennessee in the Sum of two hundred and fifty Dollars to be levied of his goods and chattles lands and tennements void on condition that Philip Coffelt make his personal appearance on the Wednesday after the second Monday in November next then and there to answer a charge the state against him and not depart the court without leave

John Cardwell } vs } Allen Collins } An execution having appeared in this case which came to the hands of John Hunt Sheriff of Claiborne County be returned he had levied the said execution on one small grey stud horse whereupon on motion it is ordered by the court that an order of sale issue to sell the said property levied on as aforsaid

John Huddleston
John Neil
John Brock

State } vs } Jacob Coffelt }

Court met according to adjournment

(p 185) Saturday August 19th 1820

State } vs }

Jacob Coffelt ) this day came the State by the solecitor General who prosecutes on behalf of the state and thereupon came the demurrer to the Scirefacias to be argued & of argument of council being heared as well as against it & the matters therein considered being duly considered & fully understood it is considered by the court that said demurrer be sustained

State
vs
Jacob Coffelt ) On motion & for reasons appearing to the satisfaction of the court the forfeture heretofore entered against the defendant be set aside & that the defendant pay all begot costs of said forfeture It is therefore considered by the court that the state recover against the defendant the costs aforesaid in form aforesaid & be in mercy & &

Ordered by the court that the following persons be appointed Jurors to the next court David Huddleston, Richard Harper, Joseph Neil, John Fergurson, Isaac Lane, William Clark, Thos. Hill, Samuel Dodson, Peter Leger, Robert Grisham, Jesse Hurst, thomas McCarty, John Riley, Henly Fugatt, Neal McNeal, Henry Sumpter, George Colehorn, Jesse Hopper, William Perevine, Elijah Harp, thomas Brasfield, Dennis Brassfield, John Doherty, Mark Cadle, Solomon Fly, James Lake

(p 186) State
vs
Philip Coffelt ) this day came the state by the Solecitor General who prosecutes on behalf of the state & thereupon came on the demurrer to the Scirefacias to be argued & on argument of council being heared as well in support of said Demurrer as against & the matters therein contained being duly considered & fully understood it is considered by the court that the demurrer be sustained

State
vs
Philip Coffelt ) On motion and for reasons appearing to the Satisfaction of the court the forfeiture heretofore entered against the defendant be set aside & that the defendant pay all legal costs of said forfeiture

It is therefore considered by the court that the state recover against the Defendant the costs aforesaid in form aforesaid & be in mercy & &

---

the state
vs
Daniel Coffelt ) this day came the State by the Solecitor General who prosecutes on behalf of the state & thereupon came on the demurer to the Scirefacias to be argued & on argument of counsil being heard as well in support of said Demurer as against it & the matters & things therein contained being duly considered & fully understood it is considered by the court that the demurer be sustained

(p 187) Saturday August 19th 1820

State
vs
Danial Coffelt ) On motion & for reasons appearing to the Satisfaction of the court the forfeiture heretofore entered against the defendant be set aside and that the defendant pay all legal costs

of said forfeiture

It is considered by the court that the state recover against the defendant the costs aforesaid in form aforesaid and be in mercy & &

State
 vs
Daniel Coffelt

this day came the state by the solecitor General who prosecutes on behalf of the state & thereupon came the Demurrer to the scirefacias to be argued and on argument of counsel being heard as well in support of said demurer as against it & the matters therein contained being duly considered & fully understood it is considered by the court that the said demurer be Sustained

State
 vs
Daniel Coffelt

On motion & for reasons appearing to the satisfaction of the court the forfeature heretofore entered against the defendant be set aside & that the defendant pay all legal costs of said forfeiture it is therefore considered by the court that the State recover against the defendant the cost aforsaid in manner & form aforsaid & be in mercy & &

(p 188) Court adjourned untill court in course

John Brock
John Neil
John Huddleston

November 13th 1820

At a court of pleas and quarter sessions begun and held at the courthouse in Tazewell for the County of Claiborne on Monday the thirteenth day of November one thousand eight hundred and twenty present the worshipful Justices to wit

John Huddleston — Marcurious Cook
John Brock — George Brock
John Neil — George Yoakum
Robert W. McClary

---

A Deed of conveyance from Robert W. McCleary and his wife Polly McCleary to John Kearn for an undivided fourth part of three certain tracts of land therein described was duly acknowledged in open court by the said Robert W. McCleary and by the said Polly McCleary on her private examination admitted to record and ordered to be

(p 189) November 13th 1820

be certified to Knox County for registration the land lying in said county

---

A deed of conveyance from James W. Glasgow to Fielding Lewis for eighty acres of land in Claiborne County was duly proved in open court by the oaths of William Brown and Dennis Condry Subscribing witnesses admitted to Record and ordered to be certified for registration -

---

A Deed of conveyance from Henry Lebow to Covington Collensworth for one hundred acres of land was duly acknowledged in open court by the maker and was admitted to record and ordered to be Registered

---

A Deed of conveyance from James W. Glasgow to Hugh Graham for thirty acres of land was duly proven in open court by the oaths of John Hunt and Reuben Rose two subscribing witnesses thereto and admited to record and ordered to be registered

---

A Deed of conveyance from James W. Glasgow to William Graham for ninety acres of land was duly proven in open court by the oaths of John Hunt & Jeremiah Cloud the subscribing witnesses thereto and was admited to record and ordered to be registered

(p 190) November 13th 1820

A Deed of conveyance from James W. Glasgow to Daniel Hobsons for one hundred and thirty acres of land was duly proven in open court by the oath of Ransom Day and Thomas Shearmon the subscribing witnesses thereto and was admitted to record and ordered to be registered -

---

A Deed of conveyance from Daniel and Ann to David Bunch Jerry Bunch, Lewis Bunch, James Bunch, Wenslow W. Bunch and Tamsey Bunch for one hundred acres of land was duly proven in open court by the oaths of Ransom Day and thomas shearmon the Subscribing witnesses thereto and was admited to record and ordered to be registered

---

A Deed of conveyance from James W. Glasgow by his attorney in fact William Brown to Nathan Moore for fifty acres of land was duly acknowledged in open court and was admited to record and ordered to be registered

---

A Deed of conveyance from Daniel and Ann Hopson to James and Winslow W. Bunch for thirty acres of land was duly proven by the oaths of Ransom Day and Thomas Shearmon and was admited to record and ordered to be registered

(p 191) November 13th 1820

A Deed of conveyance from William Baker to William Hill for one Town Lot no thirty too in the Town of Tazewell was duly proven in open court by the oaths of William Graham & Hugh Graham the subscribing witnesses thereto and was admited to record and ordered to be registered

---

A Deed of conveyance from Joel Dobbs to John Hunt for thirty four acres of land was duly proven in open court by the oath William Graham and Hugh

Graham and William Houston for one Town lot in the Town of Tazewell was duly proven in open court by the oaths of John Hunt and Charles Payne the subscribing witnesses thereto and was admited to record let it be registered

---

A Deed of Trust from Daniel Rice to Absolom Robinson for four hundred and Sixty acres of land was duly acknowledged in open court by the maker and was admited to record and ordered to be certified for registration

---

A Bill of sale from Richard Hitson to Hugh Graham for a negro boy named Adam was proven at last court by the oath of Thomas Givens and filed for further probate is now fully proven by the oath of John Hunt and admited to record and ordered to be certified for registration

---

Ordered by the court that Edward Wootton be appointed overseer of the Road leading from Tazewell to Lee courthouse that is from Wallens old field to Tazewell in room and stead of Alin McCarty and have the same hands and bounds said McCarty had.

(p 193) Monday Nov. 13th 1820

Ordered by the court that Bowyers Bullard be appointed overseer of the road in room and stead of Benjamin Capps and have the same hands and bounds said Capps had

---

Ordered by the court that John Wallis be appointed overseer of the road in room and Stead of Thomas Whitehead and have the hands as follows to wit James Brock, Jacob Cloud, Luke Perry, William Perry and William Bridges

---

Thomas Shearmon, Richard Harper, Bryant Breeding, John Hurst and Elijah Hurst who were summoned and sworn to view and lay out a road from near James Hodges Spring and to leave the said Hodges House and fince below the present new road as out and marked do report to court that said road do pass and the same to entersect the old road at or near a school house above the said Hodges House

---

Ordered by the court that the above Report of the Jury be affermed and that the same be apart of the public road

(p 194) Monday November 13th 1820

Ordered by the court one third of the acting Justices of the peace being present that the road Laid out leading from the nine mile tree near Doherty by Crockets Ironworks intersecting the valley road at John S. Hardys be made null and void and no longer considered a public road

Ordered by the court that Enos Hobbs John Riley Henly Fugatte, Hugh Mountgomery and William Bales be appointed a Jury of view to view and lay out apart of the road leading from Tazewell to Lee courthouse that is from an old school house on the said old road the nearest and best way to intersect the old road again at the top of the Hill this side of William McDowells and make report to the next Term of this court

(p 195) John S. Hardy presented to court a coppy of the last will and testement of James H. Campbell with thenecessary certificates of the clerk of KnoxvCounty of the State of Kentucky and it was ordered by the court the it filed and recorded.

——

——

John Riley Summoned to attend this term as a Juror is excused from further attendance as it appeared to the satisfaction of the court that he is an oversear of the road Solicitor General

——

——

Ordered by the court that Sterling Cocke be allowed fifty Dollars for his ex oficis services for the year 1820 and that a certificate issue for the same

——

——

Ordered by the court that Benjamin Cloud clerk fees allowed fifty Dollars for his exoficio services for the year 1820 and that certificate issue for this Same

——

——

A Deed of conveyance from James W. Glasgow to Edward Jenings for one hundred acres of land was proven in open court by the oath of William Houston and filed for further probate

——

——

Court adjourned till tomorrow 9 oclock John Brock
John Neil
John Huddleston

Tuesday November 14th 1820

Court met according to adjournment present John Huddleston, John Neal and John Brock Esquires

(p 196) Tuesday November 14th 1820

Court met according to adjournment Present the worshipful John Huddleston John Neil and John Brock and Josiah Ramsey Esqrs.

John Hunt Sheriff returned to court the venire Facias Served on the following Persons namely

| | | | |
|---|---|---|---|
| 1 | David Huddleston | 10 | Robert Grisham |
| 2 | Richard Harper | 11 | Jesse Hurst |
| 3 | Joseph Neil | 12 | John Riley |

| | | | |
|---|---|---|---|
| 4 | John Ferguson | 13 | Henly Fugatt |
| 5 | Isaac Lane | 14 | Neal McNeal |
| 6 | Wm. Clark | 15 | Henry Sumpter |
| 7 | Thomas Hill | 16 | Geo. Golahorn |
| 8 | Samuel Dodson | 17 | Jesse Hooper |
| 9 | Peter Leger | 18 | Wm Purvine |
| 19 | Elijah Harp | 22 | John Doherty |
| 20 | Thos. Brasfield | 23 | Mark Cadle |
| 21 | Dennis Brasfield | 24 | Solomon Ely |
| | | 25 | James Lake |

of whom the following persons were chosen a Grand Jury for the present Term namely

| | | | |
|---|---|---|---|
| 1 | Isaac Lane foreman | 8 | James Lake |
| 2 | Dennis Brasfield | 9 | John Doherty |
| 3 | David Huddleston | 10 | Henry Sumpter |
| 4 | Jesse Hooper | 11 | Joseph Neil |
| 5 | Peter Leger | 12 | Jesse Hurst & |
| 6 | Solomon Ely | 13 | Mark Cadle |
| 7 | Henly Fugatt | | |

who were Sworn according to Law and recived their charge - whereupon Nathan Pery was sworn as constable to attend the Grand Jury and they retired -

(p 197) Tuesday November 14th 1820

Thomas Johnson
vs
Ransom Hays } Original attachment

The plaintiff comes and dismisses his Suit, and thereupon the defendant comes and confesses Judgment for the costs whereupon it is considered by the court that the plaintiffs Suit be dismissed, and that the plaintiff recover of the defendant his costs by him about his Suit in this behalf expended and the defendant in mercy.

Robert W. McCleary
vs
John Bundron } Writ of enquiry

This cause is continued on the afidavit of the plaintiff.

George Vanbebber
vs
Wilson W. Martin } Appeal

The plaintiff in proper person comes into court and dismisses his suit and thereupon the defendant comes into court and confesses Judgment for half the cost - whereupon it is considered by the court that the plaintiffs

(p 198) Tuesday November 14, 1820

Suit be dismissed that the defendant recover of the plaintiff one half of the costs that the plaintiff recover of the defendant the other half of the costs and that Executions issue accordingly

George Vanbibber
vs
Wilson W. Martin &
James C. Martin } Debt

The plaintiff comes into court in proper person and dismisses his Suit - and thereupon the defendants come and confesses Judgment for half the costs whereupon it is considered by the court that the plaintiffs Suit be dismissed that the defendants recover of the plaintiff one half of the costs that the plaintiff recover of the defendant the other half of the costs and that execution may issue accordingly

---

Nathan Perry constable was sworn to attend on the Grand Jury at the present Term
Isd.

---

John McCubbin a constable was sworn to attend on the court
Isd.

(p 199) Tuesday November 14th 1820

William Barnwell vs Peter Smith } Petetion certiorari

It appearing to the Satisfaction of the court that the Defendant never gave Security nor obtained his writs of certiorari or Supersedeas on motion it is considered by the court that the petetion of the Defendant be dismissed and that the plaintiff recover his costs about his Suit in this behalf expended -

Henry Castor vs Robert Gibson } Trespass A. & B.

This day came the parties by their attornies and thereupon came a Jury to wit

| | | | |
|---|---|---|---|
| 1 | John Fergurson | 7 | John Richardson |
| 2 | Richard Harper | 8 | Benjamin Barney |
| 3 | Robert Grisham | 9 | Emanuel Landers |
| 4 | John S. Hardy | 10 | Archibald Eads |
| 5 | Edward Wooten | 11 | Martin Fugatt |
| 6 | Daniel Coffelt | 12 | Jacob Cloud |

who being elected, tried and sworn well and truly to try and the truth

(p 200) Tuesday November 14th 1820

to speak on the issue joined upon their oaths do say they find the defendant guilty of the Trespass assault and Battery mentioned in the plaintiffs declaration, and assess the plaintiffs damage by reason thereof to Two dollars and fifty cents besides costs whereupon it is considered by the court, that the Plaintiff recover of the Defendant Two dollars and fifty cents his damages by the Jury assessed as aforesaid, together with his costs about his Suit in this behalf expended and the defendant in mercy -

A plat and certificate of Survey for Ten acres of Land in Claiborne County in the name of Isaac Vanbebber with an assignment thereon from said Isaac Vanbebber and produced in open court, and the Executors of said assignment was duly acknowledged in open court by said Isaac Vanbebber, and the same is admitted to record

(p 201) Tuesday November 14th 1820

A power of attorney from Elizabeth Killion to George Fansett was acknowledged in open court by the said Elizabeth as her act and deed for the purposes therein expressed and it is ordered ordered by the court that the same be certified accordingly

---

Deed of conveyance from Nathaniel Davis to Fredrick Bowlinger for three hundred acres of Land was proven at May Term 1820 by the oath of Fredrick Bowlinger and filed for further probate is now fully proven by the oath of Daniel Coffelt the other Subscribing witness and was admited to record and ordered to be registered

---

A Deed of conveyance from Archibald Eads to John Crechfield for forty acres of Land was duly acknowledged in open court by the maker and was admitted to Record and ordered to be registered.

---

A Deed of conveyance from William Baker to John Hodges and Elizebeth Todd for one Town Lot in the Town of Tazewell No 33 was duly proven in open court by the oath of William Graham and Hugh Graham the subscribing witnesses thereto and was admited to record and ordered to be registered

(p 202) Tuesday November 14th 1820

A Bill of sale from William Hill to William Graham & Co. for beds and ferenture was duly proven in open court by the oaths of Tidance Lane and Charles Payne the Subscribing witnesses thereto and was admited to record and ordered to be certified for Registration

---

William Houston, Hugh Graham and John Huddleston commissioners appointed to Settle the Estate of Benjamin Posey Deceased with Susannah Posey the administratrix made their Report to court which was recived and ordered to be Recorded

---

State vs Joseph Morning } Personaly appeared in open court Joseph Morning, John Devenport and Daniel Coffelt and acknowledged themselves indebted to the State of Tennessee in the sum of five hundred Dollars for the use of the State that is to say Joseph Morning in the sum of $2.50 and John Devenport and Daniel Coffelt in the sum of $1.25 Each to be levied of their respective goods and chattals land and Tennements to be void on conditions that Joe Morning make his personal appearance & from day to Day to answer a charge of the State against him, and not depart the court without leave

(p 203) Tuesday Nov. 14th 1820

State vs } Personally appeared in open court Lewis Lay and Hardy Hughs and

Lewis Lay ) acknowledged themselves indebted to the State of Tennessee in the sum of three hundred & seventy five Dollars that is to say Lewis Lay in the sum of two hundred and fifty Dollars and Hardy Hughs in the sum of one hundred and twenty five dollars to be respective - ly Levied of their goods and chattals Lands and Tennements to be void on condition that Lewis Lay make his personal appearance from day to day to answer a charge of the State exhibited against him at the present term of this court and not depart without leave

---

State )
vs )
Henry Lower ) Personally appeared in open court Henry Lower, Jesse Devers & Peter Lower and acknowledged themselves indebted to the State of Tennessee in the sum of five hundred Dollars that is to say Henry Lower in the sum of two hundred and fify dollars and Jesse Deavers, and Peter Lower in the sum of one hundred and twenty five each

(p 204) Tuesday 14th Nov. 1820

to be respectively levied of their goods and chattals lands and Tennements for the use of the State to be void on condition that Henry Lower make his appearance from day to day to answer a charge of the State exhibited against him at the present Term and not depart the court without leave

---

A power of attorney James W. Glasgow to John Cocke was Duly proven in open court by the oaths of John Huddleston and Benjamin Cloud the Subscribing witnesses thereto admitted to record and ordered to be recorded at length

---

An article of agreement between John Cocke and James W. Glasgow was duly proven in open court by the oaths of John Huddleston and Benjamin Cloud the subscribing witnesses thereto and was admited to record and ordered to be certified to Grainger County for registration

(p 205) State of Tennessee )
Claiborne County ) On this 14th day of November in the year of our Lord 1820 personally appeared in open court it being the County Court of pleas and quarter sessions and a court of Record held for the County of Claiborne aforesaid, Joseph Evans, aged Sixty one years, Resident in the aforesaid County of Claiborne in the State aforesaid, who being first duly sworn according to Law Doth on his oath Declare that he Served in the Revelutionary War, as Follows to wit, In the Seventh Virginia Regiment commanded by Col. McClanahan in the company commanded by Captain Joseph Crockett as Set forth in an original Declaration Dated on the 28th day of May 1818 - - - - - In consiquence of which he has Recived a pension certificate of number 7045 and I Do Solemly Swar that I was a resident citizen of the United States on the 18th day of March 1818 and that I have not Since that time by gift sale or in any manner Disposed of my property or any part thereof with Intent thereby so to deminish it, as to bring myself within the provisions of an act of Congress Entitled an act to provide for certain persons ingaged in the Land and Naval Servaces of the United States in the Revolutionary War passed on the 18th of March 1818, and that I have not, nor has any person for intrust for me on property or Security

contract or Debts Due to me nor have I any income other then what is contained in the Schedule Hereunto annexd. and by me Subscribed - which is as follows to wit

(p 206) thirty acres of Land but inferior quality and modratly

| | |
|---|---|
| Improved worth say | $200.00 |
| one marr & two colts worth say | $100.00 |
| five Head of cattle worth say | $ 20.00 |
| twelve Head of Sheap worth say | $ 18.00 |
| 6 plats 1 dish 5 Knives & forks worth | $ 7.00 |
| 3 Small Sows & 12 pigs worth | $ 2.50 |
| one oven & Frying pan worth | $ 1.50 |
| Debts owing to me at this time | $ 2.75 |
| Total of Debts & property | $351.75 |
| Amount of Debts which I owe | $156.00 |
| Total amount after Deducting what I owe | $195.75 |

that he is a <u>fermer</u> by occupation & that he has not bien able to do one Days work for ten years last past - by Reason of being afflicted with the Tiphisic, that his Family is in number Three (besides himself) a weak and Sickly wife 58 years of age of a week and sickly Habbit Sworn to and Declared in open court in the year of our lord 1820

his
Joseph X Evans
mark

attest
B. Cloud clerk

(p 207) Tuesday Nov. 14th 1820

John Wallen vs James Martin } This day came the plaintiff by his attorney and thereupon came a Jury to wit

| | |
|---|---|
| Thomas Hill | Daniel Sowder |
| Thomas Brasfield | William Henderson |
| Elijah Harp | Samuel Wilson |
| William Purvine | George Cloud |
| Jonas Hill | William Wallis |
| Robert Parks | Jesse Devers |

who being elected Tried and sworn well and Truly to enquire of the damages Sustained by the plaintiff upon their oaths do say they find for the plaintiff one hundred and seven dollars and twenty three cents besides his costs Therefore it is considered by the court that the plaintiff recover of the defendant his Damages aforesaid in manner and form as by the jury assessed together with his costs in this behalf expended and that he have an order of sale to sell the property attached

(p 208) Tuesday Nov. 14, 1820

A Bill of Indictment for an assault and Battery the State against Joseph Mournin was returned by the Grand Jury <u>endorised</u> a true Bill Isaac Lane foreman

State vs Lewis Lay } Indictment for asst. & Batty.

The Grand Jury returned a true Bill

State vs Henry Lown } Indt. for asst. & Battery

The Grand Jury returned a true Bill

The court adjourned until tomorrow morning nine oclock
John Brock
Josiah Ramsey
John Neil
John Huddleston

Ordered by the court that the order of last court appointed William Graham and John Huddleston Esqrs. commissioners to settle the Estate of Alexander Southerland Deceased with William Condray the administrator be Renewed and the same commissioners make Settlement with said administrator and make Report to the next Term of this court
Isd. 30th Jany

(p 209) Wednesday November 15th 1820

Court met according to adjournment present the worshipful Josiah Ramsey John Huddleston, John Neil and John Brock Esquires

State of Tennessee }
Claiborne County }
On this 14th day of Novemoer 1820 personally appeared in open court the court of pleas and quarter sessions for said county being a court of record having been so constituted by act of asembly and exercising power of fine and imprisonment, John A. Honey commonly called Acellis Honey aged about Sixty years a citizen of said county who being first duly sworn according to Law Doth on his oath make the following declaration in order to obtain the provisions made by the act of congress of the 18th March 1818 and the 1st May 1820 and that he the said J. A. Honey enlisted for the Term of three years on or about the 16th day of November in the year immediately proceeding the Battle at Savannah as well as he recollects in Caroline County of Virginia in the company commanded by Capt. Wooslen. Wooslen died he then fell under the command of Capt Pendleton was enlisted by Coronel John White private Soldier of the First Virginia regiment of Light Dragoons as then called said regiment was commanded by Colo. Anthony W. White in the Line of the State of Virginia on the continental establishment he contimued to serve (p 210) in the said regiment the full term of three years and four days more which was discharged from the said Service at Petersburg in the state of Virginia which discharge he lost many years ago said discharge was given him by Maj. Balor Hill of said regiment in the year after enlisted applicant was in the Battle of Savannah he has no evidence now in his power of said Services other than hence with transmitted, and relinquishes all claim to a pension except the present and in pursuance of the act of 1st May 1820 I do Solemly swear that I was a resident citizen of the United States on the 18th day of March 1818 and that I have not Since that time by gift, Sale, or in any manner disposed of my property or any part thereof with intent thereby so to deminish it as to bring myself within the provisions of an act of congress entitled an act to provide for certain persons engaged in the Land and naval Services of the united states in the revolutionary war passed on the 18th day of March 1818 and that I have not, nor has any person in Trust for me, any property or securities contracts or debts due to me; nor have I any income other than what is contained in the schedule hereunto anexed and by me subscribed 1 mare at $12, 1 cow and calf 10 - 1 oven $2.50, ½ doz. plates & dish & 3 or four knives & forks $5, a table 50 cents 0

The applicants family consist of himself his wife age about fifty five years old and 3 children Sarah, Stephen & John about 16 - Sarah & stephen work from home for their own support and John talks of leaving the county to shift for himself applicant is old and inferm and his wife is daily unwell and very feeble & scarcely able to do anything for support. The applicants occupation is to a list in attending a grist mill. Applicant can not tell how soon he and his wife may be left to shift for themselves sworn and declared in open court the date first above B. Cloud Clerk

his
John A. X Honey
mark

I Benjamin Cloud, clerk of the court aforesaid, do hereby certify that the forgoing Mark oath and the schedule hereunto anexed thereby copied from the record of said court, and I do further certify that it is the opinion of the said court, that the total amount in value of the property exhibited in the aforesaid schedule is not more than thirty dollars. In testimony whereof I have hereunto set my hand and affixed the seal of said court on this 14th day of November 1820 B. Cloud clerk

(p 111) Wednesday November 15th 1820

The petition of Thomas Evans for License to keep a house of entertainment in Claiborne County was granted on the giving Bond and security and being qualified as the Law directs, which was done accordingly

The State
vs
Samuel Day

this day came the State by the solecitor general who prosecutes on behalf of the state and the defendant on his proper person and being charged on the bill of Indictment pleaded thereto guilty and submites to the court whereupon it is considered by the court that for this offence he be fined the sum of twenty five cents and it is further considered by the court that the state recover of the defendant the cost in this behalf expended and the defendant in mercy & & and on motion of the attorney for the government It is ordered by the court that said Defendant remain in custody of the sheriff untill the fine and costs aforesaid are paid or security given for the Same whereupon John Day came into open court in his proper person and with the

(p 112) Wednesday November 15th 1820

assent of the court agrees to and as the security of said Defendant confesses Judgment for the fine and costs aforesaid which is here made the Judgment of the court & the said Defendant in mercy & &

The State
vs
Peter Lower

Indt. A. B.

The grand Jurors this day returned into court the bill of Indictment drawn in in this cause found a True Bill -

The State
vs
Thomas Bundy

Assault and Battery

The Grand Jury returned a True Bill

The State
vs
David Kain

Assault & Battery

This day came the attorney General and the Defendant in his own proper person and thereupon came a Jury to wit

1 Thomas Hill 7 Miles Hodges

| | | | |
|---|---|---|---|
| 2 | Thomas Brassfield | 8 | William Ritter |
| 3 | Elijah Harp | 9 | John Harper |
| 4 | William Pervine | 10 | Alexander Hunter |
| 5 | Richard Harper | 11 | Harden Carey |
| 6 | Thomas Mays | 12 | John Richardson |

who being elected tried and sworn well and truly to try the Issue of Traverse joined upon their oaths do say, that they find the Defendant Guilty in manner and form as charged in the Bill of Indictment and the court not being advised what judgment to render the cause is continued for the court to consider thereof until tomorrow

(p 213) Wednesday November 15th 1820

James Grant vs John Umstead — Two cases

The petition of the defendant, by his agent Joseph Hart for writs of certerori and supresedas was presented to court and the prayer thereof is granted on the petitioners giving security in each case the Law directs - which is done accordingly

State vs Philips Coffelt

This cause was continued until next court for Sufficient reasons appearing in the Defendants affidavit - and it appearing that the defendant is a minor, thereupon came into open court his father Daniel Coffelt and acknowledged himself indebted to the State of Tennessee in the penal sum of Two hundred and fifty dollars to be levied of his goods and chattels lands and tenements; to be void on condition that said defendant make his personal appearance at or on next court to be held at the court house in Tazewell on the Wednesday after the second Monday of Febuary next answer the

(p 214) Wednesday, November 15th 1820

charge of the state exhibited against him by indictment, and not depart the court without leave -

State vs Peter Lower — Indictment

Personally appeared in open court Peter Lower, Reuben Flowers and Adam Jaral and acknowledged themselves indebted unto the state of Tennessee in the sum of four hundred Dollars to wit, Peter Lower in the sum of two hundred Dollars and Reubin Flowers and Adam Jaral in the sum of one hundred Dollars Each to be respectively Levied of their goods and chattals lands and tennements for the use of the use of the state void on condition that Peter Lower make his appearance from day to day at the present Term of this court to answer a charge of the state against him on bill of Indictment and not depart the court without leave -

---

William Burges vs Joseph Ferrell

the petition of Joseph Ferrell the defendant for writs of certiorari and supersedeas was granted him on giving Bond and security as the Law directs which is done accordingly

(p 215) Wednesday November 15th 1820

A Deed of conveyance from Richard Mays to Miles Hodges for seventy five acres of land was duly acknowledged in open court by the maker thereof and was admitted to record and ordered to be registered

---

A Deed of conveyance from Thomas R. McClary to John Jones for thirty acres of land was duly acknowledged in open court by the maker and was admited to Record and ordered to be registered

---

A Deed of conveyance from James W. Glasgow by his attorney in fact William Brown to Bibby Hodges for one hundred acres of Land was duly acknowledged in open court by Said attorney and was admited to record and ordered to be registered

(p 216) Wednesday 15th $N_o$v. 1820

A Deed of conveyance from James W. Glasgow to Edward Jennings for one hundred acres of land was duly proven in open court by the oaths of William Houston and John Simions the subscribing witnesses thereto and was admitted to record and ordered to be registered

---

A Deed of conveyance from Abel Lanham to Joel Dobbs for two hundred and fifty acres of Land was proven in open court by the oath of William Graham a subscribing witness there to and filed for further probate

---

Court adjourned until tomorrow morning 9 oclock

John Brock
John Huddleston
Josiah Ramsey
John Neil

Thursday November 16th 1820

Court met according to adjournment present the worshipful Josiah Ramsey John Huddleston, John Neal and John Brock Esquires

State<br>
vs } Assault and Battery<br>
Jacob Pereafile

The Defendant being charged on the Bill of Indictment say for plea thereto he is guilty and Submits to the court

(p 217) Thursday November 16th 1820

Therefore for such his offence it is considered by the court that he be fined one Dollar It is therefore considered by the court that the State recover of the Defendant the fine and costs aforesaid for which Execution may issue

State )

vs ) Assault and Battery
David Cain ) The defendant having been convicted on yesterday, and the court having taken time to consider of their Judgment, this day pronounced the same, the defendant being present as follows that the defendant be fined in the sum of Twenty dollars - and thereupon it is considered by the court that the state recover of the Defendant the fine aforesaid together with her costs about her Indictment in this behalf expended and that the defendant remain in custody until the fine and costs are paid or security given therefor

(p 218) A Deed of conveyance from Elijah Roblet to Abraham Collet for one hundred and fifty acres of land was duly proven in open court by the oaths of William Rogers and Reuben B. Rogers subscribing witnesses thereto and and was admited to record and ordered to be certified to Green County for Registration

---

State ) This day came the State by the
vs ) Solecitor General who prosecutes
Samuel Day ) on behalf of the state and the Defendant in his proper person and being charged on the bill of Indictment pleaded guilty thereto and submits to the court whereupoh it is considered by the court that for this his offence he be fined twenty five cents and it is further considered by the court that the State recover of the defendant the cost in this behalf expended and on motion of the attorney for the government it is considered by the court that said defendant remain in custody of the sheriff untill fine and cost are paid or security given for the same whereupon John Day came into open court in his proper person and with the assent of the court agrees to, and as the security of said defendant confesses Judgment for the fine and cost aforesaid and said defendants in mercy & &

(p 219) Thursday 16th Nov. 1820

State ) Personally appeared in open court
vs ) Peter Lower, Reuben Flowers, and
Peter Lower ) Adam Jaral and acknowledged them selves indebted to the state of Tennessee in the sum of five hundred Dollars to wit Peter Lower in the sum of two hundred & fifty Dollars and Reuben Flowers & Adam Jaral in the sum of one hundered & twenty five Dollars each for the use of the state to be levied of their respective goods and chattels lands and tenements void on condition that Peter Lower make his personal appearance from day to day at the present term of this court to answer a charge of the state against him on a bill of indictment and not depart the court without leave

---

State ) Indictment
vs )
Sampson Dodson ) this day came the State by the Solecitor general who prosecutes for the state and the defendant in his proper personand being charged on the bill of indictment pleaded thereto not guilty and thereupon came a Jury to wit Thomas Hill, Thomas Brasfield Elijah Harp, William Purvine, Pharaoh Rhoe, William Ritter, Jese Devers, Martin Fugatt,

Richard Moore, James Maddy Daniel Sowder & Timothy Philpot (p 220)
who being elected tried and well and truly to try and the truth to speak upon the Issue Joined upon their oaths do say they find the defendant not guilty in manner and form as charged in the bill of indictment it is therefore considered by the court that the defendant go hence without Day and that the County of Claiborne pay the cost of this prosecution

---

State
vs
Joseph Morning

Indictment

this day came the state by the Solecitor who prosecutes for the State and the defendant in his proper person and being charged on the Bill of Indictment for plea says he is not guilty whereupon came a Jury, to wit,

| | | | |
|---|---|---|---|
| 1 | Thomas Hill | 7 | James Maddy |
| 2 | William Purvine | 8 | Richard Moore |
| 3 | Elijah Harp | 9 | Daniel Sowder |
| 4 | Pharoah Roe | 10 | Edward Woolen |
| 5 | William Ritter | 11 | James Hill |
| 6 | Timothy Philpot | 12 | Allen Morris |

who being elected, tried and sworn well and truly to try and the truth to speak in the Issue of Traverse joined, upon their oaths do say, they find the defendant guilty in manner and form as charged

(p 221) Thursday November 16th 1820

in the Bill of Indictment - whereupon it is considered by the court that the defendant be fined in the sum of fifty cents - that the state recover of the Defendant the fine aforesaid and the costs about his Indictment in this behalf expended and it is further ordered by the court that the defendant be held in custody until the fine and cost or paid or security given therefor whereupon John Davenport came into court and undertook as security for the said defendant and confesses judgment for the fine and costs aforesaid for which execution may issue -

Jesse Devers
vs
John Devenport

Ordered by the court that the order of Last court to take the deposition of Reachel Devanport i in the suit wherein John Devenport is plaintiff & Jesse Deavers is Defendant be renewed

Ordered by the court that a commisioner issue to any one Justice of Whitley County Kentucky to take the deposstion of William Lay in the two Suits now pending in the court between John Devenport and Jesse Devers the plaintiff giving the Defendant ten days notice

(p 222) Thursday November 16th 1820

John Devenport
vs
David Cain

Trespass Asst. & Batty.

This day came in to court Jesse Devers and Martin Fugatt appearance Bail of said defendant and suggested to the court, that they were desireus of surrendering the defendant in custody in discharge of themselves and further suggested that said defendant was already in custody and in the prison on account of a charge of the state against him - and the same is ordered to be entered on the records and said securities released as bail

John Whiteaker
vs
Andrew Johnson

On sufficient cause shown to the court on affidavit of the defendant it is ordered by the court that the Judgment by Default entered at the Last term of this court in this cause be set aside on defendant paying the cost of this term

(p 223) Thursday Nov. 16th 1820

John Wallen
vs
Hugh White

The rule of referance in this case is set aside and the cause continued for trial at next Term

State
vs
Henry Lower

Indictment

Personally appeared in open court Henry Lower Hardy Hughs, and John Doherty and acknowledged themselves indebted to the state of Tennessee in the sum of four hundred Dollars to wit, Henry Lower in the sum of two hundred Dollars and Hardy Hughs, and John Doherty in the sum of one hundred Dollars each to be levied of their Respective goods and chattels land and tenements for the use of the State void on condition that Henry Lewer make his personal appearance at the court house in Tazewell on the Wednesday after the second Monday in February next to answer a charge of the State exhibited against him on a bill of indictment and not depart the court without leave

(p 224) Thursday Nov. 16th 1820

State
vs
Henry Lower

Indictment

Personally appeared in open court Joseph Mornnin and Lewis Lay and acknowledged themselves indebted to the state of Tennessee in the sum of four hundred Dollars that is to say Joseph Mornnin in the sum of one hundred Dollars & Lewis Lay in the sum of one hundred Dollars for the use of the state to be respectively Levied of their goods and chattels lands and tenements , void on condition that Joseph Mornnin make his appearance at the courthouse in Tazewell on the Wednesday after the second Monday in February next to prosecute and give evidence on behalf of the state against Henry Lower and not depart the court without leave

---

A Deed of conveyance from Samuel Cowan to George Shetter for one hundred and fourteen acres of land was duly proven in open court by the oath of William Rogers a subscribing witness thereto and was filed for further probate.

(p 225) Thursday Nov. 16th 1820

A Deed of conveyance from John Owens to George Shetter for one hundred acres of land was duly proven in open court by the oath of William Rogers a subscribing witness thereto and was ordered to be filed for further probate

Silas Williams Henry Hunter and Wm. Bowman who was by court appointed commissioners to settle the estate of Robert Cary Decd. with William Cary the Executor made their Report to court which is recived and inspected by the court and ordered to be filed and recorded -

State
vs
Duglass Grady

Personally appeared in open court Douglass Grady, and Reuben Day and acknowledged themselves indebted to the state of Tennessee in the sum of three hundred and fifty Dollars for the use of the state to wit, Douglass Grady in the sum of two hundred and fifty Dollars and Reuben Day in the sum of one hundred and twenty five Dollars

(p 226) Thursday 16th Nov. 1820

to be levied of their goods and chattels Lands and Tenements void on condition that Douglass Grady make his appearance at the courthouse in Tazewell from Day to Day then and there to answer a charge of the state exhibited against him on a bill of indictment and not depart the court without leave

Court adjourned until tomorrow 9 oclock

John Neil
Josiah Ramsey
John Huddleston
John Brock

Friday November 17th 1820

Court met according to adjournemnt present the same Justices as of yesterday

State
vs
Lewis Lay

Indictment

this day came the state by the Solecitor general who prosecutes on behalf of the state and the defendant in his proper person and being charged on the bill of indictment pleaded thereto not guilty and thereupon also came a Jury to wit

(p 227) Friday November 17th 1820

1 Thomas Hill
2 Elijah Harp
3 William Purvine
4 Richard Harper
5 John Crichfield
6 Timothy ________
7 Isaac Vanbebber
8 Allen Morris
9 Edward Woolton
10 William Walles
11 William Weaver
12 William Burch

who being elected Tried and sworn well and Truly to try and the truth to speak on the Issue of Traverse wherein the state is plaintiff and Lewis Lay is Defendant upon their oaths do say that the defendant is guilty in manner and form as charged in the bill of Indictment therefore it is considered that for this His offence he be fined twenty five cents and it is further considered by the court that the state recover of the defendant the cost in this behalf expended and on motion of the attorney for the government it is ordered by the court that said defendant remain in custody of the sharif untill the fine and cost aforesaid are paid or security given for the same whereupon Hardy Hughs came into open court in his proper person and with the assent of the court agrees to and as security of said defendant confesses (p 228) Judgment for the fine and cost aforsaid which is here made the Judgment of the court and the Defendants in mercy & &

---

State vs Peter Lower } this day came the state by the solecitor General who prosecutes on behalf of state and the Defendand in his proper person and being charged on the bill of indictment pleaded thereto not guilty and thereupon came a Jury to wit -

1 Thomas Hill
2 William Purvine
3 Elijah Harp
4 John Hurst
5 Joseph Hurst
6 Elijah Hurst
7 Willis Harper
8 Reuben Harper
9 William Maddy
10 Richard Moore
11 Tidance Lane
12 Jesse Carpenter

who being elected tried and sworn well Truly to try and the truth to speak on the issue of Travers wherein the state is plaintiff and Peter Lower is defendant upon their oaths do say they find the defendant guilty in manner and form as charged in the bill of Indictment therefore it is

(p 229) Thursday Nov. 17th 1820

considered by the court he be fined fifty cents and it is further considered by the court that the state recover of the Expended and the the Defendant in mercy & &

state vs John Bundron } Indictment

Personally appeared in open court John Bundron & Dennis Condray and acknowledged themselves indebted to the state of Tennessee in the principal sum of three hundred & seventy five Dollars to wit John Bundron in the sum of two hundred and fifty Dollars & Dennis Condry in the sum of one hundred & twenty five Dollars to be levied of their goods and chattals lands and Tenements void on condition that John Bundron make his personal appearance at the courthouse in Tazewell from day to day at the present term of this court and abide by and perform the Judgments of said court and not Depart without leave

(p 230) State vs Richard Mays } Indictment

Personally appeared in open court Richard Mays & Joseph McCleary and acknowledged themselves indebted to the state of Tennessee in the penal sum of three hundred and seventy five Dollars to wit - Richard Mays in the sum of two hundred & fifty dollars and Joseph McCleary in the sum of one hundred and twenty five dollars to be levied of their respective goods and chattles Lands and Tennements void on condition that Richard Mays make his personal appearance at the courthouse in Tazewell from day to day and abide by and perform the Judgment the court and not depart without leave

state vs Ransom Day } Indictment

Personally appeared in open court Ransom Day and Reuben Day and acknowledged themselves indebted to the state of Tennessee in the sum

(p 231) Thursday Nov. 17th 1820

of three hundred and seventy five Dollars to wit Hansom Day in the sum of two hundred and fifty Dollars & Reuben Day in the sum of one hundred and twenty five dollars to be levied of their respective good and chattals land and tenements void on condition that Ransom Day make his personal appearance at the courthouse in Tazewell from this court and not depart without leave -

State
vs
Douglass Grady

Indictment

this day came the state by the solecitor general who prosecutes for the state and the defendant in his proper person and being charged on the bill of indictment for plea says he is guilty and submited to the court whereupon it is considered by the court that for such his offence he be fined twenty five cents and it is further considered by the court that the plaintiff recover of the defendant the cost in this behalf . (p 232) Expended and on motion it is ordered by the court that the defendant remain in custody of the sheriff untill fine and cost are paid or security given whereupon John Bundron and Miles Hodges came into open court in their proper persons and with the assent of the court agrees to and as the security of the said defendant confesses Judgment for the fine and costs aforesaid which is here made the Judgment of this court and the Defendants in mercy & &

Ordered by the court that the following named person be appointed Jurors to the next term of this court to wit

Isd. 7 Dec.

| | |
|---|---|
| 1 William Jenkins senr. | 12 Ransom Day Jun'r. |
| 2 William Turner | 13 Willis Harper |
| 3 John Sulfrage | 14 Richard Harper |
| 4 Richard Crichfield | 15 William Cooper |
| 5 Thomas Hoskins | 16 Russell Lane |
| 6 Thomas Shumate | 17 Amos Johnson |
| 7 Jubal Lee | 18 Abel Lanham |
| 8 Robert Yoakum | 19 George Campbell |
| 9 John Henley | 20 Rice Whitaker |
| 10 Abraham Devault | 21 William Lanham |
| 11 Jacob Shoults | 22 Joseph Bishop |

(p 233) Friday 17th Nov. 1820

James A. Hamilton, Reuben Flowers Lewis Lay Elijah Jones

Ordered by the court that the following named persons be appointed Jurors to next Cercuit Court

| | |
|---|---|
| 1 Peter Huffaker | 14 John Huddleston |
| 2 George McCrary | 15 James Sims |
| 3 Andrew Crockett | 16 John Simmons |
| 4 William Ely | 17 Thomas Hurst |
| 5 Aaron Davis | 18 Richard Harper |
| 6 John Wallen | 19 David Huddleston |
| 7 Moses Davis | 20 David Rogers |

| | | | |
|---|---|---|---|
| 8 | George Yoakum | 21 | Neal McNeal |
| 9 | William Renfro | 22 | John Stakely |
| 10 | Robert Gibson | 23 | Isaac Thomas |
| 11 | Isaac Yoakum | 24 | John Lynch |
| 12 | Reuben Moss | 25 | George Evans |
| 13 | John Neil | 26 | John Riley |

Isd. 9 December

Ordered by the court that William Renfro be appointed guardian to William Vanbebber and Peggey Vanbebber minor heirs and orphans of John Vanbibber Dec'd who intered into Bond accordingly

(p 234) Friday 17th Nov. 1820

A Deed of conveyance from Abel Lanham to Joel Dobbs for two hundred and fifty acres of Land was duly acknowledged in open court by the maker and was duly admitted to record and ordered to be Registered

A Deed of conveyance from James W. Glassgow to Reuben Rose for two hundred and fifty acres of Land was duly proven in open court by the oaths of James A. Hamilton and Dennis Condray the subscribing witnesses thereto and was admitted to record and ordered to be registered

the Grand Jury is discharged from further attendance at this term

John M. Vaughan
vs
Thomas Rice, Daniel Rice & Lewis Rice

this day came the parties by their attornies and thereupon also came a Jury to wit
Elijah Hurst
Joseph Hurst
Willis Harper
Reubin Harper
William Maddy
Richard Moore
Tidance Lane
Jesse Carpenter
Thomas Hill
William Purvine
Robert Grisham
John Hurst

(p 235) Friday 17th Nov. 1820

who being elected tried and sworn well and truly to try and the truth to speak on the Issue of traverse joined on their oaths do say that the defendants have not paid the debt in the declaration mentioned as in pleading they have alledged and assess the plaintiffs damages by reason of the execution of the same to eleven dollars and twenty five cents Therefore it is considered by the court that the plaintiff recover of the defendants the debt in the declaration mentioned and also the same of eleven dollars and twenty five cents the damages aforesaid remainder and form aforesaid be the

Jury assessed together with his costs by him about his suit in this behalf expended and and the defendants in mercy & A

John Whitaker vs Andrew Johnson } On cause shewn by affidavit of the plaintiff it is ordered by the court that a commissioner issue to any Justice of the peace for Harland County, Kentucky to take the deposition of Betsy Whitaker and giving the defendants five days notice of the time and place of taking the same

Court adjournment till tomorrow 9 oclock

John Brock
John Neil
John Huddleston

(p 236) Saturday November 18th 1820

Court met according to adjournment present the worshipful John Huddleston John Neal John Brock Esquires George Martin and James Ball who have appeared the confirmation of the report of the commissioners who made petition of the Lands between the heirs and Legal representation of Benjamin Posey Deceased having dismissed and with drawn their opposition to said report of said commissioners It is considered by the court that said suit be dismissed and that the said George Martin and James Ball pay the costs thereof and that execution issue therefore

---

Ordered by the court that the report of the commissioners making Division of the Lands of Benjamin Posey Deceased between the heirs and Legal representation of said Deceased heretofore made by said commissioners to this court be in things affirmed and It is further ordered by the court that said report of said commissioners be registered in the registers office of Claiborne County

William Maddy vs Benjamin White and James W. Glassgow } The plaintiff in this cause Dismissess his Suit It is therefore considered by the court that the Defendants go hence without day and recover of the plaintiff their costs in this behalf expended and the plaintiff in mercy & A

State vs Philip Coffelt } Personally appeared in open court Jesse Devers and acknowledged himself indebted to the state of Tennessee in the sum of one hundred Dollars to be levied of his good chattels Lands and

(p 237) Saturday November 18th 1820

tenements void on condition that Martin Fugat make his personal appearance at the next term of the court of pleas and quarter of the County of Claiborne to be held on the second Monday in Feburary next on the Wednesday of said term then and there to give evidence on behalf the state and prosecute a Bill of Indictment against Philip Coffelt and not depart the court without leave

William Shumate & wife vs Armstead Brown } This day came the defendant by his attorney and the plaintiffs being solemly called to come and prosecute their suit in this behalf, came not but made default - whereupon it is considered by the court that the plainiffs be non prossed and that the defendant go hence without day, and recover of the plaintiff the costs about his suit in this behalf Expended and the plaintiff in mercy -

Josiah Smith
vs
Joshua Davison
Peter Sharp

Debt

This day came the plaintiff by his attorney and the defendant being solemnly called to come into court and defenda

(p 238) Saturday November 18th 1820

their suit in this behalf came not, but made default - whereupon it is considered by the court that the plaintiff recover of the defendant the debt in the declaration mentioned to wit, the sum of one hundred and fifty five dollars and fifty cents, together with eleven dollars and twenty seven cents damages by reason of the detention thereof besides his costs about his suit in this behalf expended and the defendant in mercy

Samuel English
vs
Thomas Bray

This day came the defendant by his attorney and the plaintiff being Solemly called to come and prosecute his suit in this behalf came not, but made default - whereupon it is considered by the court that the plaintiff be non prossed - and that the defendant recover of the plaintiff his costs about his suit in this behalf expended and the plaintiff in mercy & &

(p 239) Saturday November 18th 1820

The State
vs
Thomas Bunda

Assault and Battery

This day came the attorney General who prosecutes for the state and the defendant in his proper person who becamse he will not defend, being charged on the Bill of Indictment pleads thereto Guilty whereupon it is considered by thecourt that for such his offence he be fined in the Sum of fifty cents - and that the state recover of the defendant the fine aforesaid and the costs about his suit in this behalf expended and that the defendant remain in custody until the fine and costs and paid or security given therefor - whereupon Timothy Philpot comes into court and undertakes, that the said defendant will pay the fine and costs aforesaid or that he will do it for him, and as the security of said defendant confesses Judgment for the same upon which Execution may Issue

(p 240) Saturday November 18th 1820

State
vs
Douglass Grady

This day came the attorney General who prosecutes on behalf of the state and the defendant in his proper person, who being charged on the Bill of Indictment, pleads thereto not guilty and puts himself on the county and the state by his attorney General doth the like - Whereupon came a Jury to wit

1 Thomas Hill
2 Elijah Harp
7 John Rice
8 Thomas Whitmoore

3 Richard Harper
4 Isaac Vanbebber
5 John Murphy
6 Thomas Brassfield
9 John Fergerson
10 William Purvine
11 Samuel Dotson
12 Robert McNew

who being elected, tried and sworn, well and truly to try and the truth to speak in the Issue joined, upon their oaths do say they find the defendant not guilty whereupon it is considered by the court that the defendant go hence without day and further it is considered that the county pay the costs od this prosecution

John Davenport vs Jesse Devers — Appeals - Two cases

By consent the matters and things in thease two cases & all other matters and things actions and causes of action what so ever and refered to the final determination and arbitrament of Hardy Hughes Martin Miller, John Huddleston Esqrs. John Graves and

(p 241) Saturday Nov. 18th 1820

if they cannot agree, they the said abritators shall choose a fifth and then anexed to be made in writing on the said Saturday in January to the next term of this court to recover of the Judgement of the court

state vs Richard Mays & John Bundron — Affray

this day came the state by the solecitor general who prosecutes on behalf of the state and the defendant in proper person who being charged on the bill of Indictment plead thereto not guilty and put themselves on the county and the attorney doth the like whereupon came a Jury to wit

1 Thomas Hill
2 Elijah Harp
3 Richard Harper
4 Robert Mitchell
5 John Murphy
6 Thomas Brassfield
7 John Rice
8 Thomas Whitmore
9 John Fergerson
10 William Purvine
11 Samuel Dotson
12 Robert McNew

who being elected tried and sworn well and truly to try the issue joined upon their oaths do say they find the defendant guilty in manner and form as charged in the bill of Indictment but that as to the defendant Richard Mays they find him not guilty whereupon it is considered by the court that the defendant Richard Mays go hence wihtout day and further it is considered by the court that the defendant John Bundron be fined for his offence in the

(p 242) Saturday November 18th 1820

sum of two dollars and fifty cents, that the state recover of the defendant John Bundron the fine aforesaid together with all costs about his suit in this behalf expended and that said defendant John Bundron remain in custody until said fine and costs are paid or security given therefor whereupon Dennis Condry come into court and undertook as security for said Bundron and confessed judgment for the fine and costs aforesaid for which execution may issue -

The state vs Ransom Day Jnr.

This day came the attorney General who who produced on behalf of the state and the defendant in proper person who being charged on the Bill of Indictment pleads thereto not guilty and puts himself on the county and the state by his attorney General doth the like thereupon came a Jury to wit

| | | | |
|---|---|---|---|
| 1 | Thomas Hill | 7 | John Rice |
| 2 | Elijah Harp | 8 | Thomas Whitmore |
| 3 | Richard Harper | 9 | John Fergerson |
| 4 | Robert Mitchell | 10 | William Purvine |
| 5 | John Murphy | 11 | Samuel Dotson |
| 6 | Thomas Brassfield | 12 | Robert McNew |

who being elected tried and sworn well and truly to try the issue joined upon their oaths do say they the defendant not guilty

(p 243)

State of Tennessee
Saturday November 18th 1820

whereupon a rule is granted to shew cause why the defendant should pay the costs of this prosecuition and said rule is contunied on adverment until next court for want of a competent court and on motion a rule is granted to shew cause why the prosecution should pay the costs and the same is conuninued as above

A deed of conveyance for fifteen acres of land in Claiborne County from Charles Goin to Robert G. Parks was duly proved by the oath of Thomas R. McClary one of the subscribing witnesses who also proves the death of Anderson Watson the other subscribing witness and that he saw him sign said deed as a corresponding witness whereupon it is ordered by the court that the same be recorded and let it be registered

A deed of conveyance for fifteen acres of land in Claiborne County from William Constant to Robert G. Parks was duly proved in open court by the oaths of Thomas R. McCleary one of the subscribing witness thereto who proves the death of Anderson Watson the other subscribing witness, and that he saw him sign said deed as a subscribing witness with said Wm. Cleary whereupon it is ordered by the court that the same be recorded and that it be registered

(p 244)

State of Tennessee
Saturday, November 18th 1820

Jesse Ward
vs
John Bundron } Trespass

This day came the plaintiff by his attorney, and the defendant by his attorney also and the same is continued by consent

The report of the Jury heretofore appointed to asign and lay off to susanna Posey widow and wife of Benjamin Posey Decd. her dower which in part has been filed heretofore is now recived by the court and ordered to be recorded

Court adjourned until court in course
John Brock
John Neil
John Huddleston

(p 245)

Monday February 12th 1821

At a court of pleas and quarter sessions begun and held for the County of Claiborne at the courthouse in Tasewell it being the 12th day Justices present as follows William Graham, George Yoakum
John Huddleston Archibald Bales

John Brock
John Neil
Alexander Campbell
William Savage
Mercurious Cook
John Hurst
George Brock
Aaron Davis

A Deed of conveyance from William McBee, Isaac McBee, Samuel McBee, and Obediah Watters to James Johnson for one hundred acres of land was duly proven in open court by the oaths of William McBee and thomas Watters the subscribing witnesses and was admited to record and ordered to be registered

A Deed of conveyance from William McBee the subscribing witnesses and was admited to record and ordered to be registered

Ordered by the court that William Graham Aaron Davis and George Yoakum Esqrs. be appointed commissioners to settle the administration account of Mark Cadle Decd. with Mary Cadle administratrix of said Estate and make Report to the present term of this court

(p 246) Monday February 12th 1821

Ordered by the court that William Graham and John Huddleston Esqrs. be appointed commissioners to settle the administration account of William Jennings Decd. with William Jennings administrator and make report to the next Term of this court

Order by the court that Robert W. McClary and Archibald Bales be appointed commissioners to settle the administration account of William Mason Deceased with Robert Southern administrator and make return to the presentTerm of this court

Ordered by the court 9 Justice being present that Mary Cadle administratrix of the Estate of Mark Cadle Deceased be allowed Twenty Dollars from the Estate of said Deceased for her trouble and expence in the management of said Estate

Ordered by the court 9 Justices being present that Absalom Hurst be allowed forty Dollars for supporting 4 children of Edmond Maples for the last three months being poor of the county out of the poor funds

(p 247) Monday Febuary 12th 1821

Joel Jones Exhibited to court 9 Justices being present the sculp of a wolf over Six months old and proved he killed said wolf in the county of Claiborne and in the year 1820 and the court being satisfied therewith It is ordered that the sheriff burn the scalp and that the said Joel Jones receive from the Treasurer of East Tennessee the sum allowed by law

Ordered by the court that Jacob Nicely be appointed overseer of the road leading from Tazewell to Knoxville from the Town to the two mile post in room and stead of Thomas Rogers and have the same hands and bounds of hands that said Rogers had

William Graham and John Huddleston commissioners appointed to settle with William Condray administrator of the Estate of Alexander Southerland Deceased at this court made their report which was recived by the court inspected and ordered to be recorded

Ordered by the court that Thomas Bray be appointed overseer of the road leading from the big spring to Mulberry Gap from the spicewood hollow to John Condrays in room and stead of Hiram Edwards and have the same hands and bounds of hands said Edward had

(p 248) Monday February 12th 1821

Ordered by the court that Jesse Cain be appointed overseer of the Road in room and stead of Isaac Bowlinger and have the same hands and bounds for h hands that said Bowlinger had

Ordered by the court that Reubin Flowers be appointed overseer of the Road in room of John Strevle and have for hand the same bounds Said Strevle had

Ordered by the court that Ransom Day Jnr. be appointed overseer of the Kentucky Road from the big spring to the top of Wallens Ridge in Room and stead of Miles Hodges and have for hands the same bounds said Hodges had

Ordered by the court that William Clark be released from working on the Road that leads up sycamore creek and work on the Kentucky Road under Bibby Hodge

Ordered by the court that Solomon Ely be appointed overseer of the state road from Powels River to Wallens Branch in the room and stead of Jacob Pike and have the same bounds for hands said Pike had

(p 249) Monday February 12th 1821

Peter Huffaker, Aaron Davis, William Norvell, Lewis Huffaker, John Roddy James Mundy, William Lea, and William Crichfield or a majority of them be appointed to view and mark out that part of the Road leading from Isaac Vanbebber to intersect the Kentucky road in a direction to Lee County, thence to the State line near John Hardys the nearest and best way to injure Farm as little as may be made their Report as follows to wit

In conformity to the within order We Peter Huffaker, Aaron Davis, James Mundy, William Lea & William Norvell a majority of the Jury have viewed the road from Isaac Vanbebber near to the Virginia line and think the old road is as convenant as any new one we can find from Vanbebbers up to Wallens path leaving the road there & crossing the Kentucky Road near Wallens store House thence a streight Direction to a house where Isaac Parker formerly lived from thence the most Direct way to the old Virginia road at or near Crocketts wood cutting passing near the Sinking spring -

N. B. be it understood the old road leading thro Davises lane to the

(p 250) Monday February 12th 1821

ford of Town Creek is the road we prefer November 7th 1820 Peter Huffaker, Aaron Davis, James Munday Wm. Lea, Wm Norvell

Ordered by the court that the above report of the Jury be affirmed and made a public road of this county

Ordered the court that Dennis Condray be appointed overseer of that part of the Kentucky road from Tazewell to the top of Wallens Ridge and have the same bounds and hands to work thereon as Tennessee Margraves the last overseer had.

Ordered by the court that Beverly Marcum be appointed overseer of that part of the Kentucky road leading from Tazewell the top of the hill north and west of his old shop and so far as he formerly worked and to have the same hands and bounds as he formerly had

---

Ordered by the court that William Ely be appointed overseer of the road as now laid out by the Jury beginning at the old road at Wallens path thence crossing the Kentucky road near Wallens store house thence a strieght direction to where Isaac Parker formerly lived from thence the

(p 251) Monday February 12th 1821

most direct way to the old Virginia road at or near Crockets wood cutting passing near the Sinking spring and have for hands all that lives in the following bounds that is from Cumberland Gap to station creek between powels river and cumberland Mountain

Isd.

---

William Graham, Aaron Davis and George Yoakum who was appointed commissioners to settle the administration accounts of Mark Cadle Deceased with Mary Cadle the administratrix at the present term, has made report of their Settlement to court which was recived by the court and ordered to be recorded.

---

With leave of the court Mary Cadle was appointed Guardian to Lucinda Cadle Mahala Cadle and Squire Jackson Cadle minor heirs and orphans of Mark Dadle Deceased who entered into bond with Aaron Davis and Samuel Cloud her Securities

(p 252) Monday Feby. 12th 1821

A quit claim Deed from Dickerson Jenings to Joseph Jennings for his undivided __________ of the Lands of William Jennings Deceased was duly acknowledged in court admitted to record and ordered to be registered

---

Ordered by the court that Frederick Bolinger Junr. and Betsy Polly Bolinger be appointed administrator and administratrix of the Estate of Isaac Bolinger Deceased who Entered into bond with Amsted Kirk as Security and was sworn as the Law dericts

A Deed of conveyance from Thomas Johnson by his attorney in fact Ashael Johnson to Joseph Campbell for fifty three acres of Land was proven in open court by the oaths of Alexander Campbell and Thomas Givins two subscribing witnesses thereto admitted to record and ordered to be registered

---

A Deed of conveyance from George McNeal to Peter Clipper for Sixty acres of Land was duly acknowledged proven by the oath Alexander Campbell and ordered to be filed for further probate

A Deed of conveyance from James W. Glassgow to John Tompson for three hundred acres of Land was duly proven in open court Dennis Condray and Thomas Shearmon admitted to record and ordered to be registered

(p 253) After making proclamation the court proceeded to Election of a court of quarum for the year 1821 and after counting and compairing the votes it appears that Hercurious Cook John Brock, John Neil William Savage and George Brock had a majority of the whole number of votes and was therefore considered duly and constitutionally Elected a county quarum

---

Ordered by the court a majority of the acting Justices present that John Hunt be allowed to recive of the County Trustee three Dollars for repairs done to the court House

---

Ordered by the court that Benjamin Cloud Clerk of this Court be allowed to receive of the the County Trustee of Claiborne County fifteen dollars forty one and a fourth cents for stationary & & for the use of the office

William Graham Esqr. is appointed Chairman of the court of pleas and quarter Sessions of Claiborne County

The assignment of a plat and certificate of survey from Alexander B. Bradford to Jesee Yoakum for fifteen acres of Land was acknowledged in court which was ordered to be certified

---

The assignment of a plat and certificate of survey from Alexander B. Bradford to Isaac Vanbebber & Reuben Parrott for seventy five acres of land was duly acknowledged in open court which was ordered to be certified

(p 254) Henry Gratner vs Joab Brewer } On motion of Henry Gratner by Sterling Cocke his attorney to be discharged from further liability as security for Joab Brewer in the office of a constable for Claiborne County and it appearing to the Satisfaction of the court that the said Joab Brewer had due and Legal notice of this motion It is therefore considered by the court that the said Henry Gratner be from henceforth discharged from his obligation as security for said Joab Brewer in the office of constable is considered by the court here vacant the said Joab having failed to give additional security for the performance of the duties of said office of constable It is therefore farther considered by the court that the plaintiff recover of the Defendant the costs of this motion and the defendant in mercy & &

The court allow the sheriff of this county the sum of fifty dollars for his Exofices services for the year of our Lord 1820

(p 255) Monday February 12th 1821

A Deed of conveyance from John Cuningham, Guardian of Edward shipley to Tidence and Taltroe shipleys for two hundred acres of Land was proven by John Simmons and Hiram Hurst admitted to record let be registered

---

A Deed of conveyance from Abel Lanham to Joel Dobbs for two hundred and fifty acres of Land was duly acknowledged admitted to record let it be registered

---

A Deed of conveyance from James W. Glassgow to Thomas Mays for two hundred acres of Land was proven by Dennis Condray and Robert Mitchell admitted to record let it be registered

---

A Deed of conveyance from John Mason to Thomas Jones for thirty five acres of land was acknowledged in court admitted to record let it be registered

---

A Deed of conveyance from John Grubb to Isaac McBee for fifty acres of Land was acknowledged in court admitted to record let it be registered

---

A Deed of conveyance from samuel McBee to John Grubb for fifty acres of Land was acknowledged in court admitted to record let it be registered

(p 256) Monday Feby. Term 1821

Court adjourned untill tomorrow 9 oclock

John Brock
John Neil
Wm. Savage
George Brock
Markuies Cook

Court met according to adjournment with Leave of the court the administrator of Isaac Bowling Deceased returned into court an Inventory of said Estate which was read

---

On motion John Carr & Wm Bowman senr. are appointed commissioners to set a part out of the provisions on hand of the Estate of Isaac Bolinger one years provisions and make report of their proceedings to the next Term of this court.

Ordered by court that the administrator of the Estate of Isaac Bolinger Expose the personal estate of the sd. Isaac to sell as the law Derects.
Isd.

Christian Plank
vs
Archer Edward } In Debt

This Suit having been compromised the plaintiff in proper person by

Sterling Cocke his attorney dismisses the same and the Defendant in his proper person confesses Judgment for the costs thereof It is therefore considered by the court that the plaintiff recover of the Defendant the costs of this and the Defendant in mercy & &

(p 257) Christian Plank vs Arthur Edwards } This suit having been compromised by the parties the plaintiff by Sterling Cocke his attorney dismisses the same and the Defendant in his proper person confesses Judgment for costs

It is therefore considered by the court that the plaintiff recover of the Defendant the costs of this suit in this behalf expended and the Defendant in mercy & &

Tuesday February 13th 1821

Court met according to adjournment present the Worshipful Mercurioes Cook John Neil John Brock George Brock and William Savage Esqrs.

---

John Hunt Esquire sheriff of Claiborne County returned the venire facias Executed on the following named persons to wit

| | |
|---|---|
| William Jackson | Willis Harper |
| William Turner | William Cooper |
| John Sulfrage | Russel Lane |
| Richard Critchfield | Amos Johnson |
| Thomas Hoskins | Abel Lanham |
| Thomas Shumate | George Campbell |
| Jubal Lee | Rice Whitaker |
| Robert Yoakum | William Lanham |
| John Honly | Joseph Bishop |
| Abraham Duvalt | James A. Hamilton |
| Jacob Shoults | Reuben Flowers |
| Ransom Day Jr. | Lewis Lay |

(p 258) Tuesday February 13th 1821

| | |
|---|---|
| Elijah Jones | Richard Harper |

out of which the following named persons was balloted a Grand Jury to the present Term to wit

| | |
|---|---|
| Russel Lane foreman | Ruben Flowers |
| Richard Critchfield | William Turner |
| Robert Yoakum | Joseph Bishop |
| Amos Johnson | Lewis Lay |
| Ranson Day Jr. | John Honly |
| Abel Lanham | Willis Harper |
| Rice Whitaker | |

who was sworn as the Law dericts and recived their charge from the Soliciter General -

---

The Sheriff returned Nathan Perry as an office to attend the Grand Jury at this Term

---

A Deed of conveyance from James W. Classgow to Alfred Noel for fifty acres of Land was duly proven by the oaths of Thomas R. McClary, Robert W. McClary in open court admitted to record and ordered to be Registered

---

A Deed of conveyance from Tidance Shipley and Talbot Shipley to Huron Hurst for two hundred acres of Land was duly proven in open court by the oaths of John Harper and Thomas Hurst admitted to record let it be registered

---

A Deed of conveyance from James W. Glassgow to Reuben Harper for Two hundred acres of Land was duly proven by the oaths of William Huston and George Yoakum admitted to record and ordered to be registered

(p 259) Tuesday February 13th 1821

A Deed of conveyance from James W. Glassgow to John Tompson for one hundred acres of Land was proven by Dennis Condray and Reuben Harper admitted to record let it be registered

---

A Deed of conveyance from Nathan Perry to James Cook for one hundred acres of Land was Duly acknowledged in open court admitted to record let it be registered

---

A Deed of conveyance from John Henderson to Edward Jennings for one hundred and Eighty acres of Land was proven in open court by the oaths of Sterling Cooke and William B. Rose admitted to record let it be registered

---

A Deed of conveyance from Joseph Hart to George Hamilton was duly acknowledged in open court admitted to record let it be registered

---

A Deed of conveyance from James Dobbs to Wharlow Nunn for Two hundred and Sixty acres by the oaths of Thomas R. McClary and William Hooper admitted to record let it be registered

---

A Deed of conveyance from George McNeal to Peter Clepper for sixty acres of Land was proven by the oaths of Joseph Bishop and Alexander Campbell admitted to record and ordered to certified for registration

---

A Deed of conveyance Nathaniel M. Noble to Thomas McClain for one hundred acres of Land was duly proven by the oath of Robert Yoakum and ordered to filed for further probate

Thomas Hoskins is Excused from further attendance as a Juror to this Term

(p 260) Tuesday Feby. 13th 1821

A Deed of conveyance from James W. Glassgow to Alfred Noel for fifty acres of Land was proven by the oaths of John Hunt and Dennis Condray admitted to record and ordered to be Registered

---

Ordered by court that Frederick Bollinger Snr. be appointed Guardian to Fredereck Bolinger, William Bolinger Armsted Bolinger, Betsy Bolinger and Isaac Bolinger minor Heirs and orphans of Isaac Bolinger Deceased who Entered into Bond in the sum of five hundred Dollars with Jesse Cain and Daniel Coffelt as securities

---

After proclamation being made the court proceed to the Election of a constable for the Town Company and after counting and compairing the votes it appeared that John Ashley was duly and constitutionally Elected for the ensuing two years and thereupon Entered into Bond with Dennis Condray and Alexander Barton as his Securities

---

After proclamation being made the court proceeded to the Election of a constable in the bounds of the Town Company and after counting and compairing the votes it appeared that John McCubbins was duly elected for the Surendering Two year entered into bond with John Neil and John Hunt as Securities

---

After empaneling the Grand Jury it appeared that

| | | |
|---|---|---|
| 1 | John Sulfrage | Elijah Jones |
| 2 | Wm. Lanham | Richd. Harper & |
| 3 | Wm. Cooper | Jacob Shoults |

were retained as travers Jurors of the original pannel

(p 261) Tuesday Feby. 13th 1821

John Whitaker
vs } Slander
Andrew Johnson

This day came the parties in this cause and with the assent of the court the Plaintiff agrees to and Dismisses his suit and the Defendant assums payment of costs wherefore It is considered by court that this Suit be dismissed and that said Defendant pay the costs aforesaid in form aforesaid assumed & the said Defendant in mercy & &

---

Henry Castor
vs } certiorari
Robert Gibson

The defendant by his attorney comes and with the assent of the court entered a Rule to compell the Plaintiff to give security for costs within the siting of the present sessions or that said Suit Stand Dismised

---

Jesse Lewis ) certiorari
vs )
John Thompson ) This day came the parties in this cause by their attorney into open court and thereupon came a Jury to wit John Sulfrage, William Lanham, Wm. Cooper, Thomas Bridges, Joseph Niel, Edwd. Wooton, Thos. R. McClary, John Williams, Joseph Hurst, David Cosby, Levi Goin & George Richardson who being Elected Tried and sworn the truth to Speak upon this matter of controversey upon their oaths do say they find for the plaintiff and assess his damage to one cent wherefore It is considered by the court that the plaintiff recover of the Defendant his Damages aforesaid in form aforesaid assesed also his costs by him about his suit in this behalf Expended and the said Defendant in mercy & &

(p 262) Tuesday 13th Feby. 1821

William Killian ) Slander
vs )
Patrick Bray ) This day came the parties in this cause into open court and with the assent of the court the plaintiff agrees to and dismisses his suit and the defendant assumes payment of costs wherefore It is considered by the court that this suit be dismissed and that the Defendant pay the costs aforesaid in form aforsaid assumed and the said Deft. in mercy & &

Nathl. Cary ) In certiorari
vs )
Jas. Ellison ) This day came the parties in this cause by their attornies into open court and thereupon came a Jury to wit John Sulfrage Wm. Lanham, William Cooper, Thomas Bridges, Joseph Neil, Edwd. Wooton, Thos. R. McClary, John Williams, Joseph Hurst, David Cosby, Levy Gowin & George Richardson who being Elected tried and sworn the truth to speak upon this matter of controversy upon their oaths do say they find for the plaintiff and asses his damage to fifty four dollars and forty cents besides costs wherefore on motion of the atto. for this plaintiff, It is considered by the court that the plaintiff recover of the Defendant and his Security William Linah the aforesaid Sum of fifty four dollars & forty cents his damages aforesaid in form aforesaid assessed also his costs by him about his Suit in this behalf Expended and the said Defendant in mercy & &

Robt. W. McClary ) Trespass on the case
vs )
John Bundren ) This day came the parties in this cause by their attornies into open court and thereupon came a Jury to wit Elijah Jones, Richard Harper, John Sulfrage, Wm. Cooper, Thos. Bridges, Joseph Niel, Edward Wooton, John William, Joseph Hurst, David Cosby, Levy Goin and George Richardson who being Elected

(p 263) Tuesday 13th Feby. 1821

tried and sworn deligently to inquire of Damages upon their oaths do say they find for the Plaintiff and assess his damage to one cent besides costs therefore It is considered by the court that the plaintiff recover of the Defendant his damages aforesaid in form aforesaid assessed also his costs by him about his Suit in this behalf Expended and the Sd. Deft. in mercy & &

John Devenport } Slander
vs }
Martin Fugate } This day came Jesse Devers who was appearance bails for sd. Deft. into open court and surrendered up to the court his principal in discharge of himself which was admitted of and recd. by the court whereupon sd. Defendant is ordered in custody of the Sheriff & &

John Devenport } Slander
vs }
Martin Fugate } This day came the parties in this cause by their atto. into open court and thereupon came a Jury to wit John Sulfrage, Wm. Cooper, Elijah Jones, Richard Harper, Thos. Bridges, Joseph Neil, Edward Wooton, Jno. Williams, Joseph Hurst, David Cosby, Levy Coin & Geo. Richardson who being Elected tried and sworn the truth to speak upon this matter of constroversy upon hearing the Evidence admitted by the parties were respited untill tomorrow morning

Court adjourned until Tomorrow morning 9 oclock
John Brock
Wm. Savage
Mercurious Cook
George Brock
John Neil

(p 264) Wednesday Feby 14th 1821

Court met according adjournment present, John Neil, John Brock, George Brock, William Savage, and Mercureus Cook Esqrs.

John Devenport } Slander
vs }
Martin Fugatt } This day came the parties by their attornies and the same Jury who were respited from rendering their verdict on yesterday who upon their oaths do say they find the Defenant Guilty of speaking and publishing the false and slander our words in the plaintiffs Declaration mentioned and assess the damages by occasion thereof to Six dollars besides costs - Therefore it is considered by the court that the plaintiff recover of the defendant Six Dollars Damages aforesaid by the Jurors aforesaid as assessed together with the costs of his said Suit in this behalf Expended and for which Execution may Issue -

Personally appeared in open court John Ashly and John McCubbins who were appointed constable of yesterday for the bounds of the Town Company and took the necessary oath of office

Reubin B. Rogers
vs
Absolum Morris

Continued by consent

The State
vs
Moses Jones

Indictment

This day came the state by his solicitor General and the Defendant in his own proper person who being charged upon the Bill of Indictment pleaded Thereto Guilty

It was therefore considered by the court that that the Defendant be fined for such his offence

(p 265) Wednesday 14th Feby. 1821

five dollars besides costs and that Execution Issue for the same

---

The State
vs
James Tucker

A true Bill

The State
vs
James Tucker

Indictment

This day came the state by the solecitor General who prosecutes for the state and the defendant in his own proper person and being charged upon the bill of Indictment pleads guilty

It is therefore considered by the court that he be fined two Dollars and fifty cents for such his offence Therefore it is considered by the court that the state recover of the defendant two Dollars and fifty cents fine together with his costs in this behalf Expended and the Defendant in mercy & &

The state
vs
James Tucker

Indictment

Personally appeared in open court Reuben Flowers and took upon himself that he would pay two Dollars and fifty cents fine and the costs of said prosecution

Therefore it is considered by the court that the state recover of R^eubin Flowers two Dollars and fifty cents the aforsaid in manner and form aforesaid together with the costs in this behalf Expended and that Execution Issue

(p 266) Wednesday Feby. 14th 1821

John Devenport
vs
Jesse Davers

The rule of refferance heretofore made in said cause set aside

---

Jesse Davers
vs
John Devenport

The rule of referance heretofore made set aside

---

James Grant
vs
John Umsted

Attachment continued by consent

---

Same
vs
Same

Continued by consent

---

The State
vs
Charles Hurst

Indictment

this day come came the state by her Solicitor General Sterling Cocke and the defendant in his own proper person and being charged upon the bill of indictment pleaded thereto guilty

Therefore it was considered by the court that he be fined five Dollars for such his offence and it is further considered by the court that the state recover of the defendant the fine aforesaid together with the costs and that the defendant remain in custody of the sheriff that till fine and costs are paid whereupon personally appeared in open court Thomas Hurst and took upon himself that he would pay the fine and costs of the aforesaid prosecution

(p 267) Wednesday Feby 14th 1820

Therefore it is considered by the court that the state recover of Thomas Hurst five Dollars the fine aforesaid confessed in manner and form aforesaid together with costs of said prosecution and Execution Issue

---

William McNew
vs
Pearson Barney and Benjamin Barney

certiorari

continued by consent

The State
vs
Ambrose Dry

Indictment A. B

returned a true bill

---

A Deed of conveyance from James W. Glasgow to William Stallings for fifty acres of land was duly proven in open court by the oaths of Hugh Graham and William Houston the only subscribing witnesses thereto and was admitted to record and ordered to be Registered

---

A Deed of conveyance from John Crowley to Thomas McClain for two hundred and twenty one acres of Land was proven in open court by the oath of Henry Hunt and ordered to be recorded

(p 268) Wednesday February 14th 1821

A Deed of conveyance from James W. Glasgow to John Dobbs for one hundred and fifty of Land was duly proven in open court by the oaths of Peter Marcum and Thomas R. McClary the only subscribing witnesses thereto and was admitted to record and ordered to be registered

A Deed of conveyance from Abel Lanham to William Lanham for fifty acres of Land was duly acknowledged in open court by the maker and was admitted to record ordered to be registered

A Deed of conveyance from Larkin Fergurson to Andrew & Robert Crockets for one hundred and Sixty acres of land was duly proven in open court by the oaths of Elijah Jones and William Marcum the only subscribing witnesses thereto and was admitted to record and ordered to be registered

(p 269) Wednesday February 14th 1821

Frederick Bowlinger Guardian for the heirs of Isaac Bowlinger Deced. presented his petition to court praying devision of 200 acres of land held by said heirs in common with George Sharp and thereupon the court appointed Thomas Mc Clain David Rogers William Rogers, William Bowman and John Carr commissioners to make devision of the said 200 acres of land agreeably to Law and make out fair plats of such their Devision and make return to the next term of this court

Henry Long vs Fredrick Bolinger — On motion and for Reasons appearing to the satisfaction of the court a commissioner is award to take the deposition of Jacob Jakson to be read in evidence on the trial of the above cause to be taken before any Justice of Claiborne County no notice to be given both parties being present on behalf of the plaintiff

The State vs Andrew Crockets — Ordered that Andrew Crockett be fined two Dollars and fifty cents for contempt to court by profane swearing in presents of the court

(p 270) The state vs Philip Coffelt — Indictment

this day came the state by sterling cocke her Solecitor General who prosecuts for the state and the defendant in his own proper person and thereupon also came a Jury to wit

| | |
|---|---|
| John Sulfrage | Mathew Hamilton |
| William Lanham | Tidance Lane |
| William Cooper | Caleb Dobbs |
| James Allison | Charles Shearmon |
| Isaac Vanbebber | Spencer Edwards |

on motion a rule is Entered to shew cause why the bill of Indictment should be quashed and after argument of counsil being heard as well in support of said motion as against it and the matters and this therein contained being Duly considered and fully understood it is considered by the court that said Bill be quashed and that the county of Claiborne pay the costs of said prosecution

---

The State
vs
Samuel Hamilton

Indictment A. B.

This day came the state by her selecitor General who prosecutes for the State and the defendant in his own proper person who being charged upon the bill of Indictment pleaded thereto not Guilty and thereupon alse came a Jury to wit

| | |
|---|---|
| John Sulfrage | Tidance Lane |
| William Lanham | Caleb Dobbs |
| William Cooper | Charles Shearmon |
| Thomas Hunter | Thomas Shearmon |
| James Allison | Spencer Edward |
| Isaac Vanbebber | William Lewis |

who being Elected tried and sworn well and truly to try and the truth to say on the Issue of Traverse Joined upon their oaths do say they find the defendant not guilty

(p 271) Wednesday Feby. 14th 1821

in manner and form as charged in the bill Indictment

It is therefore considered by the court that the Defendant be discharged and that the County of Claiborne pay the costs

Court adjourned untill Tomorrow mornin 9 oclock

John Bunch
Wm Savage
George Brock
John Neil
Mercurious Cook

Thursday February 15th 1821

the same court as of yesterday met

The State
vs
Henry Lower Jr.

Indictment

This day day came the state by the selecitor General who prosecuts on behalf of the state and the Defendant in his own proper person and being charged upon the bill of Indictment pleaded thereto not guilty thereupon alse came a Jury to wit

| | |
|---|---|
| William Lanham | George Ford |
| John Sulfrage | John Critchfield |
| William Cooper | Daniel Coffelt |
| Samul Dodson | John Hurst |
| Spencer Edwards | Caleb Dobbs |
| Edmined Perry | Jesse Ward |

who being Elected tried and sworn well and truly to try and the truth to say upon the Issue of Traverse Joined wherein the state is plaintiff and Henry Lowery is Defendant upon their

(p 272) Thursday February 15th 1821

do say they find the Defendant Guilty in manner and form as charged in the bill of Indictment and the court cannot being advised what Judgment to Render the cause is continued for the court to consider thereof untill tomorrow

State
vs
Henry Lower
A Rule is granted to Shew cause why a new trial should be granted in the above cause

---

State
vs
Ambrose Day
Indictment

this day came the state by her solecitor General who prosecutes on behalf of the state and the defendant in his own proper person and being charged on the bill of Indictment for plea says he is not guilty and puts himself on the county and the state by the attorney General doth the like and thereupon came Jury to wit
Elijah Jones, Richard Harper, Jacob Shoults, John Condry, Isham Jennings, Edward Wootten, Joseph Jennings, David Huddleston, William Renfree, Martin Fugatt, Daniel Sewder and James A. Hamilton

(p 273) Thursday February 15th 1821

who being Elected Tried and sworn well and truly to try and the truth to speak upon the issue Joined upon their oaths do say they find the defendant Guilty in manner and form as charged in the bill of indictment, It is therefore considered by the court that for this his offence he be fined the sum of five Dollars and it is further considered by the court that the state recover of the defendant the fine and cost aforesaid and that the said defendant remain in custody until fine and cost are paid or security given therefor whereupon on Ruben Day came into in his proper person and with the asent of the court confesses Judgment as the security of the said defendant for the fine and cost aforesaid which is here made the Judgment of the court and the Defendants in mercy & c Taxed

---

Jesse Ward
vs
John Bundron
On motion of the plaintiff it is ordered by the court that a commission Issue to anyone Justice of the peace for Claiborne County to take the deposition William Weaver to be read evidence on behalf of the plaintiff in the above cause on giving five days notice the defendant of the time and place of taking the same Isd.

(p 274) Thursday February 15th 1821

Samuel Wilson
vs
[illegible]seph Ferrel
the plaintiff came into open court and dismisses his suit and confesses [illegible]dgment for all costs

It is therefore considered by the court that the Defendant recover of the plaintiff his cost in and about his suit in this behalf Expended and be in mercy & c

Ordered by the court that John Neil Esqr. and John Simmons be appointed commissioners to settle the administration account of William Grisham Deceased with Susannah Grisham administratrix of said Estate and make report to the next Term of this court.

Isd.

---

Ordered by the court that the following Justices be appointed to take in lists of the Taxable property and poles in the county of Claiborne for the present year to wit

John Lynch Esqr. in the bounds of Capt. Rogers Company

(p 275) Thursday Feby. 15th 1821

George Yoakum Esqr. in the bounds of Capt. Davisses Company
John Wallen Esqr. in the bounds of Capt. Browns Company
John Brock Esqr. in the bounds of Capt. Moyersses company
John Hurst Esqr. in the bounds of Capt. Moors Company
John Huddleston Esqr. in the bounds of Capt. Marcums Company
John Neil Esqr. in the bounds of Capt. Joseph Hurst Company
Robert W. McClary Esqr. in the bounds of Capt. McCartyes Company
Archibald Bales Esqr. in the bound of Captain Bales Company
Alexander Campbell Esqr. in the bound of Capt. Joab Brewers Company

---

Robert W. McClary and Archibald Bales Esqrs. who was appointed commissioners to settle with Robert Southern administrator of the Estate of William Mason Dec'd. made their report to court which was receved and ordered to be registered

(p 276) Thursday February 15th 1821

William Genings administrator of the Estate of William Gennings dec'd returned a supplement Inventory of the Estate of Decendants sworn to in open court which was Rec'd by the court and ordered to be filed and recorded

---

John Wallen<br>vs<br>David Gosby } This day came the plaintiff by his attorney and suffers non suit

It is therefore considered by the court that the Defendant go hence without day and recover a Judgment against the plaintiff for costs and that Execution Issue

---

On application it is ordered by the court John Brock and George Brock Esquires members of the court of pleas and quarter sessions for the County of Claiborne be and they are hereby appointed commissioners to take the private examination of Betsy Hamilton her husband whether she had executed a Deed of conveyance from herself and said Husband to George Cardwell for 270 acres of Land lying in prince Edward County in the State of Virginia of her own free will and accord or wheather she had executed said Deed by the threats compullion or constraint of her husband and that they there report of such examination to the present term of this court

(p 277) Friday Feby. 1821

A deed of conveyance from James Hamilton To George Cardwell for 270 acres of land Saittuate in Prince Edward County Virginia was acknowledged in open court by the said James Hamilton the Executor therein and ordered to be certified.

And therefore the other Grantor Betsy Hamilton was taken Seperate and a part from her sd. husband James Hamilton and privetly Examined by John Brock & George Brock Esqrs. who upon such examination saith that she executed said deed of her and free will and acord and not by restraint or compulsion of her her husband which is also ordered to be certified

Court adjourned untill tomorrow 9 oclock John Brock
Mercurious Cook
Wm. Savage
John Neil

(p 278) Friday Feby. Term 1821

Court met according to adjournment present Same Justices as of yesterday

State vs Jesse Devers } Jesse Devers and James Kain, Jesse Kain & David Kain personally appeared in open court and acknowledged themselves indebted to the state of Tennessee in the sum of two hundred dollars each to be levied of their Goods and chattles lands and Tenements but to be void if the above Jesse Devers and James Kain do make their personal attendance before the Circuit Court at the courthouse in Tazewell on the 3rd Monday of April next then and there to answer a Bill of indictment to be prefered against them on a charge of present court and not depart the court without leave

The state vs Jesse Devers and James Kain ) Personally appeared in open court Robert Mitchell and acknowledged himself Indebted to the state of Tennessee in sum of one hundred Dollars to be levied of his goods and chattels Lands and Tenements void on condition that he make his personal appearance before the Judge of the Cercuit Court of Claiborne

(p 279) Friday Feby. 16th 1821

County at the courthouse in Tazewell on the third Monday in April next to prosecute and give evidence on behalf of the state vs the said Defendant in a bill of Indictment and not depart the court without leave John Hunt Sheriff of Claiborne County returned into court an Execution Issued by John Huddlesten Esqr. a Justice of the peace for said County commanding said sheriff or other lawful officer that of the goods and chattles lands and tenements of Robert Grissam in his County he would make the sum of Sixty two dollars ninety three and three fourth cents which William Graham and company moved against Grissam and also the further sum of seventy five cents costs and said Sheriff having entered upon said execution that no personal property could be found in his county and that he had levied said execution on one tract of land lying on Clinch river including an island it being the land whereon said Grissam now lives the number of acres not his and the plaintiff having moved the court by William B. Reese their attorney that an order of sale Issue to sell the land levied on it is considered by the court that an order of sale do issue to sell said land, and that the plaintiff recover of the defendant the costs of this motion Isd. March 1st 1821

(p 280) Feby. Friday 1821

John Huddleston
vs
Arthur Edward and Christian Flank

On motion and it appearing that an execution under the hand of Wm. Graham Esquires had been in the hands of John Hunt sheriff for the sum of $40.40 and one dollar cost of suit that the Said Sheriff had thereupon returned no personal property found Levied on fifteen acres of land on Mulberry Creek. It was considered by the court on motion of W. B. Reese atto. for plaintiff that an order of sale issue to the said Sheriff comanding him to Expose the said land to sale for the satisfaction of the said debt as the law derects.
Isd. March 1st 1821

Thomas Johnson
vs
J. Gratner & Wm. Russell

On motion of the plaintiff By J. Peck atto. and it appearing that an Execution in the above Suit

(p 281) Friday Feby 16th 1821

came into the hand of Joab Brewer constable whereby he was commanded to make the sum of 95 dollars and nine cents and by his return it appeared that the said execution of the Suit of Johnston against the above defendants had been levied on two tracts of land on swan creek the one 38 acres the other 88 acres no personal property be found

It is therefore ordered that a Veddetive Ex ponas Issue to the sheriff of Claiborne County commanding of land to sale as the law directs to Satisfy said debt -
Isd. March 1st 1821

Wm. Graham & Co.
vs
Robert Grisham

John Hunt Sheriff of Claiborne returned into court an Execution issued by John Huddleston Esquire a Justice of the peace for said county commanding him the said Sheriff that of the goods and chattles lands and tenements of Robert Grisham in his county he make or cause to be made

(p 282) Friday Feby 1821

the sum of Sixty five Dollars and thirty nine cents which sum Wm. Graham & Co. Recovered against the said Robert Grisham before John Huddleston and the further sum of seventy five cents cost in the said suit Expended and there being no personally property to be found in my county to satisfy this execution I have levied on one tract of land lying on Clinch River including an Island being the land whereon the said Grisham now lives number of acres not known On motion of William B. Reese It is therefore ordered by the court that an order of sale issue to the sheriff of Claiborne County to expose said land to sale as the law directs to satisfy said Debt. Isd. March 1st 1821

William Graham & Co. ) John Hunt Sheriff of Claiborne
vs ) County returned into court an
Robert Grisham ) execution issue by John Huddleston Esqr. a Justice of the peace of Claiborne County for the sum of $33.35 cents costs on which execution he the sd.

(p 283) Friday Feby. 1821

Sheriff had Levied on a tract of land lying on Clinch river being the land on which sd. Grisham lives - there being no personal property to satisfy the same and thereupon a motion ofWilliam B. Reece a writ of venditive ex ponas is awarded to sell the said land or so much thereof as may Satisfy said demand and the costs of the motion

Isd. March 1821

McHenry & Preston
vs
John Casey

In case

This day came the parties by their attornies and thereupon was called a Jury to wit

John Sulfredge, Wm. Langham, William Cooper, Abr. Murphy, Elijah Hurst, Thomas Hurst, Edward Wooton, Squire Berch, Sam Cloud, Bryant Bradon, Joel Willis, Caleb Dobbs who being elected tried

(p 284) Friday Feby 1821

and sworn to try the issue Joined upon their oaths do say they find that the defendant did assume and take upon himself in manner and form as the plaintiff against him has complained and assess the plaintiff damage to ninety four dollars 71 cents besides cost Therefore it is assessed that the plaintiff recover said sum so assessed and the costs in this behalf expended for which the defendant be in mercy

John Davanport
vs
David Kain

Tresspase

This day appeared the parties by their attornies and thereupon was called a Jury to wit

John Sulfredge, Wm. Cooper, Elijah Jones, John S. Hardy, Esquire Berch John Whitacre

(p 285) Friday Feby. 1821

Thomas Hurst, Abraham Murphy, Edward Wooton, Isaac Shoults, Caleb Dobbs & Wm. Langham who being lected tried and sworn well and truly to try the Issue Joined upon their oaths do say that the Defendant David Kain is guilty of the Tresspass assault Battery and wounding in manner & form as the plaintiff against him in his declaration both complained and assess his damage by reason thereof to five hundred dollars besides costs

It was therefore considered by the court that the plaintiff recover of the defendant said sum of five hundred dollars the damage to by the Jury assessed and the cost of suit in this behalf expended and be in mercy for the same

(p 286) Friday February 1821

State ) Motion for a new tryal

vs
Henry Lower } The rule entered in this cause for a new tryal is on argument discharged - and the court for such his offence consider that he pay a fine of twenty five cents besides the costs of this prosecution for which execution may issue

Wm. Graham & A
vs
Robert Grisham } John Hunt Sheriff returned into court an execution issue by John Huddleston Esquire a Justice of the peace for Claiborne County commanding him that of the goods and chattels lands and tenements of Robert Grisham in his county he make or cause to be made the sum of Sixty Eight Dollars which sum William Graham & Co. Recovered against the said Robert Grisham before John Huddleston Esqr. and the further sum of seventy five cents cost in this behalf Expended

(p 287) Friday Feby 1821

On which Execution he the said sheriff there being no personal property found to satisfy this execution levied on one tract of land lying on Clinch River including an Island being the land whereon the said Grisham now lives on motion of William B. Reese It was therefore considered by the court that and order of sale issue to the sheriff of Claiborne County to sell the sd. land as the law Derects or so much thereof as may Satisfy said Debt and costs -

---

State
vs
Darias Shumate } Indictment
the Grand Jury returned into court a true bill founded on the presentmen

State
vs
Benjamin Housman } Indictment
the Grand Jury Returned into court a true bill founded on a presentment

State
vs
Jonathan Mays } Indictment
the Grand Jury returned into court a true bill founded on a presentment

(p 288) Friday Feby. 1821

Joseph Jennings
vs
James Asberry } The plaintiff came into court and Dismisses his Suit and confesses Judgment for the cost It is therefore considered by the court that the defendant go hence without day and recover of plaintiff the costs in this behalf Expended for which execution may issue

Ordered by the court that the following named person be appointed Jurors to the next term of this court

| | | | |
|---|---|---|---|
| 1 | Edward Wootton | 14 | Ambrose Hurst snr. |
| 2 | Hugh Mountgomery | 15 | Hurem Hurst |
| 3 | George Richardson | 16 | Richard Harper |
| 4 | John Richardson | 17 | David Huddleston |

| | | | |
|---|---|---|---|
| 5 | William McNew | 18 | William Hurst |
| 6 | Daniel Slavans | 19 | John Hurst |
| 7 | Alexander Bales | 20 | William Parker |
| 8 | Levin Busick | 21 | Jacob Adams |
| 9 | Samuel Dodson | 22 | Peter Lower |
| 10 | Robert Grisham | 23 | Peter Marcum |
| 11 | John Condry | 24 | Abraham Murphy |
| 12 | Thomas Coleman | 25 | Elijah Evans |
| 13 | James Hopson | 26 | William McCullogh |

(p 289) Friday Feby. 16th 1821

The Grand Jury and pettet Jury is discharged from further attendance at the present Term of this court

James Collensworth vs Joseph Hurst } On motion It is ordered by the court that a commission Issue to any one Justice of the peace for Claiborne County to take the Deposition of Elijah Hurst and Polly Hurst witnesses on behalf of the plaintiff on the plaintiff giveing the defendant one days notice of the time and place of takeing the same Isd. Feby. 17th, 1821

Isaac Sawyers vs John S. Hardy } On motion of the defendant a commissen is awarded him to take the deposition of Arthur L. Campbell before any one Justice of Jefferson County Kentucky on the Defendant giving the plaintiff ten days notice of the time and place of taking same Isd. 17th April

(p 290) Friday February 16th 1821

Edward Weston vs Abraham Murphy } On motion and for reasons appearing to the satisfaction of the court by affidavit of plaintiff a commission is awarded him to take Deposition of William Weaver before any two Justices of Claiborne County on three days notice given

The State vs Jonathan Mays } Personally appeared in open court John Honly and acknowledged himself Indebted to the state of Tennessee in the sum of one hundred dollars to be Levied of his goods and chattels Lands and Tenents void on condition that he make his apperance before the court at the courthouse in Tazewell on the Wednesday after the second Monday in May next to prosecute and give evidence on behalf of the state in a bill of Indictment the state against the said Mays and not depart the court without leave

The State )
vs ) Personally appeared in open court Robert Yoakum and acknowledged
James C. Martin ) himself Indicted to the state of Tennessee in the sum of one hundred dollars to levied of his goods and chattels lands and Tenements void on condition that he make his personal appearance before the Justices of our court of pleas and quarter sessions on the Wednesday after the second Monday in May next to give Evidence on behalf the state Against the said Martin in a bill of Indictment and not depart the court without leave

(p 291) Friday February 16th 1821

The state )
vs ) Personally appeared in open court John Honly and acknowledged him-
Derias Shumate ) self Indebted to the state of Tennessee in the sum of one hundred dollars to be levied of his goods and chattels Lands and Tenements void on condition that he make his personal appearance before the Justices of our court at the courthouse in Tazewell on the Wednesday after the second Monday in May next to give Evidence on behalfof the state vs the sd. Derias Shumate in a bill of Indictment the state and doth not Depart the court without leave

---

State ) Indictment
vs )
Benjamin Houseman ) Personally appeared in open court Reuben Flowers and acknowledged himself indebted to the state in the sum of one hundred dollars to be levied of his good and chattels Lands and Tenemts void on condition that he make his personal appearance before the Justices of our court on the Wednesday after the second Monday in May next to give evidence on behalf of the state ag the said Houseman in a bill of Indictment and doth not depart the court without leave

---

On petition to the satisfaction of the court filed by Joseph McCleary leave is granted him to Keep and ordimary in the Town of Tazewell for one year and thereupon the said Joseph was sworn as the Law derects and give bond and security

(p 292) Friday February 16th 1821

On petition being filed by Abraham Murphy to the satisfaction of the leave is granted him to keep an ordinary in the Town of Tazewell for one year and thereupon was swn. and give bond & security as the Law derects.

---

A Deed of conveyance from Spencer Edwards to Francis Patterson for one hundred acres of Land was duly acknowledged in open court by the maker thereof admitted to record and ordered to be Registered

---

William Graham and Benjamin Cloud Executors of the last well and Testament of Christopher Dawren Deceased returned to court a list of the amount of sales of said Estate which was Reced. by the court and ordered to be filed an recorded

Court adjourned till tomorrow

Wm. Savage
John Neil
Mercurious Cook
John Brock
George Brock

Saterday February 17th 1821

Court met according adjournment present the same Justices of yesterday &&

(p 293) Saturday February 17th 1821

Robert Kyle
vs
Robert Grisham

John Hunt Esquire Sheriff of Claiborne County returned into court an Execution at the suit of Robert Kile against Robert Grisham levied on fifty acres of land in the Caney Vally adjoining the Lands of George Barrnard and fifteem acres more lying at the Bleedlick on the waters of sycamore creek for a Judgment of Sixty two dollars & one Dollar Six & for Interest and costs said Kyle vs Grisham.

And on motion of the Plaintiff by his atto. Sterlend Cock an ordered of sale is Granted him to sale said Land or so much thereof as will satisfy the same

Taxed.

---

John McCubbens attended five Days an officer of the court at this Term for which he is allowed five Dollars

Isd. May 24th 1821

Abraham Kyle and other Executors of Robert Kyle Deceased
vs
Robert Grisham

The Defendant in his proper person appeared in open court and says he cannot gain say the plaintiff action for $100 debt and $11.50 - intrest therefore it was considered by court that the plaintiff recover the sd. sum confessed and cost of suit for which execution may issue

Taxed

(p 294) Saturday Feby. 1821

John Tucker
vs
George Jenning

The defendant being called to defend his suit came not nor prosecutes his writs of certierari and supercedeas wherefore the same is dismissed - Therefore it is considered by the court that the plaintiff recover the amount of one dollar debt and 75 - costs against the debt and Anderson Jennings his securities also costs of this suit for which execution may issue

Taxed

Same )
vs ) The deft being called to defend his suit came not for further proceeds his
Same )

writs of certiorari & supercedeas - wherefore they are Dismissed therefore the court consider that the plaintiff

(p 295) Saturday February 17th 1821

plaintiff recover his debt $6.75 and cost 75 cents against the sd. defendant and Anderson Jennings his Security and also cost in this behalf expended for which Execution may issue

Taxed

Nathan Perry a constable attended four days on the grand Jury at this term for which a certificate may issue

Isd. May 24th 1821

The court adjourned till court in course and all the cause not disposed of are continued till that time.

John Brock
Markious Cook
Wm. Savage
John Neil
John Brock

(p 296) State of Tennessee Claiborne County
Monday May 14 1821

At a court of pleas and quarter sessions Begun and held in the courthouse in Tazewell on the second Monday of May and in the year 1821 The following Justices being present to wit

| | |
|---|---|
| John Brock | John Hurst |
| John Huddleston | Aaron Davis |
| Archibald Bales | John Wallen |
| Mercurious Cook | George Yoakum |
| Josiah Ramsey | Alexander Campbell |
| William Savage | William Graham |
| Robert W. McClary | |

Ordered by the court a majority of the acting Justices present that a Jury be appointed to view and lay off a road the nearest and best way leading from the county line near Robert Smiths in Powels Vally to Cains ford on Powels river doing as little prajudice to enclosers as possible and report to the next term of this court their proceedings and that the following Jurors be appointed to review, and report

| | |
|---|---|
| Thomas McLane | James Walker |
| William McNew | David Wilson |

Isd. May 22nd, 1821

(p 297) Monday May 14th - 1821

| | |
|---|---|
| Reuben B. Rogers | William Bowman senr. |
| John Lynch | A James Rogers |

Isd. May 22 1821

Ordered by the court that Polly Dobkins be admitted to administer on all and singular the goods and chattles rights and credits of Reuben Dobkins deceased who entered into bond with Solomon Dobkins and Patrick Bray her Securities, and was qualified as the law derects.

---

Polly Dobkins administratrix of the estate of Reuben Dobkins deceased returned into court and inventory of said estate, which was received, and ordered to be recorded

---

Ordered by the court that William Houston be allowed the sum of fourteen dollars and seventy five cents for services rendered by the said Houston as commissioner and for one Blank book furnished for the use of said commissioner by said Housten
Isd. May 22nd. 1821

---

Ordered by the court Benjamin Cloud Clerk of said court be allowed the sum of eleven dollars and twenty one cent for

(p 298) Monday 14th May 1821

Books and Stationary from November 14th 1820 to May the 14th 1821
Isd. May 22nd.

---

Joel Jones Exhibits to court the sculp of a wolf 9 Justices being present and proved that said wolf was over Six months old and also proved he Killed said wolf in Claiborne County and in the year 1820 and the court being Satisfied therewith it was ordered by the court Sheriff burn the scalp and that the said Joel Jones receve of the Treasurer of East Tennessee the sum allowed by Law and that certificate Issue
Isd. May 22nd.

---

Ordered the court that John Evans and John Huddleston be appointed commissioner to settle the Estate of William Jénning Decd. with William Jenning the administrator and make report to the next Term of this court
Isd. May 22

---

Ordered by the court a majority of the acting Justices being present that that John Hunt sheriff of said county be allowed the sum of $50 for his Ex oficious services for the year 1820 and that certificate Issue
Isd. May 22nd 1821

---

Ordered by the court 9 Justices being present that Abraham Hurst be al-

lowed the sum of $40 for keeping four children the children of Edmund Maples from the last of this court up to the present term
Isd. 22nd. May 1821

(p 299) Monday May the 14th 1821

A Bill of sale from Dennis Condray to Hugh Graham & Co. for one negro boy named Dick was duly proven in open court by the oaths of Thomas R. Mc Clary & Benjamin Cloud the only Subscribing witnesses thereto and was admited to Record and ordered to be certified for Registration

---

Ordered by the court 9 Justices being present that Edmon Perry be released from the payment of $2 on the account of a stray bull by him posted
Isd. May 22d.

---

Ordered by the court 9 Justices being present that Reuben Ford be allowed $30 for keeping Catharene Ford one of the poor of this county for the Term of one year
Isd. May 22

---

Isaac Sawyers
vs
John S. Hardy

On motion of the defendant and sufficient cause shewn to the court it is ordered that a commission issue to anyone Justice of peace for Harland County in the state of Kentucky to take the deposition of William Beard and Arthur L. Campbell on the defendant given the plaintiff three days notice of the time and place of taking the same -

(p 300) Monday May the 14th 1821

Isaac Sawyers
vs
John S. Hardy

On motion and cause shewn by the defendant a commission is ordered to issue to any Justice of the peace for the County of Jefferson in the state of Kentucky to take the Deposition of Arthur L. Campbell on the defendant giving the plaintiff fifteen Day notice of the time and place of taking the same

---

The court appointed Lewis Rice a constable in the bounds of Captain Bales Company who entered into bond with Daniel Rice and William Condray for his securities and was qualified as the law derects

State
vs
William Marcum

Personally appeared in open court William Marcum and John McCubbins and acknowledged themselves indebted to the state of Tennessee in sum of one hundred and fifty dollars to wit William Marcum in the sum of one hundred Dollars and John Mc Cubbens in the sum of fifty dollars to be levied of their Respective good and chattels land and tennements for the use of the state of Tennessee to be void on condition that the said William Marcum make his appearance on the Wednesday of the present term of this of this court also from day to day to answer a charge of the state against him and not Depart the court without leave

(p 301) Monday May 14th 1821

State vs William Bryant — Personally appeared in open court William Bryant Jeremiah Cloud and Robert Mitchell and acknowledged themselves indebted to the state of Tennessee in the sum of Two hundred Dollars for the use of the state to be levied of their respective goods and chattles land and Tennements that is to say William Bryant in the sum of one hundred dollars and Jery Cloud & Robert Mitchell in the sum of fifty Dollars Each but to be void on condition that William Bryant make his appearance at the courthouse in Tazewell on the Wednesday of the present term of this court to answer a charge of the state exhibited him from day to day and not depart the court without leave

---

John Wallen, John Huddleston, John Hurst, George Yoakum, Archibald Bales, and Alexander Campbell who was by the court appointed commissioners to take list of Taxable property and poles for the year 1821 returned to court their Lists which was received and filed

(p 302) May 14th 1821

A Deed of conveyance from James Miller to David Roark for one hundred acres of land was duly acknowledged in open court by the maker thereof and was admited to record and ordered to be Registered

---

A Deed of conveyance from Amose Johnson to John Whitaker for forty acres of land was duly proven in open court by the oaths of Thomas McClary and William Houston subscribing witnesses thereto and was admited Record and ordered to be Registered

---

A Deed of conveyance from James W. Glasgow by his attorney William Brown to Robert Mitchell for forty acres of land was duly proven in open court by the oaths of Thomas B. McClary & Abraham Murphy the subscribing witnesses and was admited to record and ordered to be registered

---

Ordered by the court that Moses Davis be appointed overseer of the Road from Town Creek to Wyatts mill by Thomas Lee in room and stead of Jubal Lee and have the same hand and bound said Lee had

(p 303) Monday May 14th 1821

Ordered by the court a majority of the acting Justices being present that Fielding Lewis William Yoark Samual Moore Martin Fugatt Henry Moyers,

William Lewis and Jacob Adams be appointed a Jury of view to view and Lay out a road from Karklins hollow at or near Martin Fugatts the nearest and best way to intersect the big Valley Road at or near the sand Lick and make report to the next term of this court

---

Ordered by the court that George Poff be appointed overseer of the road from Wallens branch to Cumbland Gap in the room and stead of John Bruster and have the same bound for hands that said Bruster had

---

Ordered by the court that William Parker be appointed overseer of the Road from Blairs Creek to the top of the Russels Creek hill in the room and stead of John Whitaker and have the hands and bounds of hands that said Whitaker had

(p 304) Monday May 14th 1821

In pursuance to an order to us directed from February Term 1821 we have met at the Dwelling house of Isaac Bolinger Deceased and have set apart what provisions we think necessary for the widow and her children for one year of the provisions and stock on hand Bacon 288 lbs. one fat hog 3 troughs of soap on stand of lard one Bushell of salt two small hogs one milk cow and all the flax wool and cotton on hand 60 Bushels of corn 20 Bushels of wheat one cag of vingar one piece sole Leather Do upper and all the poultry on hand

William Bowman senr.
John Carr senr.

---

Ordered by the court that Abel Lanham Edward Jennings and Jesse Hurst be appointed commissioners to set a part so much of the stock and provisions on hand of the Estate of Reuben Dobkins Deceased as will be sufficient for the support of the widow for the Term of one year and make report to the next term of this court

---

Ordered by the court that Elijah Hurst be appointed overseer of the Road from John Hurst Esqr. leading to Tazewell in room of Thomas Shearmon and have the same hands and bounds for hands said Shearmon had.

(p 305) Monday May 14th 1821

Ordered by the court that Solomon Dobkins be appointed overseer of the road / leading from Blairs Creek to Mulberry Gap that is from the top of the hill on the north side of Russells Creek to Thomas Brays in room and stead of Ambrose Simmons and have the same hand and bounds of hand said Simmons had

---

John Ousley Deceased to John Ousley Guardian Do to money Expended in Travling two Trips to the Indinna to the County of Harrison for the collection of the heirs money $30.

Ordered by the court that Peter Marcum be allowed the sum of four Dollars and fifty cents for services as a commission in settleing county claim with Sheriff and trustee of said county.

---

Ordered by the court that William Savage be allowed Six Dollars for Services done as a commissioner in settling with the Sheriff and Trustee of said County of Claiborne

(p 306) Monday May 14th 1821

Court adjourned until tomorrow morning nine oclock

John Brock
Wm. Savage
John Neil
Mercourious Cook
George Brock

Tuesday May 15th 1821

Court met according to adjournment present John Brock, John Neil, William Savage, Mercurious Cook and George Brock

William Bowman Senr. exhibited to court 9 Justices being present the soulp of a wolf over Six months old and proved he killed said wolf in the county of Claiborne & in the year 1821 & the court being satisfied therewith, It is ordered by the court that the sheriff burn said soulp & said William Bowman receive of the Treasurer of East Tennessee the sum allowed by Law

---

The Sheriff returned Nathan Perry as a constable to attend on the Grand Jury at this Term who was sworn as the Law derícts

(p 307) Tuesday May 15th 1821

William Rutledge
vs
Isaac Vanbebber

Debt - On motion of the Defendant & By consent of the parties it is ordered by the court, that commissions issue to some Justice of the peace for sullivan County to take the depositions of James Phagan and Jacob Snapp to be read as witness in this cause the defendant giving the plaintiff five days notice of the time and place of taking the same

---

William Cincaid for the use of Absalom Morris
vs
William Maddy

This day/came the parties by their attornies and therefore came a Jury to wit

1 Thomas R. McClary
2 James Vanbebber
3 David Wright
4 William Walles
7 John Bullard
8 Ambrose Day
9 David Huddleston
10 Daniel Slavens

5 Anson L. Carden | 11 John Hurst
6 Peter Marcum | 12 Joseph Cloud

who being Elected tried and sworn well & truly to try and the truth to speak upon the issue Joined in this cause do say they find the defendant has paid the Debt in the

(p 308) Tuesday May 15th 1821

Declaration as in pleading he hath alledged and assess the plaintiff Damages by reason of the detention of that Debt to fourteen Dollars and twenty five cents besides his cost It is therefore considered by the court that the plaintiff recover of the defendant the sum of one hundred Dollars the Debt in the declaration mentioned together with his Damages aforesaid in form aforesaid assessed besides his costs in this behalf expended and the defendant in mercy & & -

---

State
vs
Joseph Ferrell

Indictment

Personally appeared In open court Joseph Ferrell and Jacob Vanbebber and severally acknowledged themselves indebted to the state of Tennessee in the sum of two hundred Dollars that is to say Joseph Ferrell in the sum of one hundred Dollars and Jacob Vanbebber in the sum of one hundred Dollars to be severally and Jointly levied of their goods and chattels land and Tenements to the use of the state

(p 309) Tuesday May 15th 1821

void on condition that Joseph Ferrell makes his personal appearance at the courthouse in Tazewell from Day to day and not Depart the court without leave

---

Mathew McClury
assignee of Thomas L. Williams
vs
William Norvell

Debt

This day came the plaintiff by his attorney and the defendant in proper person who withdrew his plea and confessed Judgment for the sum of one hundred dollars the debt in the declaration mentioned and the further sum of fourteen dollars and ninety five cents damages on account of the detention of said debt together with all costs -

Whereupon it is considered by the court that the plaintiff recover of the defendant the sum of one hundred dollars the debt and the further sum of fourteen dollars and ninety five cents the damages confessed as aforesaid and also his cost about his suit in this behalf expended and the defendant in mercy & &

(p 310) Tuesday May 15th 1821

Richard Moore
vs
Daniel Sowder

Appeal

This day came the parties by their attornies, and thereupon came a Jury to wit

1 Isaac Lane | 7 Anson L. Carden
2 Tidance Lane | 8 John Bullard

| | | | |
|---|---|---|---|
| 3 | Thomas R. McCleary | 9 | David Huddleston |
| 4 | James Vanbebber | 10 | Daniel Slavens |
| 5 | David Wright | 11 | John Hurst & |
| 6 | William Wallen | 12 | Joseph Cloud |

who being elected, tried and sworn well and truly to try the matter of controversy now before them on their oath do say they cannot agree whereupon it is ordered by the court with the consent of the parties that a mistrial be entered and the cause conimued untill next court

James Collinsworth }
vs } Case
Joseph Hurst } This day came the parties by their attornies and on cause shewn by the defendants affidavit, it is ordered by the court that this cause be contimued untill next court

(p 311) Tuesday May 15th 1821

James Vanbebber & Isaac Vanbebber Executors of John Vanbebber decd. vs Jonathan Austin } Appeal

This day came the parties in proper person and by their consent with the assent of the court this cause is refered to the award and determination of Marcellus Moss, Henry Hunter, David Rogers, Daniel Huff and William Hagan and their award to be the final Judgment of this court

Henry Long }
vs } Appeal
Frederick Belinger } By consent of the parties this cause is contimued untill the next Sessions of this court -

Herrod Hopson }
vs } Appeal
Ambrose Day } The day came the parties and the plaintiff dismisses his suit and the defendant assumes the cost - whereupon it is considered by the court that said Suit be dismissed and that the plaintiff recover of the defendant

(p 312) Tuesday May 15th 1821

his costs by him the defendant confessed and asumed as aforesaid and the defendant in mercy -

Thomas Bray }
vs } Case
John McCellem } This day came the plaintiff in proper person and dismisses his suit and thereupon came Anderson Barton and assumed the costs and confessed Judgment therefor

Whereupon it is considered by the court that said Suit be dismissed and that the plaintiff recover of the said Anderson Barton his costs about his Suit in this behalf expended assumed and confessed as aforesaid

---

John Hunt Sheriff returned into court the venire facias executed on the following named person to wit

| | | | |
|---|---|---|---|
| 1 | Edward Wooton | 7 | Alexander Bules |
| 2 | Hugh Mountgomery | 8 | Leven Rusick |
| 3 | George Richardson | 9 | Samuel Dodson |
| 4 | John Richardson | 10 | Robert Grisham |
| 5 | William McNew | 11 | John Condray |
| 6 | Daniel Slavens | 12 | Thomas Coleman |

(p 313) Tuesday May 15th 1821

| | | | |
|---|---|---|---|
| 13 | James Hopson | 20 | William Parker |
| 14 | Ambrose Day Sr. | 21 | Jacob Adams |
| 15 | Hiram Hurst | 22 | Parter Lower |
| 16 | Richard Harper | 23 | Peter Marcum |
| 17 | David Huddleston | 24 | Abr. Murphey |
| 18 | William Hurst | 25 | Elijah Evans |
| 19 | John Hurst | 26 | Wm. McCullough |

Jurors remaining of the original pannel as follows to wit

| | | | |
|---|---|---|---|
| 1 | William Hurst | 5 | Ambrose Day sr. |
| 2 | William McCullough | 6 | Daniel Slavens |
| 3 | John Richardson | 7 | David Huddleston |
| 4 | Samuel Dodson | 8 | John Hurst |

---

James C. Martin vs Robert Finly } Attachment

Jesse Yoakum a garnishee in this case after being duly sworn states that he Executed a note to Robert Finly for the sum of nine Dollars and fifty cents

(p 314) Tuesday May 15th 1821

The time of giving said note he does not recollected but he believes that is is Due and payable on the 25th Day of December 1820 and that he has not paid said note nor no part thereof and further state that he knows not who has the possession of said note

---

John Neel and Robert W. McClary who was by the court appointed commissioner to Take lists of Taxable property and poles for the year 1821 returned in to court their lists which was recorded and filed

---

A Deed of conveyance from Mathew Hunter to Andrew Hunter for one hundred and thirty acres of land was Duly proven in open court by the oaths of David Wright and Squire Hunter the subscribing witnesses thereto and was admited to record and ordered to be registered

---

A Deed of Relinquishment from Hugh Graham & Co. to William Hill for one Town Lot in the Town of Tazewell was Duly proven in open court by the oaths of Robert Southern and Abner Yarbor the subscribing witness thereto and was admited to record and ordered to be Registered (p 315) Tuesday May 15th 1821

A Deed of conveyance from William Hill to Thomas L. Walker for one Town Lot in the town of Tazewell Number 32 was duly acknowledged in open court by the maker and was admited to record and ordered to be registered

---

A Deed of conveyance from Edward Jennings to William Condray for one hundred acres of land was duly acknowledged in open court by the maker and was admited to record and ordered to be registered -

---

A Deed of conveyance from John Grubb to Abraham Boyers for one hundred acres of land was duly proven in open court by the oaths of Hugh Vance and Joseph Boyers the subscribing witnesses thereto and was admited to record and ordered to be Registered

---

A Bill of sale from Benjamin Lankford to Reuben Rose for a negro Girl was duly proven in open court by the oath of William Graham & Peter Marcum the subscribing witness and was admited to records and ordered to be certified for Registration

(p 316) Tuesday May 15th 1821

A Bill of sale from Daniel Burkett to John Guthery for sundry articles was proven in open court by the oath of William Norvell and was filed for further probate

---

James Walker
vs } Appeal
Daniel Coffett

this day came the parties by their attornies and thereupon also came a Jury to wit

| | |
|---|---|
| William Hurst | Mathew Hamilon |
| John Richardson | Tidance Lane |
| William McCullah | John Fergerson |
| Samuel Dodson | Isaac Lane |
| John Whitaker | Jubal Lee |
| Briant Breeding | Tidance Lane jr. |

who being Elected tried and sworn well and truly to try and the truth to speak upon the matter in dispute wherein James Walker is plaintiff and Daniel Coffett is defendant

It is therefore considered by the court that the defendant go hence with out day and recover of the plaintiff his costs by him in this behalf Expended and have Execution

---

Of the Jurors attending that were returned on the venire at this court the following persons were balloted a Grand Jury to wit, Hiram Hurst who was appointed forman, Hugh Montgomery Alexander Bales William Parker, James Hopson

Jacob Adams

(p 317) Tuesday May 15th 1821

Thomas W. Coleman, John Condry, George Richardson, Edward Wooton, Richard Harper, William McNew & Leven Buick, who were sworn and returned under the charge of an officer to consider of their presentment

---

---

Martin Fugate )
vs )
John Davenport and Lucy his wife )

On motion of the defendant by attorney, and it appearing to the satisfaction of the court that the prosecution bail in this case has absconded or removed, it is ordered by the court that the plaintiff give other and sufficient security for prosecuting this suit on or before the second day of next term of this court or the suit shall stand dismissed

Court adjourned till tomorrow nine oclock John Neil
Wm. Savage
John Brock
Marcurious Cook

(p 318) Wednesday May 16th 1821

Court met according to adjournment present the worshipful
John Neil ) John Brock
Wm. Savage ) Mercurious Cook

Henry Hinton )
vs )
James Williams )

John Whitaker appearance bail in this case brought into open court the body of James Williams the defendant and surrenders him in discharge of himself and thereupon came the plaintiff, by his attorney and dismisses his suit whereupon came the defendant in his proper person and confesses Judgment for the costs it is therefore considered by the court that the plaintiff recover against the defendant his costs by him about the prosecution of his suit expended in manner and form as by the defendant confessed for which execution may issue

State )
vs )
Jonathan Mays )

This day came the state by the attorney General and the defendant in his proper person who being charged upon the bill of indictment

(p 319) Wednesday 16th May 1821

for plea thereto says he is guilty it is therefore considered by the court that for such his offence he be fined twenty five cents and that the state recover of the defendant the fine aforesaid together with the costs in and about the prosecution in this behalf Expended and that the defendant remain in custody till fine and costs are paid or security giveing

State )

vs ) This day came the state by
David Shumate ) the attorney General and the defendant in his own proper person and being charged upon the bill of indictment for plea thereto says he is guilty; it is therefore considered by the court that for his offence he be fined the sum of twenty five cents and that the state recover against him the fine aforesaid together with the costs in this prosecution expended and that defendant remain in custody till fine and costs are paid or security and thereupon came into court Mark Shumate and confessed Judgment for the fine and costs, it is therefore considered that the state recover against the said Mark the fine & cost aforesaid

State ) This day came the state by
vs ) the attorney General and the
Ansen L. Gardon ) defendant in his own proper person and being charged upon the bill of indictment for plea

(p 320) Wendesday 16th May 1821

thereto says he is not guilty and puts himself upon the country & the attorney Genl. doth the like and thereupon came a jury to wit William Hurst, William Mc Cullough, John Richardson, Samuel Dotson, Richard Moore, Robert Yoakum, James Williams, Jacob Vanbebber, Jacob Cloud, Jesse Carpenter, William Ritter, John Whitaker who being elected tried and sworn well and truly to try and the truth to speak on the issue joined upon their oaths do say they find the defendant not guilty in manner and form as charged in the bill of indictment whereupon on motion of the attorney Genl. and do sufficient cause appearing to the satisfaction of the court it is considered by the court that the state recover against the defendant the costs in this behalf expended and remain in custody till the same are paid or security given

State ) Indictment for an affray
vs )
Wm. Briant )
& ) This day came the state by
William Marckum ) the attorney General and the defendant in their proper person and being charged on the bill of indictment for plea thereto say they are guilty It is therefore considered by the court that for such their offense they be fined the sum of five dollars each and that the state recover against them the

(p 321) Wednesday 16th May 1821

the fine aforesaid in manner and form as against them severally assessed as also the costs in this prosecution expended and that the defendant remain in custody untill fine and costs are paid or security given and thereupon came into court Jeremiah Cloud Peter Marckum and confessess judgment for the fine and costs It is therefore considered by the court that the state recover against the said Jeremiah and Peter the fines and costs in manner and form as by them confessed for which execution may issue

---

This day came John Ashly a constable of Claiborne County and returned and execution issued by John Huddleston Esqr. a Justice of the peace on the 14th Apl. 1821 against James Williams for the sum of twenty dollars debt and

and seventy five cents cost in favor of and to satisfy a judgment obtained by William Graham against said Williams return thereon indrosed that he had levied the same on a tract of land lying on Powels river adjoining lands of John Whitaker and others being the tract on which the said Williams now lives no personal property being found in his county wherefore on motion of William Graham, by William B. Reese his attorney it is ordered by

(p 322) Wednesday 16th May 1821

the court that an order of of sale issue to expose to public sale the said tract of land to satisfy the said William Graham his debt and costs aforesd. the costs of the motion

State
vs
Benjm. Houser

Affray

This day came the state by the attorney General and the defendant in his proper person and the defendant being charged on the bill of indictment for plea thereto says he is not guilty in manner and form as charged in the bill of indictment and of this puts himself upon the country and the attorney General having done the like thereupon on came a Jury to wit

1 William Hurst
2 William McCullough
3 John Richardson
4 Samuel Dotson
5 Richard Moore
6 James Williams
7 Jacob Vanbebber
8 Jacob Cloud
9 Jesse Carpenter
10 William Ritter
11 John Whitaker
12 Harden Carey

who being elected tried and sworn well and truly to try and the truth to speak on the issue joined on their oaths do say the defendant is not guilty in manner and form as charged in the bill of indictment It is therefore considered by the court that the County of Claiborne pay the cost of this prosecution

(p 323) Wednesday 16th May 1821

Jesse Devers
vs
John Davenport

In this cause heretofore by rule of court and consent of the parties referfered to arbitrators an award was returned into court with words and figures following to wit

"State of Tennessee
Claiborne County

We the arbitrators chosen and sworn to try a certain matter of controversy wherein Jesse Deaver is plaintiff and John Davenport is defendant, and it being duly considered by us that find for the plaintiff five dollars forty one and a forth cents debt and the plaintiff and defend each and pay their own cost Giving under our hands the 16th day of March 1821

James Bice
Thomas Jackson
Wm. Bullard
James Brown"

It is therefore considered by the court that the said Jesse Deaver recover against the said John Davenport the said sum of five dollars forty one

(p 324) Wednesday 16th May 1821

and a fourth cents the sum by the said arbitrators awarded in manner aforesaid and that the plaintiff and for which execution may issue

John Davenport )
vs )
Jesse Deavers ) This cause by rule of court and consent of parties heretofore assessed to arbitrators an award in the following words and figures was this day returned into court:

"State of Tennessee )
Claiborne County ) We the arbitrators chosen and sworn to try a certain matter of controversy wherein and defendant and the matters and things relative to the same being duly considered by us we find for the plaintiff twelve dollars debt and the plaintiff and defendant each one pay their own cost Giveing under our hand the 16th day of March 1821

James Brown
Wm. Bullard
James Rice
Thomas Jackson"

It is therefore considered by the court that the plaintiff recover against the

(p 325) Wednesday 16th May 1821

defendant the said sum of twelve dollars in manner and form as by the arbitrators awarded and that the plaintiff and defendant each pay his own costs for which execution may issue

---

Thomas Johnston )
vs )
William McCullough ) The plaintiff in his own proper person comes into court and dismisses his suit It is therefore considered that defendant go hence without day and recover against the plaintiff his cost in and about his defence in this behalf expended for which execution may issue

Jesse Devers ) Motion
vs )
James Haddy ) This day came the parties by their attorneys into open court and said plaintiff by his counsel moved the court for a Judgment against the defendant as a constable and his securities for the sum of dollars and on account of an Execution placed in the hands of said defendant in favor of the plaintiff against a certain Daniel Brukil and the evidence and argument being heard

(p 326) Wednesday May 16th 1821

and understood by the court it is considered that the plaintiff take nothing by his motion, that the defendant go hence without day and recover of the plaintiff his costs about defence in this behalf Expended and the plaintiff in mercy

John Anthony ) Original attachment
vs )
Arthur L. Campbell ) This day came the plaintiff by his attorney, and the defendant failing to appear, replevy and defend this suit, On motion it is considered by the court that Judgment by default be entered against the defendant, but because the court is not advised what damages the plaintiff has sustained in this behalf it is further considered

and ordered by the court that a Jury come at the next sessions of this court to enquire of the plaintiff damages -

In this cause it is further ordered by the court a commission issue for the plaintiff to take the deposition of Luke Lea, directed to any Justice of the Peace for Knox County, on giving the defend- Isd. July 2nd 1821

(p 327) Wednesday May 16th 1821

ant, or his agent John S. Hardy Ten days notice of the time and place of taking the same - said deposition to be read as evidence in the above cause

---

A paper porporting to be the last will and testament of James Lemar Deceased was duly proven in open court by the oaths of Jesse Cain & John Lynch the subscribing witnesses thereto who swor they saw the said James Lemar sign publish and declare the same to be his last will and testament and that the will was executed at the time it bares Date that they were called upon by the said James Lemar and in his presents did witnessethe same and that the said James Lemar was of sound mind and disposing memory at the time of executing the same

---

A paper porporting to be the last will & Testament of John Gray deceased was duly proven in open court by the oaths of Nathan Perry & Elijah Harp the only subscribing witnesses thereto who swor they saw John Gray sign seal & publish & declare the same to be his last will & testamant that the will was executed at the time it bears date that they were called upon by the said John Gray & in his presents did witness the same & that the said John Gray was of sound mind & disposing memory

(p 328) Wednesday May 16th 1821

at the time of Executing the same

State } Indictment
vs }
James C. Martin } this day came the state by the solecitor general who prosecutes on behalf of the state and the defendant in his own proper person and being charged on the bill of Indictment for plea says he is guilty

It is therefore considered by the court that he be fined the sum of three dollars and that the state recover against him the fine aforesaid together with the cost in this behalf expended and that the Defendant remain in custody till fine and cost are paid or security given therefore whereupon Isaac Vanbebber came into court and confessed Judgment for the fine and cost aforesaid it is therefore considered by the court that the state recover of the said Isaac Vanbebber the fine and cost aforesaid and the defendant be in mercy & &

---

Magdeline Vanbebber minor heir of John Vanbebber Deceased came into court and being over the age of fourteen years was admited to choose her guardian whereupon she made choice of George Vanbebber who entered into bond with Jacob

Vanbebber and Dennis Condry for his securities

(p 329) Wednesday May 16th 1821

A Deed of conveyance from Squire Hunter to Andrew Hunter for one hundred and twenty three acres of land was duly proven in open court by the oaths of Joseph Powell and David Wright and was admited to record and ordered to be registered

---

A Deed of conveyance from John Word to David Snuffer for two hundred acres of land was duly proven in open court by the outh of Thomas R. McClary one of the subscribing witnesses thereto and filed for further probate

---

A Deed of conveyance from William Acklin to John McCubbins for one hundred acres of land was duly acknowledged in open court by the maker and was admited to record and ordered to be registered

---

A Deed of conveyance from James W. Glassgow to John McCubbens for twenty acres of land was duly proven in open court by the oath of Thomas R. McClary one of the subscribing witnesses thereto and filed for further probate

---

A Deed of conveyance from Thomas Cunningham to John Sanders for one hundred and fifty acres of land was duly proven in court by the oath of John Evans & Jesse Sanders the subscribing witnesses thereto admited to record let it be registered

(p 330) Wednesday May 16th 1821

A Deed of gift from David Brooks to Gidian Brooks was Duly proven in open court by the oaths of Hezikiah Brooks and Armsted Brooks the only Subscribing witnesses thereto and was admited to record and ordered to be regestered

---

A Deed of conveyance from Jesse Powers to William Sparks for eighty acres of land was duly acknowledged in open court by the maker and was admited to Record and ordered to be registered

---

A Deed of conveyance from Samuel Boroff to Jesse Powers for one hundred and eighteen acres of land was duly proven in open court by the oaths of John Brock and Spencer Edwards two subscribing witnesses thereto and was admited to record and ordered to be registered

---

A Deed of conveyance from James W. Glasgow to John Hurst for fifty acres of land was duly proven in open court by the oaths of John Huddleston and Fielding Lewis the only subscribing witnesses thereto and was admited to record and ordered to be registered

(p 331) Wednesday May 16th 1821

A Deed of conveyance from James W. Glasgow to Elijah Hurst for fifty acres of Land was proven by John Hurst and William Hooper subscribing witness es thereto Let it be registered

---

William Retter presented to court his petition praying leave to keep an ordinary in the County of Claiborne and the court being satisfied that the said William was and is a man of good Demeanor do grant said petition and thereupon the said William Retter Entered into bond with Dennis Condray as his Security and thereupon was sworn as the Law derects.

---

Susannah Posey presented to court her petition praying leave to Keep an ordinary in the County of Claiborne and the court being satisfied that the petitioner is a person of good Demanor do grant said petition and thereupon the sd. Susanah came into court and Entered into bond with John Bullard her security and was sworn as the Law derects

---

A Deed of conveyance from Thomas Johnson by his atto. in fact Ashael Johnson to William McCullah for one hundred acres of Land was duly acknowledged in open court by the Grantor therein named admitted to record and ordered to be registered

---

John Lynch Esqrs. who was appointed to receve lists of Taxable property and poles for the year 1821 returned his list which was recd. by the cort ordered to be filed and recorded

Court adjourned till tomorrow 9 oclock

John Brock
Wm. Savage
Mercurious Cook
John Neil

(p 332) Thursday May 17th 1821

Court met according to adjournment present same court as on yesterday

John Crichfield
vs
James Maddy &
George Eades

Appeal

This day came parties by their parties by their attornies

and thereupon came a Jury to wit

1 William Hurst
2 William McCullough
3 John Richardson

7 Jesse Carpenter
8 John Rice
9 John Barnes

| | |
|---|---|
| 4 Samuel Dodson | 10 Jacob Cloud |
| 5 Caleb Dobbs | 11 Samuel Cloud |
| 6 John Dobbs | 12 Lewis Morris |

who being elected tried and sworn well and truly to try and the truth to speak on the matter of Dispute between the parties upon their oaths do say they find for the Defendant

It is therefore considered by the court that the Defendant go hence & recover of the plaintiff and his security his costs by him about his Defence in this behalf Expended and the said plff. in mercy & &

State
vs
James Bunch } Indt. assault & Battry.

The grand Jurors returned into court the bill of Indictment in this cause found a True Bill

State
vs
John Bunch } Indt. A.B.

The Grand Jurors retd. into court the bill of Indictment in this cause found a true bill

(p 333) Thursday 17th May 1821

John Wallen
vs
Hugh White } Original Attachment

This day came the parties in this cause by their attorneys into open court and thereupon came a Jury to wit

| | |
|---|---|
| Ambrose Day Sen | Tidance Lane |
| David Huddleston | Joseph Hust |
| John Hust | Edwd. Jennings |
| Jacob Vanbebber | David Rogers |
| Joseph Cloud | Jesse Devers & |
| Isaac Vanbebber | John Bunch |

who being Elected Tried and sworn the Truth to speak upon this matter of controversey upon their oaths do say they find for the plaintiff and assesses his damage to fifty seven dollars whereupon It is considered by the court that the plaintiff Recover of the Defendant and his securities Robert Gibson & Henry Anams the debt aforesaid sum of fifty seven dollars his damages aforesaid in form aforesaid assessed also his costs by him about his suit in this behalf Expended from which verdict and Judgment the Deft. by his attorney prays an appeal to the next term Cercuit Court of this County Enters into bond & security files his reasons and the appeal is granted -

---

Edward Jennings
vs
Jeremiah Cloud
and Richard Mays } Appeal

This day came the parties in this cause together with their attorney into open court and thereupon came a Jury to wit

| | |
|---|---|
| Ambrose Day Sen | Tidance Lane |
| David Huddleston | Joseph Hust |
| John Hurst | Daniel Coffett |
| Jacob Vanbebber | David Rogers |
| Joseph Cloud | Jesse Devers & |
| Isaac Vanbebber | John Bunch |

who being

(p 334) Thursday 17th May 1820

Elected tried and sworn the truth to speak upon this matter of controversey upon their oath do say they find for the plaintiff the sum of seventy Dollars wherefore on motion of the plaintiff by his attorney It is considered by the court that the plaintiff Recover of the sd. Defendant and his security Thomas Berry the aforesaid sum of Seventy Dollars together with Twelve and half percent Interest on the same amounting in the whole to seventy Eight dollars & Seventy five cents also his cost by him about his Suit in this behalf Expended and the said Deft. in mercy & &

John Matlock
vs
Thomas Hunter

Aaron Hurst a constable of Claiborne County produced in court an execution issued by John Neil Esqr. in favor of and to satisfy a Judgment obtained by John Matlock against Thomas Hunter for the sum of six dollars debt and eighteen cents interest and seventy five cents costs with his return thereon endorsed that no goods or chattels are found in his county and that he had levied the same on a tract of land situate in said county as the estate of Thomas Hunter lying on the north side of Powels river bounded by the lands of Andrew Hunter the number of acres not known and thereupon on motion of John Matlock by his attorney Wm. B. Reese it is considered by the court that an or-

(p 335) Thursday 17th May 1821

der of sale issue to expose to publick sale said tract of land or so much thereof as Shall be sufficient to satisfy the debt and costs as aforesaid as also the costs of this motion

Edward Jennings assignee of Dennis Condray
who is assignee of Anderson Barton
vs
Jeremiah Cloud and Richard Mays

This day came the parties by their attornies and thereupon came a Jury to wit

| | |
|---|---|
| 1 William Hurst | 7 Jesse Carpenter |
| 2 William McCulleugh | 8 John Rice |
| 3 John Richardson | 9 Jacob Cloud |
| 4 Samuel Dodson | 10 Lewis Morris |
| 5 Caleb Dobbs | 11 Samuel Cloud |
| 6 William Wallice | 12 Isaac Vanbebber |

who being elected tryed and and sworn well and truly to try and the truth to speak in this matter in dispute do say they find for the plaintiff forty five Dollars besides his cost It is therefore considered by the court that the plaintiff Recover of the Defendant Jeremiah Cloud, Richard Mays, and Thomas Berry their Security the sum of forty five Dollars the sum by the Jury in form aforesaid assessed together with the further sum of four Dollars Six ¼ being twelve and one half percent interest on the 9th of August 1820 the time of the appeal from the Justices Justices Judgment also the cost in this behalf expended for which execution may issue

(p 336) Thursday May 17th 1821

State
vs
James Bunch

Assault and Battery

This day came the state by the

State by the solecitor General and the Defendant in his proper person and the Defendant in his proper person and the Defendant being charged on the bill of Indictment saith for plea thereto he is guilty

It is therefore considered by the court that It is therefore considered by the court that that for such his offence he forfeit and pay the sum of twenty five cents besides the cost in this behalf expended and thereupon James Hopson comes into court in his proper person and confesses Judgment for the fine and costs of this prosecution for which execution may issue

State
vs
John Bunch

Assault and Battery

This day came the state by the solecitor General and the Defendant in his proper person and the Defendant being charged on the Bill of Indictment for plea thereto saith he is Guilty

It is therefore considered by the court that for Such his offence he forfeit and pay the sum of twenty five cents besides the costs in this behalf expended, thereupon James Hopson in his proper person comes into court and confesses Judgment for the fine and costs of this prosecution for which Execution may issue

(p 337) Thursday May 17th 1821

James W. Glasgow
vs
Thomas P. McClellan

Covenant

This day came the parties, by their attornies and the Demurrer to the plaintiffs declaration coming on to be argued, and the court being fully advised thereon it is considered that said demurrer be sustained that the plaintiff take nothing by his Suit that the defendant go hence without day and recover of the plaintiff his costs about his defence in this behalf expended for which execution may issue

Hugh Young
vs
John Wallen
John Doherty & George Doherty

Case -

On motion of the plaintiff by his attorney it is ordered by the court that anplenis capias respondendum issue against John Doherty one of the defendant dericted to the Sheriff of Franklin County

(p 338) Thursday May 17th 1821

William Rogers, William Bowman, Thomas McLain, John Carr and David Rogers, who were at last court appointed commissioners to make partition of a certain Tract of Land in Claiberne County between The Heirs of Isaac Bolinger deceased and George Sharp, this day made report to the court of their proceedings in this behalf in making the partition aforesaid according to the acts of assembly in such cases made and provided and the court being satisfied there with It is considered and orderedby the court that said report be confirmed and the same be certified for registration as the Law dericts and it is further considered by the court that the claimants pay the costs about the petition in this behalf expended for which execution may issue - and said commissioners are allowed three dollars each for their services as commissioners and that William Rogers be allowed four dollars for his services as surveyor

A Deed of conveyance from John Ward to David Snuffer for two hundred acres of land which was proven yesterday by the oath of Thomas R. McClary and filed is now fully proven by the oath of Elijah Evans and admited to record and ordered to be Registered

(p 339) Thursday May 17th 1821

Jesse Ward vs John Bundron } Trespass assault & Battery

This day came the parties by their attornies and thereupon came a Jury to wit

| | |
|---|---|
| 1 William Hurst | 7 Jesse Carpenter |
| 2 William McCullough | 8 John Rice |
| 3 John Richardson | 9 Jacob Cloud |
| 4 Samuel Dodson | 10 Samuel Cloud |
| 5 Caleb Dobbs | 11 Lewis Morris |
| 6 William Wallis | 12 Isaac Vanbebber |

who being elected tried and sworn well and truly to try the Issue joined on their oaths do say they find the defendant guilty of the Tresspass assault and battery in manner and form as charged in the plaintiff declaration and assess the plaintiff damages by reason thereof to twenty five dollars It is therefore considered by the court that the plaintiff recover of the defendant the sum of twenty five dollars the damages assessed as aforesaid and also his costs about his suit in this behalf expended for which execution may issue -

(p 340) Thursday May 17th 1821

William Renfro Guardian of Peggy Vanbebber and William Vanbebber minor h heirs of John Vanbebber Deceased presented to court his resignation as guardian which was recived by the court and ordered to be Recorded

John Brock Esquires who was by the court appointed to take List of Taxable property and poles for the year 1821 Returned into court his list which was received by the court and ordered to be recorded

---

Reuben Rose presented to court his petition praying leave to keep an ordinary or house of public intertainment at his house in the Town of Tazewell and County of Claiborne and the court being satisfied that he is a man of good demeanor ordered that a License issue accordingly gave bond and Security and took the oath presented by law

---

Court adjourned till tomorrow morning 9 oclock John Brock
Wm Savage
George Brock

(p 341) Friday 18th May 1821

Court met according to adjournment present the worshipful John Brock, George Brock & Wm. Savage

It is ordered by the court that Abraham Murphy returned by the sheriff as a Juror for this day be fined two dollars for non attendance for which execution may issue

Robert G. Parks
vs
James Hill and William Hill } Debt

This day came the parties by their attornies and thereupon came a jury to wit

| | | | |
|---|---|---|---|
| 1 | William McCullough | 7 | Danl. Coffelt |
| 2 | John Richardson | 8 | Wm. Lynch |
| 3 | John Hurst | 9 | Anderson Barton |
| 4 | Joseph Ferrell | 10 | Caleb Dobbs |
| 5 | Jacob Vanbebber | 11 | John Rice |
| 6 | John Dobbs | 12 | Eli McVay |

who being elected tried and sworn well and truly to try and the truth to speak on the issue joined on their oaths do say they find the defendant have not paid the debt in the declaration mentioned as in pleading they have alledged and assess the plaintiff damage by reason of the detention thereof to fourteen dollars and security costs besides his cost It is therefore considered by the court that the plaintiff motion of the defendants the debt in the declaration mentioned and also the damages

(p 342) Friday 18th May 1821

foresaid in manner and form as by the Jury assessed together with his costs by him about his suit in this behalf expended and defendant in mercy & & from which verdict and judgment the defendants pray an appeal to the next Cercuit Court to be holden for the County of Claiborne files reasons gives bond and security and the appeal is granted

Wm. Hurst
vs
Joseph Hurst } Debt

This day came the parties by thier attornies and thereupon came a jury to wit

| | | | |
|---|---|---|---|
| 1 | William McCullough | 7 | Daniel Cofflet |
| 2 | John Richardson | 8 | Anderson Barton |
| 3 | John Hurst | 9 | Caleb Dobbs |
| 4 | Joseph Ferrel | 10 | John Rice |
| 5 | Jacob Vanbebber | 11 | Wm. Lynch |
| 6 | John Dobbs | 12 | Eli McVay |

who being elected tried and sworn well and truly to try and the truth to speak on the issue joined on their oaths do say they find the defendant has not paid the debt in the declaration mentioned as in pleading he has alledged and assess the plaintiffs damage by the detention thereof to ten dollars Sixty two and one half cents besides his costs It is thereupon considered by the court that the plaintiff recover of the defendant the debt in the declaration mentioned as also the damages

(p 343) Friday 18th May 1821

aforesaid in manner and form as by the jury assessed together with his cost in and about suit in this behalf expended and the defendant in mercy & & from which judgment the defendant prays an appeal to that next Cersuit Court to be holden for the County of Claiborne

John Bullard assignee of Dennis
Condray who is assignee of
Anderson Barton
vs }

Jeremiah Cloud } Appeal
Richard Mays } This day came the tha parties by their attornies and thereupon also came a Jury to wit

| | | | |
|---|---|---|---|
| 1 | William McCullough | 7 | Daniel Coffelt |
| 2 | John Richardson | 8 | Anderson Barton |
| 3 | John Hurst | 9 | William Lynch |
| 4 | Joseph Ferrell | 10 | Isaac Vanbebber |
| 5 | Jacob Vanbebber | 11 | John Rice |
| 6 | John Dobbs | 12 | Eli McVay |

who being elected tried and sworn well and truly to try and the truth to speak on the matter matter of dispute upon their oath do say they find for the plaintiff the sum of fifty Dollars the amount of the Judgment rendered by the Justice of the peace It is therefore considered the by court that the plaintiff recovur of defendants and their security the sum aforesaid assessed together with his costs in and on half six cent intrest and in and about this suit in this behalf expended & the defendant in mercy & &

(p 344) Friday 18th May 1821

James Walker
vs
Stephen Con, Henderson & Beatty } Reuben R. Rodgers a constable for the County of Claiborne proceeded in court an execution issued by William Graham Esqr. a justice of the peace for said County in favor of and to satisfy or judgment obtained by James Walker before Joseph Peterson Esqr. a Justice of the peace for Campbell County against Stephen Con, Henderson and Beatty, the execution of which judgment in said County was regularly certified according to law & ~~thereupon~~ the first mentioned execution was issued, which first mentioned execution so as aforesaid produced in court commanded any campal officer said county of the goods and chattels lands and tenements of the said defendant to make the sum of seventy five dollars twelve and one half cents debt with the interest ther eon proven the 10th day of September 1819 the date of said judgment as also fifty costs upon which execution the said Reuben

(p 345) Friday 18th May 1821

R. Rodgers constable made his return that he had levied the same on a tract of land lying at Cumberland Gap as the property of Martin Beatty one of the defendants and that no personal property was found in his plaintiff James Walker, by his attorney William B. Reese, it is ordered by the court that an order of sale issue to expose to public sale the tha said tract of land so levied on or so much thereof as shall be sufficient to satisfy the plaintiff his debt and cost aforesaid and also the costs of this motion

---

Ordered by the court one third of the acting Justices of the peace being present that rates of the Taxation in this county be and remain in all respects the same this year that It was the last

Squire Hunter } Certiorari
vs
Geo. Tate } This day came the plaintiff in this cause together with his attorney as well as the Defendant by his into open court and thereupon came a Jury to wit

| | | | |
|---|---|---|---|
| 1 | Wm. Hust | 7 | Alexr. Bales |
| 2 | John Richardson | 8 | Geo. Richardson |

| | | | |
|---|---|---|---|
| 3 | Saml. Dodson | 9 | John Condry |
| 4 | Ambrose Day | 10 | Hugh Montgomery |
| 5 | David Huddleston | 11 | Hyram Hust & |
| 6 | John Hust | 12 | Wm. Parker who being Elected |

tried and sworn the truth to speak upon this matter

(p 346) Friday 18th May 1821

of controversey upon their oaths do say they find for plaintiff the sum of Twenty dollars and fifty cents whereupon It is considered by the court that the plaintiff recover of the defendant the sum aforesaid by the Jury assessed together with his cost in and bout his suit in this behalf Expended and the defendant in mercy & &

---

State vs John Day } In'd & assault and battery

the Grand Jurors returned into court the bill of Indictment in this cause found true Bill

Reubin B. Rogers vs Absalom Morris } Trespass vict armus

This day came into open court the parties aforesaid together with their attorneys and thereupon came a Jury To wit

| | |
|---|---|
| Thomas Coleman | William Henderson |
| Richard Harper | Andw. Hunter |
| Edward Wooton | Mitchel Henderson |
| Swan Busick | Geo. Barnard |
| James Hopson | Jacob Adams & |
| David C. Posey | Thomas R. McClary |

who being Elected tried and sworn the truth to speak upon this Issue Joined upon their oaths do say they find the defendant is guilty of Trespass assault and Battery in manner and form as the plaintiff hath complained in his declaration and that the defendant

(p 347) Friday May 18th 1821

is not justified as in pleading he hath alleged and assess the plaintiffs damage to Three dollars and fifty cents and the demurrer of the plaintiff to the third plea of the Defendant being argued and understood by the court it is considered that the demurrer be sustained - It is therefore considered by the court that the plaintiff recover of the defendant the sum of Three dollars and fifty cents the damages assessed as aforesaid, and also his cost about his suit in this behalf expended for which execution may issue -

John Henly vs Anderson Jennings } Appeal

This day came the parties in their proper person and the plaintiff Dismisses his suit and the defendant confessed Judgment for the sum of three Dollars & fifty cents the amount of the Justices Judgment It is therefore considered by the court that the plaintiff recover of the defendant the sum aforesaid confessed together with his cost in this behalf Expended and the defendant in mercy & &

---

The Grand Jury is discharged from further attendance at the present term of this court

---

William Hurst is discharged by the court from further attendance as a Juror at this term

(p 348) Friday May 18th 1821

Ordered by the court that the following named persons be appointed Jurors to the next Cercuit Court for Claiborne County

| | | | |
|---|---|---|---|
| 1 | William Bails | 14 | William Norvell |
| 2 | Thomas Henderson | 15 | David Snuffer |
| 3 | Alexander Richie | 16 | James Vanbebber |
| 4 | George McNeil | 17 | Isham stinnet |
| 5 | Josiah Ramsey | 18 | John Carr |
| 6 | Jesse Hust | 19 | Jonas Hill |
| 7 | Henly Fugate | 20 | John S. Hardy |
| 8 | Robert McClary | 21 | Solomon Baker |
| 9 | John Mitchell | 22 | Henry Sumpter |
| 10 | Michael Pearson | 23 | James Eastage |
| 11 | Jacob Shoults | 24 | Abraham Hurst |
| 12 | John Roody | 25 | George Brock |
| 13 | John Lea | 26 | John Evans |

(p 349) Friday May 18th 1821

Ordered by the court that the following named person be to Jurors to the next term of this court

| | | | |
|---|---|---|---|
| 1 | John Mason | 14 | John Jinkins Senr. |
| 2 | Solomon Dobkins | 15 | Richard Harper |
| 3 | Thomas Maze | 16 | David Huddleston |
| 4 | Jonah Moore | 17 | John Bradon |
| 5 | Spencer Edwards | 18 | Arther Noah |
| 6 | Jacob Coots | 19 | Christian Sharp |
| 7 | John Long | 20 | Abram Devault |
| 8 | Nathan Moore | 21 | Joab Hill |
| 9 | Sampson Caps | 22 | Isaac Lane |
| 10 | Jesse Critchfield | 23 | Thomas Hurst |
| 11 | James Hoskins | 24 | Drury Herrell |
| 12 | Jubel Lea | 25 | George Treese |
| 13 | Richard Moore | 26 | John Harper |

---

State of Tennessee } May Session 1821
Claiborne County } On this 18th day of May 1821
personally appeared in open court being a court of Record for said County Eli McVay Resident in the County of Claiborne aforesaid aged about 58 year who being first duly sworn according to Law doth on his oath Declare that he served in the Revolutionary War as follows (viz) in the Regiment commanded by lot Lytle in the company commanded by

(p 350) Friday 18th May 1821

Captain Hall in the north Carolina line that he enlisted under captain Dixon on the continental establishment and that he served Two years in said Service that his original Declaration was made out at the november session 1818 of the court of pleas & quarter sessions for the County of Hawkins in state aforesaid, and that he has now in his possession a certificate issued from the war Department of Number 14,842 to which original Declaration this Declarant refere d for a more particular account of his Service and I do solemnly swear that I was a Resident citizen of the United States on the 18th day of March 1818 and that I have not Since that time by Gift sale or in any manner disposed of my property or any part thereof with intent thereby so to diminish it as to bring myself within the provission of an act of Congress Entitled an act to provide for certain persons Engaged in the Land and Naval Service of the United States in the Revolutionary War passed on the 18th day of March 1818 and that I have not nor has any person in trust for me any property or securities contracts or debts due to me nor have I any income other than what is contained in the schedule hereunto annexed and by me subscribed (viz) 1 cow $10, 3 sows and 10 pigs $2 - 6 peuter plates & 1 Dish $3.50 6 Japanned Tumblers 75, 4 wooden stools & 1 sifter 1.25

50½ 4 spoons 4 knives and forks .50
1 mare and colt $30.
1 sugar Bowl & 1 coffee pot .50
1 peper box 4 cups & saucers $55.75

(p 351) Friday May 18th 1821

That I am by occupation a common Labourer and am not now able to obtain a subsistance by my daily Labour being frequently afflected with the Rheumatism and labouring under considerable <u>delibity</u> that I have a wife aged 49 years who is of a weak constitution two children one a Boy aged about ten years the other also a Boy aged about seven year sworn to and subscribed to in open court
Eli McVay

State of Tennessee }
Claiborne County } I Benjamin Cloud clerk of the court of pleas and quarter sessions for the County of Claiborne aforesaid do hereby certify & make Known that the foregoing oath and the schedule thereto annexed are truly copied from the record of said court and I do further certify that it is the opinion of said court that the total amount in value of the property Exhibited in the aforesaid schedule is to wit

In Testimony whereof I have hereunto set my hand and affixed my seal private seal having no public seal of office in Tazewell this day of May 1821
Benj. Cloud Clk.

---

the grand Jury is discharged from further attendance at the present term of this court

(p 352) Friday May 18th 1821

Court adjourned until tomorrow morning 9 oclock
John Brock
Wm. Savage
John Neil
Mercurious Cook
George Brock

Saterday May 19th 1821

Court met according to adjournment present the worshipful John Brock William Savage, John Neal Marcurious Cook and George Brock Esquires

Robert Kyle
vs
Robert Grisham and Dennis Condray his security

In this case and Execution having issued signed by William Grayham a Justice of the peace for said County of Claiborne in favour of Robert Kyle against Robert Grisham and Dennis Condray his security for the sum of Sixty two Dollars Debt and one Dollar Six and a fourth cents Interest besides costs & & which Execution was at last term returned to court levied on fifty acres of Land adjoining the lands of George Barnard also on fifteen acres of Land lying at the Blood lick and thereupon an order of sale haveing been issued to sell said lands & & and it appearing said lands were sold for $52.50 forty four Dollars and forty Eight of which was applied to the plaintiffs Debt whereupon on motion it is ordered by the court that a procedendo issue to William Grayham Esquire commanding him to issue a scirefacias in favour of said plaintiff against said Defendant for the residue of said plaintiffs Debt

(p 353) Saturday May 18th 1821

Nathan Perry
vs
Nancy Warren

Petition

This day came the plaintiff in his own proper person and dismisses his suit and confesses Judgment for the cost it is therefore considered by the court that the defendant go hence without day and recoverof the plaintiff her costs in this behalf expended for which execution may issue -

---

Edward Wooten
vs
Abraham Murphy

Covenant

This day came the parties & by there this cause is continued and by consent a commission is awarded to the plaintiff derected to any Justice of Peace of McMinn or of Claiborne County to take the deposition of William Weaver to be read in this cause - the plaintiff giveing the defendant Ten days notice of the time and place of taking said deposition if taken in McMinn County and two days if taken in Claiborne County

Isd. July 7 1821

---

Hugh Graham & Co. assee.
vs
William Wallis

certiorari

On motion of the defendant by his attorney, a rule is granted him to shew cause why the writ of certiorari should be dismissed

(p 354) Saturday May 19th 1821

at last court the Jury appointed at the previous court to lay off and assign Dower to the widow of Peter Vanbebber deceased Eleanor Vanbebber returned their report to court according to Law assigned to have the following described Dower to wit Begining on a small spanish oak & running thence No. 61 E. 100 poles thence N. 23 west 114 to a stake thence S. 61 W 100 poles to a dead black oak in the field, thence S. 23 E. 114 to the begining which contains seventy one acres and forty poles also includes the dwelling house spring and orchard which report was confirmed by the court and a writ of possession awarded to the petition and it is further considered by the court that the petitioner pay the costs of her petition in this behalf and let said report be certified for registration

---

Thomas Johnson vs Jesse Carpenter } Certiorari

On motion of the plaintiff Thomas Johnson by his attorney a rule is granted him to shew cause why the petition of the defendant and his writ of certiorari should be dismissed

(p 355) Saterday May 19th 1821

Alfred Noel vs Dennis Condray } Appeal

This day came the parties By their attornies and thereupon also came a Jury to wit

1 William McCullough
2 John Richardson
3 John Hurst
4 Samuel Dodson
5 Ambrose Day
6 David Huddleston
7 Samuel Cloud
8 Francis Patterson
9 Robert Yoakum
10 George Tate
11 William Wallis
12 William Hooper

who being elected tried and sworn well and truly to try and the truth to speak in the matter of dispute between the parties upon their oaths do say they cannot agree and by consent of the parties by their attorney to a miss trial was ordered to be entered and the jury discharged from rendering their verdict

Alfred Noel vs Dennis Condray } Appeal

The plaintiff in his proper person came into court Therefore it is considered by the court the Defendant recover of the plaintiff his cost in this behalf expended and go hence without day and that execution issue for the cost

(p 356) Saterday May 19th 1821

State vs John Day } Indictment assault & Battery

This day came the state by her solecitor General who prosecutes on behalf of the state and the defendant in his own proper person and being charged on the bill of indictment for plea saith he is guilty and submits to the court It is therefore considered by the court that for this his offence he be fined the sum of twenty five cents togather with the cost in this behalf Expended and remain in custody untill fine and cost are paid or security Given whereupon came into court Ransom Day ser. as security of the defendant and confesses Judgment for the fine and cost aforesaid confessed & the defendants in mercy & &

Walter Evans by his agent
James Grant
vs
John Umstead
Christian Plank

Original Attachment

certiorari

On motion of the Defendant by his attorney on his plea in this cause it is considered by the court that the original attachment in this cause be quashed abated and for nothing held that the defendant go hence without day and recover of the plaintiff his costs & about his defence in this behalf expended -

(p 357) Saterday May 19th 1821

James Grant
vs
John Umstead

Original attachment

certiorari

On motion of the defendant by his attorney and for sufficient reasons appearing to the court in the plea of the defendant it is considered by the court that the original attachment in this cause be abated quashed and for nothing held that the defendant go hence without day and recover of the plaintiff his costs about his defence in this behalf expended for which execution may issue

John Bullard assignee of
Dennis Condray
vs
Jeremiah Cloud

On motion and sufficient reasons appearing to the court it is ordered by the court that a new trial in this cause be granted because it appears to the court that Anderson Barton the original obligee was one of the Jury in this case who passed on the trial thereof

Edward Jenings assee. & &
vs
Jeremiah Cloud
Richard Mays & Thomas Berry

In this cause the defendants pray an appeal to next Cercuit Court enter into bond with approved security and the appeal is Granted reasons having been previously filed.

(p 358) Saterday May 19th 1821

Court adjourned until court in course

John Neil
Mercurous Cook
John Brock
Wm. Savage
George Brock

(p 359) Satterday (Blank)

(p 360) Monday August 13th 1821

At a court of pleas and quarter sessions begun and held for the County of Claiborne at the court house in Tazewell on the second Monday of August 1821 The following Justices being present John Brock, John Neil, William Savage, George Brock, Mercurious Cook, Aaron Davis, John Wallen, John Huddleston and William Graham

---

John Lea a constable in the bounds of Captain Browns Company Tenders his resignation which is Rec'd. by the court

—

—

After proclamation being made the court proceeded to the Election of a constable in the bounds of Captain Browns Company and after compairing the votes it appeared that John Hunt was duly and constitutionally Elected for the Insueing two years and also was sworn as the Law directs and Entered to bond with George Brock and Robert Gibson as securities

—

—

Ordered by the court that Joel Jones be appointed a constable in the bounds of Captain Browns Company for the Insuing two years and thereup was sworn as the Law directs and Entered into bond with William Hogan, and William Beaty as securities

(p 361) Monday August 13th 1821

Ordered by the court that Isaac Ously be appointed overseer of the road from Bullards Mill to the Sandlick in room and stead of Jacob Coots and have the same hands and bounds that said Coots had

—

—

Ordered by the court that Jesse Lynch be appointed overseer of the road leading up and down powels vally begining at the branch below James Rogeres t thence up to the Haw Branch in room and stead of John Bowman and have the same hands and bounds for hands that said Bowman had

—

—

Ordered by the court that William Lewis be appointed overseer of the big vally road from Lewis road to hunting creek in room and stead of Reubin Flowers and have the same hands and Bounds for hands that said Flowers had.

—

—

Fielding Lewis, Henry Moyers, Jacob Adams, Samuel Moore, and William Yoak who were appointed a Jury to view and lay out a road from Kerlins Hollow at or near Martin Fugats the nearest and best way to intersect the big vally road near the sandlick made their report in the following words and figures to wit in compleyance with an order of the worshipful court met at the house of Martin Fugates and viewed and marked said ground agreeable to the within order the big vally road at the lower end of Fielding Lewis plantation ground Fielding Lewis, Henry Moyers, Jacob Adams Samuel Moore and William Yoak Jurers

(p 362) Monday August 13th 1821

which report being inspected by the court a majority of the acting Justices being present It is ordered that the road as laid out by the Jury aforesaid be established and made a public road and it is further ordered that John Breaden be overseer to open the new road as viewed and marked by the Jury aforesaid leading from Martin Fugate to intersect the big vally road at or near the sandlick that is from Fugats to the hollow near Sparkses and have the following bounds for hands that is all the hands living in the bent of powels river thence by David Lays taking him in thence a derict course to the river ridge the north side of clinch river thence up said ridge taking in Peter Lower thence up Little Baron to Lickliters field thence a derict course taking in powers and cootses thence down Camp Crek to Powels river to the said big bent

---

And also it is further ordered by the court that Spencer Edwards be appointed overseer to open the new above recited road as viewed and marked from the cross hollow near [illegible] to the said lick and have the following bounds for hands that is beining at the mouth of Camp Creek leaving cootses and powers out then to the mouth of the cross hollow down little baron to the mouth There up clinch river to John Bullard taking him - then along the road from Bullards to the sandlick so as to include all the hands living on Lewis old place then from the sandlick up the big vally to John Hursts Esqr. then Including the Bridges and the [illegible] then taking

(p 363) Monday August 13th 1821

in the Hoppers and then to the mouth of Camp Creek

---

Polly Dobkins administratrix of Reubin Dobkins Deceased reterned to court the amount of sales of the Estate of Deceased which appears to be $249.41½ Polly Dobkins her mark which was Recd. by the court and ordered to admistrx to be filed and recorded

---

Betsey P. Bolinger and Frederick Bolinger admistratrix and administrator of Isaac Bolinger Deceased returned to court an Inventory of the amount of sales of the Estate of said Deceasants which was rec'd by the court and ordered to be filed and recorded.

---

John Huddleston and John Evanes Esqrs. clks were heretofore appointed commissioners to settle the Estate of William Jenings Deceased with William Jenings administrator of of the same returned to court on account of their settlement which was Inspected and recived by the court and ordered to be certified

(p 364) Monday August 13th 1821

Ordered by the court that John Johnson be appointed overseer of the Jennings Ferry road from the top of Clinch river Hill to Holts ford on Clinch River in room and stead of Ralph Shelton and have the same hands said Shelton had

---

Ordered by the court that Solomon Dobkins be appointed overseer of the road leading from Blairs Creek to Mulberry Gap as heretofore appointed, that is from the top of the hill on the north side of russels creeks to Thomas

Brays ~~in-room-and-stead-of-Ambrose-Brays~~ in room and stead of Ambrose Temmons and have the same hands and bounds of hands said Temmons had and the hands of Edward Jenings and John Jones in addition to the same
Isd.

Ordered by the court that Ezekiel Herril be appointed overseer of the Jenings Ferry road from the top of the river ridge to John Simmones in room and stead of Coventon Collensworth and have the same bounds for hands said Collensworth had
Isd.

Ordered by the court that Jess Shipley be appointed overseer of the upper Bullard Ferry road from the old garrison to the forks of said road near William Grahams fince in room and stead of Isham Jenings and have the same hands and bounds for hand said Jenings had
Isd.

Ordered by the court that Jacob Shoults be appointed overseer of the Kentucky road between Big and little sycamore creek in room and stead of Bibby Hodges and have the same hands and bounds of hands said Hodges had
Isd.

(p 365) Monday August 13th 1821

Ordered by the court that Green Jones be appointed overseer of the road in room and stead of William Stallins resigned and have the same hands and bounds for hands that said Stallins had

Abel Lanham Edward Jennings and Jesse Hurst who was at last Term appointed commissioners to set aprt so mach of the stock and provisions on hand of the Estate of Reuben Dobkins Deceased as will be sufficient for the support of the widow of the said Decad for the Term of one year makes the following report
Agreeable to an order of court at May sessions we the undersigned hath set a part the following articles To wit.
Seven Barrals of corn and seven midlings of Bacon one hundred Lb. of pork one cow one bushel of salt and ten bushels of wheat given under our hand this 13th day of August 1821

Edward Jennings
Abel Lanham
Jesse Hurst

(p. 366) Monday August 13th 1821

With leave of the court George Campbell is admited to administrer on all and singular the goods and chattels rights and credits of Hezekiah Rynons Deceased who entred in to bond with Elias Harrison his security and was qualefied accordingly and also returned an Inventory of said Estate which was received by the court and ordered to be filed & recorded.

The following is an account of the guardianship of William Walles who is guardian of the Estate William James and John James minor heirs of Thomas James Deceased for the last year to wit

Receive of the estate of said ward from Polly Wallis the administratrix on the second Day of May 1821 fifty one dollars which is Still on hand $50

Said guardian has made the following Disbustments to wit

expences for guardianship to the clerk of Claiborne County $1

and clerk of Russells County Virginia for copy of administration account and settlement $2.50

Expences to Russells County Virginia on the buisness of said ward ---------------------------------------- $3.75

Do to Russell County Virginia on the business of said ward --- $3

Do at last Russell County Court Virginia $3.80

(p 367) Monday August 13th 1821

Paid to Sterling Cocke Esquire for his attention to the buisness of said wards $2.50

Paid Jeremiah Cloud clerk for copies of Records on behalf of said ward $5.80

Sworn to in open court Wm. Wallis

B. Cloud Clerk

Deed of conveyance from William Bowman sr. to William Bowman Jnr. for one hundred and forty two and one half acres of land was duly acknowledged in open court by the maker and was admited to record and let it be registered

---

A Deed of conveyance from William Bowman snr. to Cornelious Bowman for one hundred and forty two and one half acres of land was duly acknowledged in open court by the maker and was admitted to record and ordered to be registered

---

A Deed of conveyance from William Bowman ser. to John Bowman for one hundred acres of land was duly acknowledged in open court by the maker and was admited to record let it be registered -

---

A Deed of convenance from Dennis Condray to Peter Marcum for four town lots in the Town of Tazewell was duly proven in open court by the oath of Thomas R. McClary and Thomas L. Walker the only subscribing witnesses thereto and was admited to let it be registered

---

(p 368) Monday August 13th 1821

A Deed of conveyance from Jacob Cloud to Andrew Davis for Sixty acres of land was duly acknowledged in open court by the maker and was admited to record let it be registered

---

A Deed of conveyance from Thomas Shearmon to John Gray for one hundred acres of land was Duly acknowledged in open court by the maker and was admited to record let it be registered

---

A Deed of conveyance from Jacob Jackson to William Stinnet for fifty acres of land was duly proven in open court by the oath of Abraham Murphey and William Murphey subscribing witnesses thereto and was admited to record let it be registered.

---

A Deed of conveyance from James ?. Glasgow to Isaac Ousley for fifty acres of land was duly proven in open court by the oath of William Houston and Hugh Graham the subscribing witnesses and was admited to record let it be Registered

---

A Deed of conveyance from John Jennings to Joseph Jeninngs for three hundred acres of land was duly proven in open court by the oaths of Sterling Cooke and Samuel Cloud the only subscribing witnesses thereto and was admited to record let it be registered

(p 369) Monday August 13th 1821

A Deed of conveyance from Thomas Shearmon to John Gray for thirty acres of land was duly acknowledged in open court by the maker and was admited to record let it be registered

---

A Deed of conveyance from George Campbell to Barney Campbell for Seventy five acres of land was duly acknowledged in open court by the maker and was admited to record and ordered to be registered

---

Rachel Davis
vs
Ransom Hays and others } This day comes here into court Joshua Davis agent for the plaintiff and the Defenants in their proper persons and thereupon the said plaintiff by his said agent dismisses his suit and agrees to pay the costs and the Defendant agrees to confess Judgement for their costs

It is therefore considered by the court that the plaintiff recover of the Defendant their costs in this behalf expended and that the Defendant recover of the plaintiff his costs in this behalf expended for which Execution may issue

(p 370) Monday August 13th 1821

State
vs
William Beaty and others } In this case the Defendant

William Beaty being charged on the Bill on Indictment for plea thereto saith he is guilty

It is therefore considered by the court for such his offence he be fined twelve and one half cents and pay the costs in this behalf expended for which Execution may issue

---

William Hoskins
vs
Peter Elrod

Certiorarri

In this case the plaintiff in his proper person comes into court and Dismisses his suit

It is therefore considered by the court that the Defendant recover of the plaintiff his costs by him in this behalf expended for which Execution may issue

Jacob Vanbebber
vs
William Maddy

Certiorarri

The Defendant having Exhibited in open court a petition praying writs of certiorarri and supercedeas in the suit Jacob Vanbebber administrator as Executor of Peter Vanbebber Deced. against him and the court being Satisfied that said petition contains merrets direct the prayer of said petition to be granted and that said writs issue accordingly

(p 371) Monday August 16th 1821

Ordered by the court that John Fergerson be appointed overseer of the Road in the room and stead of James A. Hamelton and to have the same bounds for hands that said Hamelton had with the addition of Henry Richardson Joel Dobbs and Thomas England

Isd. Aug. 14, 1821

---

Ordered by the court that William Graham and Elias Harrison be appointed commissioners to settle with William McNew administrator of John McNew Deceased and make report to the present term of this court

---

Ordered by the court a majority of the acting Justices being present that John Roddy, Andrew Crockett, Peter Clark, William McHenry, Ralph Mitchell and John McKee are appointed a Jury of view to view and lay out a road from Dennis fields to intersect the road leading from Roddy Ferry to Lee courthouse at or near Crocketts Iron Work

(p 372) Monday August 13th 1821

so as to injure individuals as little as possible and make report to the next term of this court and also that the road from sd. Dennis fields to the Virginia line as at present marked out be no longer a public road of this county -

Court adjourned till tomorrow 9 oclock John Brock

Mercurious Cook
Mercurious Cook
John Neil
Wm. Savage
George Brock

Tuesday August 14th 1821

Court met according to adjournment

A Deed of conveyance from Michael Cammon to Thomas Johnson for forty Six ½ acres of land was duly acknowledged in open court by the maker and was admited to record and ordered to be registered

---

A Deed of conveyance from Thomas Johnson by his attorney Ashel Johnson to Michael Cammon fifty acres of land was duly acknowledged in open court by the maker and was admited to record let it be registered

(p 373) Tuesday August 14th 1821

A Deed of conveyance from James W. Glasgow to Jonah Moore for one hundred and Sixty acres of land was Duly proven in open court by the oaths of Thomas R. McClary and Charles Payne the subscribing witnesses thereto and was admited to record let it be registered

---

A Deed of conveyance from James W. Glasgow to Jonah Moore for thirty five acres of land was duly proven in open court by the oath of Thomas R. McClary and Charles Payne the subscribing witnesses and was admited to record and ordered to be registered

---

A Deed of conveyance from James W. Glasgow by attorney William Brown to Jonah Moore for one hundred and thirty acres of land was duly proven in open court by the oaths of Thomas R. McClary and Charles Payne the subscribing witnesses there and was admited to record let it be Registered

---

A Deed of conveyance from Thomas Johnson and Jacob Peck to John Brock for three hundred and fifty acres of land was acknowledged at August Term 1820 by Peck and filed for further probate

(p 374) Tuesday August 14th 1821

Is fully acknowledged at this Term by Ashal Johnson attorney for Thomas Johnson and was admited to record and ordered to be registered -

---

A Deed of conveyance from James W. Glasgow to John Bullard for five hundred acres of land was duly proven in court by the oaths of Thos. L. Walker and Sterling Cocks the subscribing witnesses thereto and was admited to record let it be registered

---

A Deed of conveyance from James W. Glasgow to William Bullard for one hundred acres of land was duly proven by the oaths of Thomas L. Walker and Sterling Cocks the Subscribing witnesses thereto and was admited to record let it be registered -

---

A Deed of conveyance from John James to William Muncus for forty four acres of land was duly proven in open by the oaths of Henry Sharp and filed for further probate

(p 375) Tuesday August 14th 1821

A Deed of conveyance from Thomas Whitehead to Jonah Moore for eighty one acres of land was duly proven in open court the oaths of Nathan Perry and Richard Harper the subscribing witnesses thereto and was admited to record let it be registered -

---

John Hunt Sheriff of Claiborne County returned to court the venirefacias executed on the following named persons to wit

John Mason
Thomas Mays
Jonah Moore
Spencer Edwards
Jacob Coots
John Long
Nathan Moore
Sampson Caps
Jesse Critchfield
James Hoskins
Jubal Lee
Richard Moore
John Jinkens sr.
Richard Harper
David Huddleston
John Brendon
Arthur Nash
Christian Sharp
Abraham Devault
Joab Hill
Isaac Lane
Thomas Hurst
Drury Herrell
George Trease
John Harper

(p 376) Tuesday August 14th 1821

out of which venirefacias the following named persons were balloted a Grand Jury to the present were balloted a Grand Jury to the present term

1 Joab Hill foreman
2 John Mason
3 Jacob Coots
4 Arthur Nash
5 John Jinkins
6 Abraham Devault
7 John Harper
8 Isaac Lane
9 Spencer Edwards
10 Richard Moore
11 Jonah Moore
12 Nathan Moore
13 Jesse Crichfield

who were sworn as the Law directs Recieved their charge from the solecitor General and retired to considerof their presentments - Jurors Remaining of the original pannel as follows to wit

1 David Huddleston
2 Drury Herrell
5 Thomas Mays
6 Sampson Caps

3 Richard Harper 7 James Hockins
4 Jubal Lee 8 Thomas Hurst

who were sworn for the Term
Isd. Aug. 23rd 1821

(p 377) Tuesday August 14th 1821

Ordered by the court that Abel Lanham Edward Jennings and William Cunningham be appointed commissioners to set a part so much of the stock and provisions on hand of the Estate of Hezekiah Runyans Deceased as will be sufficient for the support of the widow and orphans for one year and and make report to next court
Isd. Aug. the 30th 1821

---

Ordered by the court that an order of sale Issue to George Campbell administrator of the Estate of Hezekiah Runyans Deceased to Expose to sale as the Law dericts the personal property of said Estate and and make return to next court
Isd. Aug. the 30th 1821

---

Ordered by the court that John Evans and John Simmons be appointed commissioners to settle with Sally Jennings administratrix of the Estate of Hezakiah Jennings Deceased and make report to the next term of this court

---

Ordered by the court that Thomas L. Walker, Thomas R. McClary and Peter Marcum be appointed commissioners to settle with William Graham and Benjamin Cloud Executors of the last will and Testement of Christopher Dameron Deceased and make report to the next term of this court Isd. Aug. the 30th 1821

(p 378) Tuesday August 14th 1821

William Graham and Elias Harrison who were appointed commissioners at the present Term to settle with William McNew administrator of John McNew Deceased made their report to court which was received and ordered to be filed and recorded -

---

Nathan Perry was appointed a constable to attend on the Grand Jury and was sworn accordingly -

---

The assignment of a plat and certificate of survey for one hundred acres of land from Burrell G. Sallivant to James M. McVay was duly proven in open court by the oaths of Josiah Ramsey and Danial Rice the subscribing witnesses and ordered to be certified

---

Thomas Baker one of the acting Justices presents the scaps of three wolves over four months old and proves that he killed said wolves in the County of Claiborne and in the year 1821 and the court being satisfied there with ordered that he be allowed according to Law and that the sheriff burn the scaps and that certificate issue
Isd. Jany 4th 1820

(p 379) Tuesday August 14th 1821

Ordered by the court that William McNew be appointed guardian to John McNew, Frederick McNew, Sally McNew and Finetta McNew minor heirs and orphans of John McNew Deceased who entered into bond with William Rogers for his security

---

William Rutledge
vs
Isaac Vanbebber } Continued as on affidavit and the rule to Take the deposition of James Phagan and Jacob K. Snapp made at the last term of this court is on motion of Deft. renewed with the same notice as therein mentioned

Martin Beaty & Co.
vs
Armsted Brown } Debt
this day came the parties by their attornies and thereupon came a Jury to wit

| | |
|---|---|
| David Huddleston | Tidance Lane |
| Richard Harper | David Rogers |
| Jubal Lee | Conrod Stiner |
| Thomas Mays | Edward Wootton |
| John Bartlett | Henry Cratner |
| James Overton | Luke Perry |

who being elected tried and and sworn well and truly to try and the truth to speak upon the Issue Joined

(p 380) Tuesday August 14th 1821

upon their oaths do say that the defendant hath not paid the Debt in the declaration mentioned as in pleading he hath alledged and assess the plaintiff Damage by reason of the Detention thereof to thirteen dollars and fifty three cents besides cost

It is therefore considered by the court that the plaintiff recover of the defendant the debt in the declaration mentioned and the damages aforesaid in form aforesaid assessed together with the cost in and about prosecuting their suit in this behalf Expended and the defendant in mercy & &

---

Richard Moore
vs
Daniel Sowder } Appeal
this day came the parties by their attornies and thereupon came a Jury to wit

Richard Harper, Jubal Lee, Thomas Mays, John Bartlet, James Overton, Edward Wootton, Henry Gratner, Daniel Coffelt, Dennis Condray, James Ellison,

Luke Perry & James Hoskins, who being elected tried and sworn well and truly to try and the truth to say on the matter in despute wherein Richd. Moore is plaintiff and Daniel Sowder is Defendant upon their oaths do say the find for the plaintiff Ten dollars and Twenty five cents besides costs

It is therefore considered by the court that the plaintiff recover of the Defendant Ten Dollars and Twenty five cents Debt together with his costs

(p 381) Tuesday August 14th 1821

in this behalf Expended and the Defendant in mercy & &

---

Alfred Noel
vs
Dennis Condray

This day came the plaintiff in his own proper person and Dismisses his suit and confessed Judgment for costs

It is therefore considered by the court that the Deft go hence without day and recover of the plaintiff his costs by him about his suit in this behalf Expended and the Deft. have Execution

State
vs
Conrod Stoner

Bastardy

This day came the defendant into open court who is charged on the oath of Rebecca Lemmons of being the father of a bastard child begotten on her body and likely to become chargable to the court of Claiborne County and the state by the attorney General, and the said Conrod Stoner entered in bond with Danl. Sowder, Mathew Owens and John Henly as his securities indemnify the County of Claiborne from the maintenance of sd. bastard child - It is therefore considered by the court that the state recover against the said defendant the costs in this behalf expended & defendant in mercy & &

Martha Fugate
vs
John Davenport & Lucy his wife

This day came the parties by their attorney and on petition of the plaintiffs counsel

(p 382) Tuesday August 14th 1821

and with the assent of the court the plaintiff suffers a non suit and on motion of the plaintiff a rule is granted him to shew cause why the non suit should be set aside

Isaac Sawyers
vs
John S. Hardy

Appeal

This day came the parties by their attornies and and thereupon came a Jury to wit David Huddleston, Richard Harper, Jubal Lee, Thomas Mays, John Bartlett, James Overton, Tidance Lane, David Rodgers, Conrod Stoner, Edward Wooton, Henry Gratner and Luke Perry who being elected tried and sworn well and truly to try and the truth to speak on the matter of contreversy between the parties retired to consider of their verdict and returned into court that they cannot agree Thereupon with the consent of the parties and the assent of the court a mistrial is entered and the cause continued till the next term of this court

---

A bill of sale from Dennis Condry to William Savage for a negro woman named Frazen was duly acknowledged in open court by the bargainor admited to record let it be registered

(p 383) Tuesday August 14th 1821

Court adjourned till tomorrow morning 9 oclock

John Brock
John Neil
Marcurious Cook
George Brock
Wm. Savage

Wednesday November 15th 1821

Court met according to adjournment present the worshipful John Neil, Marcurious Cook, John Brock, George Brock and William Savage, Esquires

State vs Mordica Cunningham } for assault and Battery on Absolom Horst

The Defendant being charged on the Bill of Indictment in the case pleads thereto guilty and submits to the court whereupon It is considered by the court that for such his offence he be fined ten Dollars and pay the costs of this prosecution in this behalf expended whereupon Joab Hill and John Bartlet comes into court and confesses a Judgment for the fine and costs in this behalf expended for which execution may issue

State vs Mordeca Cunningham } On assault and Battery and David Kesterson

The Defendant being charged on the bill of Indictment for plea thereto saith he is guilty It is therefore considered by the court that for such his offence he be fined five Dollars and pay the costs in this behalf expended whereupon Joab Hill and

(p 384) Wednesday August term 1821

John Bartlet comes into court and confesses a Judgement for the fine and costs in this behalf expended for which an execution may issue

State vs John Rice & Samuel Hamilton } Indictment

The grand Jury returned into court a bill of indictment against sd. defendants endorsed a true bill

---

State vs John Bundon & James Morgan } Indictment

This day the grand Jury returned into court a bill of indictment endorsed a true bill

State vs John Bundron and James Morgan } Indictment

this day the grand Jury returned

into court a bill of indictment endorsed a true bill

William McNew
vs
Person Barney & Benjamin Barney

certori

This day came the parties by their attornies and thereupon came the following Jury to wit David

(p 385) Wednesday 15th August 1821

Huddleston, Richard Harper, Thomas Mays, George Richardson, John Dobbs, Caleb Dobbs, James Maddy, Mathew Hamilton, Thomas Harp, Thomas Hurst, John Bartlett and Sampson Caps who being elected tried and sworn well and truly to try and the truth to speak in the matter of dispute between the parties on their oaths do say the find for the plaintiff fifty three dollars & forty one cents and on motion considered by the court that the plaintiff recover against the defendant and also his securities Peter Lower and David Lay the said sum of fifty three dollars and forty one cents found by the Jury aforesaid together with his costs by him about his suit in this behalf expended & & -

State
vs
Arthur L. Campbell

Personally appeared in open court James Laches and acknowledged himself indebted to the state of Tennessee in the sum of one hundred dollars to levied of his goods and chattels lands and tenements but to be void on condition that he make his personal appearance at the court house in Tazewell on the Wednesday of the second Monday of November next

(p 386) Wednesday 15th August 1821

then and there to prosecute and give evidence on behalf of the state in a bill of indictment the state vs Arthur L. Campbell and not depart the court without leave

Thomas McClain
vs
James and Isaac Vanbebber
administrators & &

This day came the parties by their attornies and thereupon came the same Jury as in the case of McNew vs Person & Benjamin Barney Jury on motion of the plaintiff by his attorney and with the assent of the court a non suit is entered in cause and on motion a rule is granted the plaintiff to shew cause why the non suit should be set aside

Richard Moore
vs
Danl. Sowder & Jacob Cloud

This day came the parties by their attornies and on motion of the plaintiff by his consent it is considered by the court that the plaintiff recover against the sd. Jacob

Cloud the security for the prosecution of the appeal the sum of ten dollars dollars and twenty five cents the amt. found by by the jury as yesterday

(p 387) Wednesday 15th August 1821

and also against the said defendant and his security intrest at the rate of twelve and one half percent per annum or the sum of $962 from the 17th day of June 1820 the date of the judgment below to this time amounting to the sum of one dollar & thirty two cents as also his costs in this behalf expended

---

On affidavit of Jubal Lee one of the venire for the present term he is excused from attending during the balance of this court

---

Wm. Lane } Petition for certiorari
vs }
Aaron Davis } On petition of Aaron Davis and sufficient cause shewn on affidavit of the petition it is ordered by the court that writs of certiorari and supercedens issue according to the prayer of the said petition on petition giving bond and security according to law

---

Hugh Young } On motion of the plaintiff by
vs } his attorney and consent of de-
John Wallen & Col } fendant a commission is awarded
him to take the deposition

(p 388) Wednesday 15th 1821

of Peter A. Young of Baltimore before any judge justice or mayor on giving the defendant John Wallen forty days notice of the time and place of taking the same

---

State of Tennessee } County Court
Claiborne County } August Sessions 1821

Personally appeared in open court the court of pleas and quarter sessions for said county in said State the same being a court of record made so by the statute of said state Conrod Kegg a citizen of sd. county and in due form of law made oath that he enlisted as a private soldier in the year one thousand seven hundred and seventy seven in the service of united states engaged in the revolutionary war for three years from the date of his enlistment that he enlisted in North Hampton County in the state of Pensylvania in Capt. Isaac Korens Coren; company in Col. James Proctors Regiment of artillery in the Pensylvania line that he was in the battle of Brandy-wine and Germantown served his full term of enlistment and was honorably dis-

(p 389) Wednesday 15th August 1821

charged about the 15th of June in the year one thousand sevenhundred and eighty by his sd. Capt. Koren (or Coren); that he has long since lost his original discharge. "And I do solemnly swear that I was a resident citizen of the United States on the 18th day of March 1818 and that I have not since that time by gift sale or in any manner disposed of my property or any part thereof with intent thereby so to dimenish it as to bring myself within the provisions of an act of Congress entitled an act of provide for certain persons engaged in the land and navel services of the United States in the revolutionary war passed on the 18th of March 1818 I have not nor has any person in trust for me any property securities contracts or debts due to me nor have I any income other than what is contained in the schedule hereunto annexed and by me subscribed (viz)

| | |
|---|---|
| 1 mare and colt the mare 16 years old, | $30 |
| One other mare and colt mare younger -------------------- | 40 |
| 10 small hogs -------------------------------------------- | 5 |
| 4 old chairs --------------------------------------------- | 1 |
| 10 peuter plates | 2 |
| 2 pots and one oven -------------------------------------- | 4 |
| 3 pails (old) -------------------------------------------- | 1 |
| | $123 |

(p 390) Wednesday 15th August 1821

sworn to in open court
B. Cloud Clerk

his
Conrod X Kegg
mark

That I am justly indebted to defendant Jurors in the aggregate sum of one hundred and seventy dollars that I am by occupation a common labourer and am Sixty Six years old and am unable to obtain a subsistance by my daily labor, am frequently afflicted with the rheumatism that my family consists of my wife aged about fifty six years, tolerably healthy, and a son who is of age and doing for himself I have raised fourteen childern but they have all left me and am doing for themselves those of them who surrive sworn to and subscribed by me in open court

his
Conrod C Kegg
mark

Sworn to in open court
B. Cloud clerk

The court having seen and inspected the above schedule are of opinion that the property therein set forth and described is worth not more than the sum of one hundred and twenty three dollars and the clerk is ordered to certify the same accordingly

(p 391) (Blank)
(0 392) Wednesday August 15th 1821

A Deed of conveyance from Walter Alvis to the heirs of John McNew Deceased was duly acknowledged in open court by Mercellus Moss attorney in fact for said Alvis and was admited to record let it be registered

---

A Deed of conveyance from Enoch Vanbebber to Jacob Vanbebber for twenty seven acres of land was duly proven in open court by the oaths of George Yoakum and James Maddy the only subscribing witnesses thereto and was admitted to recorded let it be registered

---

A Deed of conveyance from John James to William Munvus for forty four acres of land was duly proven in open court by the oaths of Henry Sharp and William Drummonds and was admited to record let it be registered

---

A Deed of conveyance from James W. Glassgow to David Huddleston for one hundred & fifty acres of land was duly proven in open court by the oaths of Dennis Condray and John Huddleston the only subscribing witnesses thereto and was admited to record let it be registered

(p 393) Wednesday August 15th 1821

A Deed of Gift from David Chadwell ser. to Eliza Chadwell was duly acknowledged in open court by the maker and was admited to record and ordered to be certified for registration

---

A Power of attorney from Daniel Root to Enoch Umstead was duly acknowledged in open court by the said Daniel Root the maker thereof and was admited to record and ordered to be certified for registration to the state of Maryland

---

A Deed of conveyance from John Cardwell to John Claypole was duly proven in open court by the oaths of Perrion Cardwell and John Cardwell the only subscribing witnesses thereto and was admited to record let it be Registered

---

A Deed of conveyance from John Rily to Henly Fugate for two hundred acres of land was duly acknowledged in open court by the maker thereof and was admited to record let it be registered

(p 394) Wednesday Au ust 15th 1821

State of Tennessee }
Claiborne County } August Sessions 1821

Personally appeared in open court being the court of pleas and quarter sessions for said county, and the same being a court of record made so by the statutes of said state David Brooks a citizen of said county and made oath in due form of Law, that about the year one thousand seven hundred and seventy seven or eight he was enlisted by as he believes Lieut. Marton in Prince Edward County Virginia as a private soldier in the service of the United States during the revolutionary war, for the term of three years from the date of his enlistment and was attached to Capt. Rogers Company in the eighth regiment commanded by Colonel Wood of the Viriginia line that he was with the army at the battle of Mammoth court house but was confined to his quarter by the small pox after this battle he marched with General Woodford and under his command to the south and continued with him until the seige and surrender of Charlestown south Carolina which he was taken prisoner by the British put on board a prison ship, and then detained untill he was with others Exchanged in the year one thousand seven hundred and Eighty or Eighty one he was landed at James Town Virginia and was afterwards peace time not recollected discharged Honorably at the Expiration of the Term of his enlistment at William borough from the services of the United States he has it not in (p 395) his power to produce and annex his original discharge and dose not at present recollect by that particular officer he was discharged I do sollemly swear that I was a resident citizen of the United States on the 18th day of March 1818 and that I have not since that time by gift sale or in any manner disposed of my property or any part thereof within intent thereby so to deminish it as to bring myself within the proisions of an Act of Congress Intitled an act to provide for certain persons ingaged in the land and navel services of the United States in the revolutionary war passed on the 18th day of March 1818 and that I have not nor has any person intrust for me any property or securities contracts other than what is contained in this schedule hereunto and by me subscribed (viz)

| | |
|---|---|
| 15 acres of Land not Improved or in a state of cultivation | $25 |
| one mare and colt mare 17 years old | 25 |
| one yearling calf | 2 |
| 15 hogs of diferent sizes | 30 |
| 1 cow and calf | 12 |
| 2 ovens and two pots and 1 Kettle | 19 |
| 1 peuter dish peuter Bason four plates | 2 |
| Some old worn out Knives and forks (say from) | 50 |
| 1 tub 1 pail 1 small piggin 1 churn | 2 |
| 1 old cask boxes 1 old muskit | 8.50 |
| 1 hoe 2 pr old drawing chains | 5 |
| 2 old chairs 1 sad Iron | 1 |
| | $132.__ |

his
David Brooks
mark

That I am by occupation a common labourer that I am now frail and feeble and unable to acquire my daily subsestance by labour I am Sixty five years old my family consests of only myself and wife aged about Sixty years and unable to do much labor sworn to and subscribed by me his
Sworn to in open Court, B. Cloud Clerk David X Brooks
mark

(p 396) And the court having seen and inspected the above schedule are of opinion that the property therein set forth and described is worth in all not more than the sum of one hundred and thirty two dollars and the clerk is ordered to certify the same accordingly

Court adjourned till tomorrow morning 9 oclock

John Brock
Wm. Savage
Mercurious Cook
John Neil
George Brock

Thursday August16th 1821 Court met according to adjournment present the same court as or yesterday

Henry Long vs Frederick Bolinger } Appeal

This day came the parties by their attornies and thereupon also came a Jury to wit

| | |
|---|---|
| Bryant Breeding | Joel Dobbs |
| Thomas Mays | Thomas Hurst |
| Charles Shearmon | Jesse Lewis |

| | |
|---|---|
| Sampson Capps | John Fergerson |
| Jacob Cloud | John Wallis |
| James Hoskins | Larkin Fergerson |

who being Elected tried and sworn well and truly to try and the truth to speak in the matter in dispute wherein Henry Long is plaintiff and Frederick Bolinger is Defendant upon their oaths do say they find for the plaintiff five Dollars besides costs

It is therefore considered by the court that the plaintiff recover of the defendant five Dollars Damage in manner and form aforesaid by the Jurors aforesaid assessed together with his costs by him in this behalf Expended and have Execution & &

(p 397) Thursday 16th 1821

James Collensworth )
vs ) Case
Joseph Hurst ) On motion of the plaintiff a commission is award him to Take the deposition of Isaac Lane before anyone Justice of the peace for Claiborne County on giving the defendant five days noticeof the time and place of takeing the same

Susannah Posey admr. & & )
vs ) Certio.
Larkin Ferguson ) This day came the parties by their attornies and thereupon came a Jury to wit

| | |
|---|---|
| David Huddleston | Isaac Vanbebber |
| Richard Harper | Willis Harper |
| Anderson Barton | William Henderson |
| Daniel Coffelt | William Hill |
| Samuel Cloud | Sampson Caps |
| George Vanbebber | |
| Luke Perry | |

who being elected tried and sworn well and truly to try and the truth to speak on the matter of dispute between the parties and after argument of council being heared and before the Jury retired from the bar the plaintiff came and Suffers non suit

It is therefore considered by the court that the defendant go hence and recover of the plaintiff his cost in and about his suit

(p 398) Thursday August 16th 1821

in this behalf expended and that Executién Issued

---

The State )
vs ) Indictment
Mordica Cunningham ) On motion of the Defendant by his attorney A. B. Bradford and for reasons appearing to the satisfaction of the court it is therefore considered by the court that the fine of five Dollars on yeasterdayassessed against the Defendant be reduced to the sum of one dollar

---

The State ) Indictment
vs )

Mordica Cuningham ) On motion the defendant by his attorney Alexander B. Bradford and for reasons appearing to the satisfaction of the court It is therefore considered by the court that a fine assessed on yeasterday against the Defendant for Ten dollars be reduced to four Dollars

---

John Bullard assignee )
vs )
Jeremah Cloud and Richard )
Mays )

Debt appeal

this day came the attorney and the Defendant in their own proper person and confesses Judgment for the sum of fifty Dollars the amount of the Justices Judgment

It is therefore considered by court that the Justices Judgment be affermed and that the plaintiff recover of the defendant the sum aforesaid confessed together with twelve & one half percent Interest from the condition of the

(p 399) Thursday August 16th 1821

Justices Judgment besides his cost in and about his defence in this behalf expended for which execution may Issue

Court adjourned till tomorrow morning 9 oclock

John Brock
Wm. Savage
Mercurious Cook
John Neil
George Brock

Friday August 17th 1821

This day the court met according to adjournment present the worshipful

John Brock )
Wm. Savage )
Mercurious Cook ) Esqr.
John Neil & )
George Brock )

Nathaniel Davis )
vs )
Daniel Cofflet )

This day came the plaintiff by his attorney and dismisses his suit; It is therefore considered by the court that the said cause be dismissed that the defendant go hence without day and recover of the plaintiff his costs by him about his suit in this behalf expended

(p 400) Friday August 17th 1821

George Mills )
vs )
William Hagan )

This day came the plaintiff into open court and dismisses his suit; it is therefore considered by the court that this cause stand dismissed, that the defendant go hence without day and recover of the plaintiff his costs by him about his defence in this behalf expended & &

Solomon Sailer for Britons <u>case</u> )

vs )
William Norvell ) In this case the demurrer in this cause having come demurrer in this cause having come an to argument the court are ofopinion that the Demurrer be sustained; It is therefore considered by the court that the plaintiff Recover of the Defendant his Debt in the Declaration mentioned together with his Damages by the Jury in this case assessed also his costs by him in this behalf expended for which execution may issue

(p 401) Friday August17th 1821

from which Judgment the Defendant prays an appeal to the next Cercuit Court to be holden for the County of Claiborne at the courthouse in Tazewell on the third Monday in October next and gave bond and security and filed reasons according to law and the appeal is granted herein

---

Martin Fugate )
vs )
John Davenport & his wife Lucy ) This day came on to be argued the rule entered to shew cause why the non suit should be set aside, and the court having heard and fully understood the matter it is considered by the court that the rule be discharged that the defendant go hence without day and recover of the plaintiff their costs by them about their defence in this behalf expended for which execution may issue

---

James Campbell ) Debt
vs )
Mathew Owens ) This day came the parties by their attornies and thereupon came the following

(p 402) Friday 17th August 1821

Jury to wit

| | | |
|---|---|---|
| | Joab Hill | John Harper |
| | Jacob Devault | Richard Moore |
| | John Jenkins | Arthur Nash |
| | Isaac Lane | Jesse Chritchfield |
| | John Mason | Jacob Coots |
| | Jacob Moore | Spencer Edwards |

who being elected tried and sworn well and truly to try and the truth to speak on the issue joined on their oaths do say they find the defendant has notpaid the debt in the declaration mentioned as in pleading he has alledged and assess his damage to five dollars and Sixty nine cents

It is therefore considered by the court that the plaintiff recover against the defendant the debt in the declaration mentioned and his damages by the jury assessed as also his costs by him about his suit in this behalf expended & deft. in mercy & &

---

Ordered by the court that the following named persons be appointed Jurors to the next term of this court (to wit)

(p 403) Friday August 17th 1821

1 Moses Willis
2 Barnabas Butcher
3 Isaac Smith
4 John Long
5 Elijah Harp
6 Samuel Shelby
7 David Moore
8 Richard Harper
9 James Cook
10 Allen Brock
11 James Brock
12 Gidian Ferris
13 Philip Nance
14 Jacob Cook
15 George Trees
16 John Lea Jnr.
17 Alfred Critchfield
18 Thomas Shearmon
19 Joudin Smith
20 William Hagon
21 Thomas Norvell
22 George Richardson
23 John Richardson
24 Edward Wooton
25 William Killian
26 William Hurst

State,
vs
Jesse Hopper &
Reuben Flowers

Indictment

Personally appeared in open court Jacob Coots and acknowledged himself indebted to the state of Tennessee in the sum of one hundred dollars for the use of the state to be levied of his goods and chattels lands Tennements to be void on condition that he make his appearance at the courthouse in Tazewell on the Wednesday after the second Monday of November next to give evidence on behalf of the state

(p 404) Friday August 17th 1821

against Jesse Hopper and Reuben Flowers on a bill of Indictment and not depart the court without Leave

---

State
vs
Samuel Hamilton &
John Rice

Indictment

Personally appeared in open court Jesse Chrechfield and acknowledged himself indebted to the state of Tennessee in the penal sum of one hundred Dollars for the use of the to be levied of his goods and chattels Lands and Tennements to be void on condition that he make his appearance at the courthouse in Tazewell on the Wednesday after the second Monday of November next to give evidence on behalf of the state against Samuel Hamilton and John Rice on a bill of Indictment and not depart the court without Leave

State
vs
John Bundron &
James Morgan

Indictment

Personally appeared in open court Jonah Moore and acknowledged himself Indebted to the state of Tennessee in the sum of one

(p 405) Friday August 17th 1821

hundred dollars for the use of the state to be levied of his goods and chattels lands and tenements to be void on condition that he make his personally appearance at the courthous in Tazewell on the Wednesday after the second Monday of November next then and there to Give Evidence on behalf of the Sate against John Bundron and James Morgan on a bill of indictment and not depart the court without leave

State )
vs )
Ambrose Murry & Rebecca Lemmons ) Personally appeared in open court Spencer Edwards & Nathan More and acknowledged themselves indebted to the state of Tennessee in the sum of one hundred Dollars each to be levied of their goods and chattals lands and Tennements to the use of the State to be void on condition the said Spencer Edwards and Nathan Moore doth make their personal appearance on the Wednesday after second Monday in November next then and there to give evidence on behalf of the state on a charge the state against Ambrose Murry and Rebeca Lemmons and not depart the court without leave

(p 406) Thomas McClain )
vs )
Isaac Vanbebber and James Vanbebber )
administrators of John Vanbebber )
Deceased )

The Rule to set aside the non Suit in this case came on to be heard and after argument of counsel being heard It is considered by the court that the said Rule be made absolute and on motion of the plaintiff it is considered by the court that said plaintiff have leave to amend his warrant against said Defendant by eraseing the ward administrators and enserting the ward executors in Lieu thereof on the condition that he pay the costs of this term for such amendment

Hugh Grayham )
vs )
William Wallice ) Rule to dismiss writs of certiorari and Supercedeas

The Rule in this case haveing came on to be heard after agreement of counsel It is considered by the court that said Rule be discharged to which opinion of the court the Defendant by his attorney excepts in Law and tenders his Bill of exception the court which is Signed Anally the court and ordered to be made part of the Record in this cause

(p 407) Ruben Rose for Lewis Morris use )
vs )
John Ashley and Dennis Condray )
and Anderson Barton his executors )

On motion of the plaintiff by Alexander B. Bradford his attorney for a Judgement against John Ashley constable security for money collected by him as constable on an execution in favour of Reuben Rose against Robert Grisham, and John Ashley for twenty seven Dollars which came to his hands and which he has failed to return within the time registered by the act of assembly and the court being Satisfied from the proof produced on said motion that said Execution was not returned with the proper time It is therefore considered by the court that the plaintiff in this motion recover against the said John Ashley constable and his securities the aforesaid sum of twenty seven Dollars the amount of said Execution together with the costs of this motion for which Execution may issue

(p 408) Friday August 17th 1821

Hugh Graham assignee & & )
vs )
William Wallis ) Certiorari

Be it Remembered that on the 17th Day of August 1821 one thousand eight hundred and twenty one the above cause came on to be argued on rul by the defendant to Dismiss the certiorari on the courts affidavit marked A on argument of councel being heard on both sides it was considered by the court that the rule be discharged and that the defendant take nothing by the motion to which opinion of the court the defendant by his attorney in law excepts and tenders this his bill of exception on which he prays may be Signed and Sealed by the court and made a part of the record

John Neal (Seal)
William Savage (Seal)
George Yoakum (Seal)

(p 409) Friday August 17th 1821

Court adjourned until court in course

John Brock
Mercurious Cook
George Brock
John Neil
William Savage

www.ingramcontent.com/pod-product-compliance
Lightning Source LLC
Chambersburg PA
CBHW080419270326
41929CB00018B/3084

* 9 7 8 0 7 8 8 4 9 0 4 1 5 *